Environmental Management in the Hospitality Industry

A Guide for Students and Managers

Kathryn Webster

CASSELL

Cassell
Wellington House   370 Lexington Avenue
125 Strand   New York
London WC2R 0BB   NY 10017-6550

First published 2000

British Library Cataloguing-in-Publication Data
A catalogue record for this book is available from the British Library.

ISBN 0-304-33232-1 (hardback)
       0-304-33234-8 (paperback)

Typeset by Pantek Arts, Maidstone, Kent
Printed by Cromwell Press Ltd, Trowbridge, Wiltshire

Contents

List of tables   vii

List of figures   ix

Acknowledgements   x

Preface   xi

Part 1: Challenges to the earth's ecosystem

 1 **Background issues in environmental management**   3

 2 **National and international action**   31

Part 2: The hospitality industry

 3 **Refrigeration**   49

 4 **Energy management**   60

 5 **Water**   90

 6 **Green technology in the hospitality industry**   109

 7 **The product**   118

 8 **Packaging and disposable products**   134

 9 **Waste management**   151

10 **The Green consumer**   175

11 **Transport**   186

Part 3: The business environment

12 **Environmental business tools**   203

13 **The environmental audit**   225

14 **Reporting on environmental performance**   239

15 **Conclusions**   254

Index   261

List of tables

Table 1.1   Significant dates in the earth's history in millions of
             years   5

Table 1.2   The typical chemical composition of fossil fuels   6

Table 1.3   The composition of the atmosphere   11

Table 1.4   Sources of carbon dioxide emissions in the UK   14

Table 2.1   Current prices of alternative energy compared with
             conventional sources, 1998   41

Table 3.1   The potential damage to the ozone layer and
             contribution to global warming of a number of
             refrigerants in common use   52

Table 4.1   Required levels of illumination, in lux   65

Table 4.2   The relative levels of energy efficiency provided by a
             range of lighting   66

Table 4.3   Comparison between illumination levels of standard
             bulbs and compact fluorescents   67

Table 4.4   Typical energy ratings for equipment used in the
             preparation, cooking and serving of a meal   74

Table 4.5   An example of a spreadsheet showing usage of a range
             of equipment   77

Table 4.6   An example of gas rates, 1994   82

Table 5.1   The predicted increase in demand for public water
             supplies in 2021 over demand in 1990   94

Table 5.2   Benchmarks for daily water consumption by
             department   104

Table 5.3   Benchmarks for daily water consumption by hotel   104

Table 5.4   Example of water usage in a large international
             hotel   105

Table 6.1   Comparison between the costs of running conventional
             cooking equipment and methods and combination
             steamers and combination microwave   112

Table 8.1   End uses of plastics production   141

Table 9.1   The hierarchy of waste management options   152

List of tables

Table 9.2   Cost comparisons of various methods of waste
            disposal   155

Table 9.3   Recycling levels achieved by some key industrial
            sectors   157

Table 10.1 Consumer priorities in the late 1980s/early 1990s   178

Table 11.1 The growth in road freight in the UK, 1950–90   195

Table 12.1 A comparison of the environmental performance of
            Ecover and Inter-Continental Hotels   207

List of Figures

Figure 1.1   The carbon cycle   7

Figure 1.2   How measured concentrations of carbon dioxide in
              the atmosphere have increased over time   8

Figure 1.3   The water cycle   11

Figure 1.4   Average annual carbon dioxide emissions, in billions
              of tonnes, in the UK   12

Figure 1.5   The logarithmic rate of growth of the world's
              population   20

Figure 4.1   The hospitality and catering industry – number of
              outlets in the UK, 1996   62

Figure 4.2   Use of energy by cost in hotels, 1983   63

Figure 4.3   500 lux using twin 75 W battens plus diffusers   70

Figure 4.4   500 lux using PSM 258 luminaires with TLD 58 W
              fluorescent lamp   70

Figure 4.5   A wind farm in the West Country   87

Figure 7.1   The RSPCA Freedom Food logo   120

Figure 7.2   The Soil Association symbol   121

Figure 8.1   The rise in reported cases of food poisoning in the
              UK, 1980–98   136

Figure 9.1   Recycling bins in the UK   158

Figure 9.2   The calorific value of plastics compared with more
              conventional sources of fuel   162

Figure 13.1   An example of a score system for an environmental
              audit   234

Acknowledgements

With thanks to Adrian Carpenter for assistance with diagrams and computers!

Preface

The price of failing to meet the environmental challenge will be that bankers will not lend, insurers will not insure, institutions will not invest, public authorities will not licence, politicians will not support, customers will not purchase, and staff will not stay.

> Michael Heseltine, Environment Secretary, speech to the
> CBI conference, Bournemouth, November 1991

Although it is a cliché to say that today's students are tomorrow's managers, it is indeed true that they will one day be in a position to influence policy and decision-making within their own companies. It is therefore vital that they are made aware of the opportunities for business success that a closer attention to environmental issues will bring.

In February 1993 the Toyne Report, *Environmental Responsibility: An Agenda for FHE*,[1] was published. The report stressed the importance of the integration of environmental issues across all areas of the curriculum in further and higher education, and its ultimate objective was to raise environmental awareness in the workforce. The report recommended that across *all* business sectors, students should understand the following basic issues:

1 The way in which the physical and biological systems of the local and global environment operate in order to make them habitable.
2 How and why human activities are placing the environment under considerable pressure.
3 The major specific issues, such as population growth, global warming or waste disposal, arising as a result of human activity, and how these problems could be addressed.
4 The responsibility of the individual in relation to these issues.

The hospitality industry itself has slowly responded to environmental or 'Green' issues, albeit mostly on an individual and fragmented basis. May 1993 saw the launch of the International Hotels Environment Initiative (IHEI), hosted by the Forte company, and addressed by HRH the Prince of Wales, Lord Forte and Jonathon Porritt. The catering press have published a number of articles that describe the 'greening' process undertaken by catering establishments, and their results. There has also been a positive response from suppliers to the hospitality industry right across the board, from the manufacturers of detergents, dishwashers and ovens to the suppliers of disposables.

At the same time public interest in, and concern about, environmental issues continues to manifest itself in a variety of ways. The success of the Body Shop chain, the ban on CFC-containing aerosols in the late 1980s, and more recently, the refusal of the major cross-channel ferry operators to transport animals destined for slaughter in Europe are just a few examples that point to a considerable public interest in environmental issues. In the case of the ferry operators it was the influence of shareholders, the majority of whom were more than likely to be middle-class, who were influential in the outcome. The middle classes also joined the ranks of the protestors against the export of live calves to Europe for the production of veal in the winter of 1994/95. Green consumerism, in its many guises, has become an established feature of the UK economy.

It is hoped that this book will at least be a start for those hospitality lecturers who would like to incorporate environmental issues into their curriculum. Several of the chapters include a reading list of texts which the author has found of particular value. The essential message of this book is that it makes sense to be Green, not only at a personal level, but also in order to achieve business success. We have a responsibility to future generations who will be left to sort out the environmental problems which this generation have created. Hopefully they will be able to appreciate that even in the most difficult of trading climates there were many who were still able to stand back and to consider the greater good.

There are a number of themes that reoccur throughout this book:

1 It makes sound commercial sense to become Green.
2 It is the large companies which have the spending power to initiate research, or to originate new systems or processes; they are the trendsetters.
3 Small companies will benefit from the learning experiences of the large companies.
4 In many cases there are no absolutes in the environmental debate, and in the business context there has to be some room for compromise.[2]
5 A company is very unlikely to implement a policy which does not make commercial sense unless it is forced to do so – by legislation or similar constraints.[3]

We should not forget, however, that for every one company that publicizes its environmental activities there are many more companies which are quietly implementing environmental systems into their operations which are not publicized other than to their own staff. This could be because, however innovative a company might be, there will always be room for improvement, and it is very easy for critics to highlight the weaker aspects of a policy rather than its strengths. McDonald's has suffered severe adverse publicity by critics who claim that the company is partially responsible for the destruction of the Amazonian rainforests, an allegation which it has worked hard to refute. The Body Shop was accused by US environmentalists of not being as Green or animal-friendly as it claimed at the end of 1994, and for a time the value of its shares on the international stock markets was reduced. The point being made here is that being Green is a compromise between the requirements of daily trading activities to operate profitably, what the customer is prepared to accept, investment costs and payback periods, and ethical considerations. In business it is the 'bottom line' that counts!

However, financial considerations will increasingly dictate the imperative for businesses to adopt environmental policies. Governments of all persuasions favour the use of taxation, or 'economic instruments', as the tool to change practices in favour of protecting the environment. A price will be placed on the environmental impact of the operation of a business which may or may not be passed on to the customer. It would be better if all businesses adopted methods of operating that reduced the pressures on the environment, thereby saving themselves heavy costs and also passing these savings on to the customer; in today's competitive trading climate it is these businesses that will be the winners.

Becoming Green not only involves effort, but in its initial stages it can also involve some considerable financial investment. In difficult trading times it is hard to justify the purchase of a dozen (or many dozen) energy-saving light bulbs at £10 each if the savings will take some time to recoup. The installation of new equipment, which again will take a number of years to pay for itself before offering large savings, is also difficult to accept if the business is barely surviving. This book aims to show both students and the industry that by using less polluting technology and techniques it is possible to produce goods and services of equal if not better standards than those of their competitors, and at a saving to the business itself. As the volume of environmental regulation increases, companies will be forced to purchase less polluting equipment and implement less polluting trading practices: the company that already has strong environmental management systems in operation will have the trading advantage over the company which has to act at the last moment in response to legislation, at considerable cost and inconvenience to that business.

As the problems of waste disposal increase, costs will soar and all companies will be seeking ways to minimize their creation of waste, or to reject potentially waste-generating materials from their suppliers. The Environmental Protection Act 1990 has already made many companies consider the costs of disposing of all types of waste. As Chapter 9 shows, this is an issue of particular relevance to the hospitality industry, and it is envisaged that recycling will become a more attractive and profitable alternative.

In the USA and in some member states of the European Union, legislation has already forced companies to consider product and packaging disposal, and they have been made responsible for the costs of this disposal. In Germany companies are required by law to run recycling schemes for their packaging which is paid for by a levy on the products. In other words, the consumer pays. But there will understandably be resistance if prices are increased to make the consumer pay for unnecessary waste.

The Report of the Royal Commission on Environmental Pollution[4] in November 1994, with its sweeping recommendations on transport use, is also likely to have a considerable impact upon the patterns of trading and supplying businesses, even if only half of its recommendations are taken on board by the Government.

The final section of the book addresses the management control systems that a company can utilize to improve its environmental performance. Such systems are applicable across a range of businesses and those appropriate to the specific needs of a business should be selected. Examples of good practice are highlighted, and the fact that there is no standard way to conduct an environmental assessment is stressed. Systems for independent verification are also discussed in some detail.

Finally, no textbook would be worth its name if it did not include a range of exercises. Each chapter ends with a selection of exercises for students to attempt, and there are also a number of issues for debate and discussion to challenge the session.

CONCLUSION

It is hoped that having read this book, students and managers in the industry will realize that although it makes sound commercial sense to implement environmentally-friendly policies in their business, this is an entirely separate issue from any moral or ethical debates to do with the environment. The company which implements such strategies is more likely to earn the loyalty of its staff, particularly its younger members, to engender customer loyalty and also to satisfy its shareholders.

NOTES

1 The Toyne Report, *Environmental Responsibility: An Agenda for FHE*, London: HMSO, 1993.
2 A good example of this is Forte's decision to demand frequent deliveries of small quantities of stock, perishable or otherwise, in order to minimize their own levels of wastage. This has to be balanced against the potential damage to the environment caused by the delivery vehicles. See Chapter 11 for a more extensive discussion of this dilemma.
3 An example of this is Forte's policy of small but regular deliveries of goods from a central distribution depot. See Chapter 11 on transport for a discussion of this policy.
4 The Royal Commission on Environmental Pollution, 18th Report, *Transport and the Environment*, London: HMSO, 1994.

This book is dedicated to the memory of my mother

Part 1

Challenges to the earth's ecosystem

Background issues in environmental management

Pressures resulting from unrestrained population growth puts demands upon the natural world that can overwhelm any efforts to achieve a sustainable future. No more than one or a few decades remain before the chance to avert the threats will be lost and the prospect for humanity immeasurably diminished.

The Union of Concerned Scientists[1]

OBJECTIVES

1 To describe the range of threats to the natural environment as a result of human activity on a global scale.
2 To demonstrate an understanding of the issues in the current scientific debate about population growth and global warming.
3 To describe the concept of 'sustainability'.

Some environmental dilemmas

● The UK agreed to cut greenhouse gas emissions at the Kyoto conference in Japan in 1997. At the moment gas supplies 25 per cent of the UK energy market (1 per cent in 1990), and it is cheaper and cleaner to burn gas than it is to generate our electricity from coal. But when gas supplies run out the UK will have to rely on imports of gas or coal.

   Note that there is a moratorium on building gas-fired power stations and there is a target for 10 per cent of our electricity to be generated from renewable sources by 2010. The question is, should the coal industry die?

● VAT on insulation has been reduced but only as part of a UK Government energy efficiency programme. The VAT reduction on domestic fuel to help the poor will encourage energy consumption, depositing an extra 300,000 tonnes of carbon into the atmosphere (0.2 per cent of the UK total).

● If every wind farm in the world relocated to the UK their combined output would generate only 10 per cent of the country's requirements. However, if a barrage was built in the Severn Estuary its water turbines would provide 7 per cent of our energy needs; but birdwatchers are against this proposal.

- The nuclear industry is set to decline as power stations end their useful life. An extra 4 million tonnes of carbon a year will be produced if nuclear-powered stations are replaced by gas-fired power stations, or 8 million tonnes of carbon if replaced by coal-fired power stations.
  These figures may double by 2020 due to increased energy demands. How does one balance the risks to the environment against the benefits?

- One suggestion would be to impose a carbon tax. Why was there such a public outcry when the Government imposed VAT on domestic fuel? Its proceeds could be used to fund public transport, renewable energy sources, even nuclear energy.

- World energy demand is expected to double by 2030, making it hard to stabilize greenhouse gases at present levels.

- The car is a major producer of greenhouse gases in the UK, yet the number of cars in the UK is predicted to increase by 30 per cent by 2010.

Some facts and figures

One hundred species of animals or plants are made extinct every day due to human activities.

Fifty million acres of tropical rainforest are destroyed each year.

In 1982, 8 per cent of European forests showed damage by acid rain; by 1988 this figure had increased to 52 per cent.

Approximately 1.25 tonnes of carbon per person in the world are deposited into the atmosphere every year.

The earth's mean surface temperature in the 1980s was 0.2 °C higher than in the 1940s.

Since 1970:
(i)   Over 200 million hectares of tree cover has been lost – equivalent to an area the size of the European Union.
(ii) There has been an increase in desert of 120 million hectares – this is more than the entire cultivated land mass of China.
(iii) Approximately 480 billion tonnes of topsoil has been lost – equivalent to the cultivated land mass of India.

INTRODUCTION

During the 1990s, a significant share of the international debate has been about the implications of industrial growth on the planet. Not only the scientific community, but also the politicians of the industrialized world have agreed that if the current rate of economic growth continues, and if the countries of the former Soviet bloc and the Third World achieve the same levels of economic growth, then the extent to which natural resources are lost forever, and the damage sustained by the earth's delicate ecosystem, will not permit the world as we know it to survive. This chapter will briefly consider the most significant of these threats and examine the strength of the evidence that radical and conspicuous action must be taken now, by everyone.

In the industrialized world we have come to expect a certain standard of living which involves, among other things, the use of the motor car, electricity at the flick of a switch, clean water on tap, and an extensive range of brightly coloured, extensively packaged consumer goods which rapidly go out of fashion and need to be 'upgraded'. These goods are created from raw materials that originated in the earth or in its atmosphere, and human beings have acted as if there were a limitless supply. Industrial growth has been primarily concerned with profit rather than with sustainability. It has been assumed that all resources are limitless, and that the dumping of waste is permissible anywhere. Industrial society is a disposable society.

In fact, industrial society is less than 200 years old, but the environmental impact has within that time been enormous. Scientists have been able to measure the quality of the earth's atmosphere back across the centuries to the Ice Ages by cutting a core sample of ice from the Antarctic, and what they have discovered is that the level of pollutant gases, dissolved in the

Table 1.1 Significant dates in the earth's history in millions of years

4500	The origin of the earth
3500	First life on earth (bacteria) appears
2000	Plants appear
600	Invertebrates appear
465	Vertebrates appear
300	Amphibians appear
280	Reptiles appear
200	Dinosaurs appear
165	Birds appear
65	Dinosaurs become extinct
2	Humanoids appear

Source: Into Science, Module 4, Open University (1994).

water as it fell as snow, has increased dramatically since the the beginning of the Industrial Revolution, which is estimated to have started around the 1750s in Britain. What is the source of these pollutant gases, why are they harmful, and can their effects be reversed?

FOSSIL FUELS

The major cause of atmospheric pollution is the burning of fossil fuels. These include natural gas, oil and coal. These fuels were formed millions of years ago as the result of partial decomposition. When plants and animals die the end product of their decay is normally carbon dioxide which is released into the atmosphere. In the case of fossil fuels this process of decay was interrupted as the trees, plants and animals from which they were formed were covered with sediments of sand and clay, and the carbon remained stored in the earth.

Oil and natural gas were formed about 150 million years ago from the semi-decomposed bodies of small plants and animals that lived in the sea. This organic matter was covered in sediment and over time gradually changed into rock. Pressure from the rock caused chemical changes to take place whereby oil and gas were formed. Over time these fluids found their way to the surface of the earth. Coal was formed 300 million years ago when dead trees and ferns were covered by sediments in swampy ground before they had time to completely decompose. As the sediments of clay and sand compressed to form rocks over millions of years, the pressure they exerted on these dead plants forced out the water and they were transformed into carbon. Again with time, movements of the earth and weathering brought these deposits closer to the surface, where they are mined as coal.

Table 1.2 shows that natural gas is the 'purest' of the three fossil fuels. The sulphur contained in coal and oil is converted into sulphuric acid when these products are burnt; this, of course, is one of the main constituents of acid rain.

Table 1.2 The typical chemical composition of fossil fuels (as percentages)

Element	Coal	Natural gas	Oil
Carbon	85	80	85
Hydrogen	5	20	12
Oxygen	0	0	0
Sulphur	variable	0	variable
Nitrogen	variable	0	variable
Total	100	100	100

Adapted from Into Science, Module 2, Open University (1994).

It is estimated that the burning of fossil fuels contributes approximately 5 billion tonnes of carbon dioxide to the atmosphere each year, and that forest fires contribute another 2 billion tonnes. This 7 billion tonnes equates to an annual increase in atmospheric carbon dioxide of 0.93 per cent, although the actual observed rate of increase is only 0.48 per cent. This means that approximately half of the carbon is being reabsorbed, mainly in the form of calcium carbonate at the bottom of the oceans. However, this rate of increase still means that there is an increase in carbon dioxide concentration in the earth's atmosphere of 5 per cent every decade, which makes it the major cause of global warming.

THE CARBON CYCLE

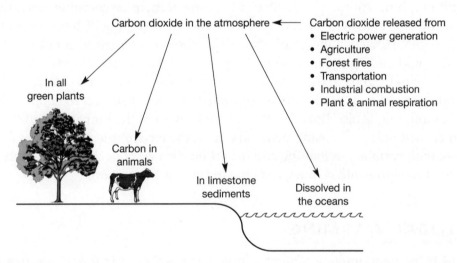

Figure 1.1 The carbon cycle. This shows how carbon is circulated through the different environments of the earth in a self-replenishing fashion. It is the fact that the volume of carbon that is 'locked up' in various 'sinks' is being released at a rate greater than other sources of carbon can be 'locked up' that creates an imbalance which is leading to global warming.

There is a natural exchange of carbon between plants and animals which is self-regulating over time (see Figure 1.1). However, post-industrial society is unbalancing this cycle by adding carbon dioxide to the atmosphere by burning fossil fuels.

If we look at Figure 1.2, it is possible to extrapolate figures for the year 2000 and beyond from this graph as follows. Between 1950 and 1990 the

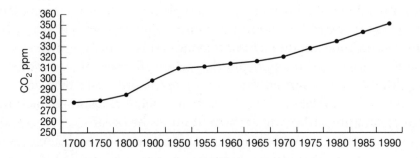

Figure 1.2 How measured concentrations of carbon dioxide in the atmosphere have increased over time – in parts per million (ppm)

Source: Into Science, Module 4, Open University (1994).

average annual increase in carbon dioxide concentrations is 1.05 parts per million (ppm). We can project that if this rate of increase continues then the reading for 1995 will be 357.25 ppm, and in 2000 it will have risen to 362.5 ppm. However, the graph shows that the rate of increase is not steady, so it would perhaps be more accurate to extend the estimated concentration to 375 ppm by 2000. Extrapolation is not a certain science, however, as the production of carbon dioxide by human activities is subject to changes in behaviour and is also linked to the rate of growth of the human population which will place increasing demands upon the environment. What we can state with certainty is that the rise in carbon dioxide concentrations started in the late eighteenth century with the Industrial Revolution.

GLOBAL WARMING

This is the phenomenon whereby there has been a gradual but significant increase in the average annual temperature of the earth due to its inability to maintain a balance between the amount of heat that it generates and its ability to lose excessive heat to outer space. The world's climate has increased in temperature by an average of 0.5 °C over the past 150 years. But there are many uncertainties attached to the predictions that the temperature will continue to rise, although it is now agreed that there will be increases; the question is by how much.

The earth obtains its energy in the form of heat which is transmitted by the sun. This energy is absorbed by plants which convert it into leaves and seeds which are consumed by animals, many of whom form part of a food chain. Every time a plant or animal is consumed some energy is lost to the atmosphere, helping to maintain the earth's temperature equilibrium.

Energy has also been stored in plants in the form of carbon for millions of years. In prehistoric times the earth was covered by forests. As these forests decayed they turned into coal and oil, locking up the carbon inside them. When burnt they release this energy. In addition, massive expanses of modern forest, in particular the tropical rainforests, have been destroyed, usually by a process known as 'slash and burn' to clear land for agricultural purposes. The energy released when burning is not used, but the carbon that is also released forms carbon dioxide in the atmosphere. Carbon dioxide is known as a greenhouse gas as it acts as an insulator and prevents the loss of excessive heat from the earth.

Heat is lost from the earth at the two Poles, particularly from the South Pole where 90 per cent of the earth's water is stored in the form of a 3 km deep ice cap. Projections by the Intergovernmental Panel on Climate Change (IPCC) indicate that if greenhouse gas emissions are not reduced there will be an average increase of global temperatures of 0.2 °C to 0.5 °C every decade for the next century. A consequent rise of 2 °C would mean average world temperatures not known on Earth for 125,000 years, and a rise of 3 °C would mean temperatures not found on earth for 2 million years. Inevitably even a small increase in temperature will result in the melting of polar ice caps, leading to an increase in the level of the sea which would cause coastal flooding, disease, increases in the number and severity of storms, and hot spells and droughts. It has been estimated that a 1.5 metre rise in sea levels will result in the flooding of Bangladesh, much of the Netherlands, many island states, Egypt's Nile Delta and London. A 3 metre rise in sea levels, which some scientists predict is possible by the year 2070, would cause even greater devastation.

Uncertainties in temperature measurements

The earth's mean surface temperature in the 1980s was 0.2 °C higher than in the 1940s; there are a variety of reasons for this, only one of which is carbon dioxide emissions. It is important not to underestimate the complexity of the climate system; there are many complex interactions, although carbon dioxide is the major climate factor that will affect temperatures in the next 100 years.

The Framework Convention on Climate Change established at the Earth Summit in Rio in 1992 adopted the 'precautionary principle' in its attitude towards the emission of greenhouse gases. This means that although there is no absolute proof at present that the emission of these gases is contributing to global warming, the body of circumstantial evidence is extensive and strong enough to indicate a prudent or precautionary approach; indeed, to reduce the emissions can only be beneficial. In 1993 the UK ratified the Convention, thereby committing itself to implement a programme to limit national emissions of greenhouse gases and to protect carbon sinks,[2] such as forests, to reduce the country's carbon dioxide emissions by 2000 to 1990 levels, and to assist developing countries to achieve reductions in their emissions of greenhouse gases.

In 1990 the UK population's contribution to carbon dioxide emissions was equivalent to 158 million tonnes of carbon – this was approximately 2.6 per cent of world carbon dioxide emissions from fossil fuel burning. In contrast, the USA produces 18 per cent of total world carbon dioxide emissions.

How does the burning of fossil fuels contribute to global warming?

Table 1.2 (p. 6) showed the main chemical constituents of coal, oil and natural gas, and we can see that the major element is carbon in each instance. When these fuels are burnt to provide heat they combine with oxygen in the atmosphere to form carbon dioxide, and in the case of oil and gas the hydrogen which they contain combines with oxygen to produce water vapour. Does the production of these gases affect the composition of the atmosphere?

Water vapour is already a major constituent of the earth's atmosphere. Figure 1.3 shows how water is constantly recycled between the land and the sea, and how the concentration of water in the atmosphere will vary according to location and also to temperature. The warmer the air, the more water in the form of vapour it will hold.

In contrast to water vapour, carbon dioxide makes up only 0.035 per cent (or 350 parts per billion) of the atmosphere, so any addition will increase this volume proportionally. Carbon dioxide acts as an insulator, and is called a greenhouse gas; it is estimated that emissions of carbon dioxide contribute 50 per cent to global warming.

For every gram of carbon that is burnt 3.67 grams of carbon dioxide are produced. If coal is composed of 85 per cent carbon, then every kilogram of coal contains 850 grams of carbon. When this is burnt this will produce 850 x 3.67 grams of carbon dioxide = 3119 grams or 3.119 kilograms.

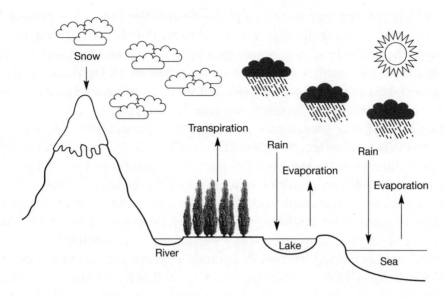

Figure 1.3 The water cycle

Table 1.3 The composition of the atmosphere

Gas	Percentage
Nitrogen	79
Oxygen	20
Carbon dioxide	0.035
Other gases	0.965

Greenhouse gases

There are four greenhouse gases, three of which occur naturally, although their major effect upon the atmosphere is due to human activity. The gases are carbon dioxide, methane and nitrous oxide. The fourth greenhouse gas, chlorofluorocarbon, or CFC, is entirely man-made. They are currently present in the atmosphere in the following quantities:

Carbon dioxide	55 per cent
CFCs 11 & 12	17 per cent
Methane	15 per cent
Other CFCs	7 per cent
Nitrous oxide	6 per cent

All heat is radiated from the sun, and one-third of this energy is immediately reflected back into space; the remainder is absorbed by the air, the land, plants and water before in turn being re-radiated back in the form of infra-red radiation. In this way the earth maintains an energy equilibrium. The presence of the four greenhouse gases prevents the efficient return of this heat, and as a result the average temperature of the earth is gradually increasing.

The production of greenhouse gases has been particularly intense over the past 40 years. Between the years 1870 and 1991 the global concentration of carbon dioxide increased from 290 parts per billion (ppb) to 355 ppb, an increase of 22 per cent, mainly as a result of the burning of fossil fuels including wood, coal and oil, and of deforestation. Some scientists predict that this concentration could double between 2030 and 2050 if fossil fuel consumption continues to increase at a similar rate as it is doing today.

Global climate models by the UN-sponsored Intergovernmental Panel on Climate Change (IPCC) predict that average global temperature increases will be 0.5 °C per decade – or 3 to 8 °C over the next century. This would lead to major environmental changes, including many of the world's grain producing areas, such as the US Grain Belt, turning into arid desert, and the melting of the Polar ice caps would increase sea levels causing major flooding of many densely populated parts of the world. Agricultural patterns would change radically so that the US and Canada, currently the two major exporters of grain, would become major importers, the majority of Africa would become desert, yet in other parts of the world there would be much more rainfall. The consequences of such dramatic climatic changes could be

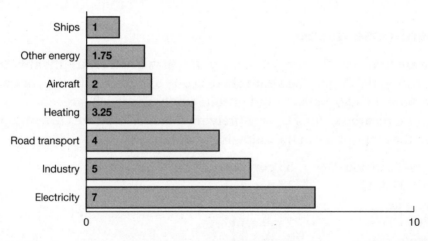

Figure 1.4 Average annual carbon dioxide emissions, in billions of tonnes, in the UK
Source: Website of the Department of the Environment, 1998.

war, more refugees, and the spread of infectious diseases. Increased numbers of forest and grassland fires would in turn increase the effects of global warming by releasing even more carbon dioxide into the atmosphere. This vicious circle would generate even more hurricanes and severe floods, while warmer seas would affect the weather patterns to produce more storms, thus destroying crops globally.

The sea currently acts as a major reservoir of carbon dioxide, but the warming of the seas would reduce its solubility, throwing more gas into the atmosphere and aggravating the global warming.

Currently over half the world's population live in coastal cities; these include Miami, New Orleans, Bangkok, Hamburg, St Petersburg, Shanghai, Sydney, Alexandria and Dhaka.

The Intergovernmental Panel on Climate Change (IPCC) predicts a rise of between 12 and 43 inches in sea level by 2100.

There would also be tremendous changes in the nature and locations of flora and fauna; temperate regions such as Northern Europe would favour tropical species which are currently found in the Southern Mediterranean areas, and the beech trees of Northern Europe would become extinct.

The latest model of the effects of global warming suggests that crop production could fall by as much as a third in countries that are located at low altitudes, or which are prone to drought. This would be balanced by increased crop production in other areas of the world. Hence Brazil would lose 35 per cent and Egypt 30 per cent of their total crop output over the next 50 years. However, China would increase its wheat production by 15 per cent, and Canada and parts of the south of the former Soviet Union would also increase their production.

Biffa Waste Services harvests the methane produced by landfill sites which it manages at Redhill in Surrey, Howley Park and Ufton, and burns it to produce electricity. In 1997/98 the company generated 56,340 MWh.

One model indicates that the rate of temperature increase will be twice the rate at which the world's ecosystems will be able to adapt. The latest models are able to allow for the cooling effects of sulphur dioxide emissions, which reflect rays from the sun away from the earth. As a result of these new models, the prediction is that there will be an increase in global temperature of 0.2 °C per decade. However, if sulphur dioxide emissions were to be reduced or terminated in an effort to prevent other forms of pollution, the 'benefits' of reflection would soon be lost and the earth's temperature would then increase by 0.3 °C per decade.

A number of factors may combine to counteract some of the major effects of global warming. Increased cloud cover would result in more sunlight being reflected back into space before it hits the earth. Increased levels of particulates in the atmosphere generated by forest fires, and dust particles generated by storms, would also cause sunlight to be reflected back into space. In addition, the loss of ozone from the lower stratosphere will result in cooling and hence buffer the effect by approximately 20 per cent.

Other evidence for global warming includes the fact that glaciers continue to recede.

Table 1.4 Sources of carbon dioxide emissions in the UK

Industry and agriculture	35 per cent
Households	26 per cent
Road transport	21 per cent
Commercial and public sector	15 per cent
Other transport (shipping, aircraft)	3 per cent

A study by the IPCC published in 1998 estimated that aircraft may be responsible for 5–6 per cent and perhaps as much as 10 per cent of the warming caused by greenhouse gases, with aircraft emissions doubling every ten years. Aircraft consume 3 per cent of the fossil fuels burned worldwide, one-sixth as much as motor vehicles, and thus emit carbon dioxide, but they also produce nitrogen oxides that are converted to ozone in the upper troposphere (extending 9–13 km from the earth's surface) where most aircraft cruise.

Climate change and the UK

A report issued by the Department of the Environment, Transport and the Regions in October 1998 stated that world average temperatures were expected to rise by 3 °C in the next century, resulting in an increased incidence of hot, dry summers in the south-east of England and wetter, windier summers in the north-west of England. One consequence could be an increase in extreme weather patterns, including severe drought in south-east England once every decade on average, rising sea levels and strong winds resulting in damage to property. Agriculture will also be severely affected.

THE OZONE LAYER

The ozone layer is located in the upper stratosphere 9–50 km above the surface of the earth. Ozone, a form of oxygen, acts as a filter to reduce the quantity of ultraviolet radiation from sunlight reaching the earth. The ozone layer has been depleted due to the action of chlorofluorocarbons (CFCs) used in aerosol cans and refrigerants, and for insulation, and also by jet planes cruising in the stratosphere.

It used to be thought that CFCs were inert gases, which means that they did not react with other chemicals in the environment to form undesirable breakdown products, and that they would remain reliable over a very long period of time. However, it has now been shown that they release chlorine as they break down in the ozone layer, destroying ozone molecules.[3]

Industry Case Study

Trusthouse Forte took its first environmental initiative in 1982 when its Chairman, Lord Forte, became aware of media concern to do with the impact of aerosol sprays on the ozone layer. He decided that even if scientific claims against CFCs had yet to be substantiated, the use of disposable aerosols was a wasteful practice, and that it would make commercial sense to change to less expensive ways of dispensing cleaning materials. The buyers negotiated with their suppliers, who were at first reluctant, to supply the same materials in trigger-squeeze bottles. In the first year alone the company saved £250,000. They also set an example for other companies.

In 1985 a massive hole was discovered in the ozone layer above Antarctica by the British Antarctic Survey team (who had been monitoring ozone levels since 1957), and since then many monitorings have shown extensive holes above south-east England, Europe and the USA. In 1988 it was confirmed that since 1969 the ozone layer in the Northern hemisphere had declined by between 1.7 and 3 per cent, and that in the Antarctic since 1979 there had been a total reduction of 5–10 per cent in total annual ozone concentration. Each year since then the breadth and depth of the holes in the ozone layer have increased. Scientific data indicates that the ozone layer is thinning all over the world, at a rate of 3 per cent per decade in the mid-latitudes in both hemispheres, and by 8 per cent in the northern part of these latitudes (which includes the UK). The winters of 1992 and 1993 both recorded very low ozone levels over Europe, which were associated with exceptional and protracted weather patterns.

The effects of ozone depletion mean that more ultraviolet light is transmitted through the stratosphere to the earth. It is predicted that this excessive exposure as a result of the thinning of the ozone layer will increase the risk of skin cancer. An excess of ultraviolet light can also weaken the immune system, making people less resistant to infection, and it can damage the retina of the eyes leading in some cases to blindness.

Ultraviolet light is also dangerous to plants: an excess of it can reduce the yield of staple crops, including rice (the world's largest staple), wheat and root crops. Bacteria are also destroyed by it, including bacteria beneficial to human existence. Ultraviolet radiation can penetrate the oceans to a depth of 60 metres, and studies in Antarctica have shown that levels of phytoplankton – microscopic plants at the start of the marine food chain – will be reduced as the result of its increased presence.

It has been predicted that the 10 per cent decrease in the ozone layer which is expected by the end of the twentieth century will result in 300,000 extra deaths from skin cancer, and an extra 1.6 million extra cases of cataracts globally.

The good news is that the ozone layer has the ability to repair itself if no more chlorine and bromine are transmitted to it. But this will take time and a change in human industrial activities. It takes about 15 years for CFCs to migrate into the stratosphere; this means that there are a number of years before the maximum levels reach this level before their destructive effects can be reduced. Given the millions of tonnes of CFCs already in the stratosphere, and the fact that it can take as long as 100 years for them to totally degrade to harmless substances, it will be well over a century before the ozone layer will begin to return to its 'normal' concentration.

Acid rain

This is the description given to very acidic rain which can turn lakes acidic, corrode buildings, damage forests and crops, and kill fish and other aquatic organisms. Normally rain is very mildly acidic, but as a result of human activities quite strong sulphuric or nitric acid is being deposited not only on mountains, lakes and forests, but also on towns and cities, sometimes hundreds of miles away from the source of the sulphur or nitrate discharge. Approximately 70 per cent of sulphur is produced as the result of burning coal in power stations, and nitrogen oxides are created due to the burning of fossil fuels in power stations, or by the combustion of petrol and diesel fuel in cars and lorries. Carried across seas and land by winds, these substances are dissolved in water vapour and are deposited either as rain or snow, or mix with the moisture droplets in fog and smog; sulphur and water become sulphuric acid, and nitrogen oxide gases and water become nitric acid.

Is it possible to reduce or reverse these harmful processes? It is possible to install 'scrubbers' in power station chimneys that can remove these contaminants, or to use alternative fuels such as gas to fire power stations. Car and lorry emissions can be reduced by the installation of catalytic converters in all new vehicles, and by cutting the volume of traffic generally. However, it is better in the long term to remove the cause rather than to treat the effects!

The by-products of the combustion of fossil fuels, whether in power stations, for domestic heating or for transport, include water vapour, carbon dioxide, sulphur, nitric oxides and 'PM10s'. These materials contribute to the greenhouse effect and hence global warming, and cause acid rain which can harm trees and buildings, and damage human and animal health, especially the lungs.

PM10s

PM10 is a term used to describe the tiny black particles which are emitted as the result of burning diesel. Often invisible to the naked eye, they are breathed into the lungs where they embed themselves and can cause significant irritation to those who are already sick or vulnerable. It has been estimated that these particulates contribute to the premature death of 10,000 UK citizens each year; these people already have pre-existing heart or lung disease, and the particulates exacerbate the thickening of the blood and breathing problems and contribute to heart failure.

POPULATION GROWTH: INTRODUCTION

It is generally acknowledged that one of the most significant pressures on the earth's resources is caused by the relentless growth of the world's population, particularly over the past 200 years. Figure 1.5 (p. 20) shows that there was a steady increase in the world's population until the mid-eighteenth century, but from this date there was a sharp increase. Although this trend started in England, it was rapidly followed by the rest of Europe. Historians maintain that the reason for this has to do with changes in both agricultural and industrial methods of production whereby more efficient processes were developed. These included scientific principles of crop rotation and the use of the newly invented threshing machines. New varieties of root vegetables, such as carrots, swedes, parsnips and turnips, were imported for cultivation from the Low Countries, potatoes were more extensively cultivated and land which had previously been cultivated as smallholdings by peasants on large estates was enclosed by the landowners for the purposes of more efficient production. Common land was enclosed with the support of Acts of Parliament. At the same time, industrial production in the cities was increasing and many people who had been forced to leave the countryside due to the enclosures found work in factories. Although living and working conditions were appalling, the infant mortality rate gradually reduced, which meant that more people survived to reproductive age, although overall expectation of life remained low at approximately 40 years. This inevitably led to an increase in population size. Throughout the nineteenth century a range of public health measures was implemented in the cities to reduce the levels of disease caused by lack of sanitation and clean water, and inadequate housing. These improvements eventually resulted in a further reduction in the incidence of illness and premature death, life expectancy increased, and as a result population sizes continued to grow.

During this same period the colonial powers of Europe expanded their international spheres of influence, and 50 million people migrated to the New World, especially to America, Australia, New Zealand and Canada. These countries accommodated the expanding populations of Europe, and also provided new markets for the goods produced in Europe; prosperity increased all round.

The change in the structure of the populations of Europe over the 150 years between 1750 and 1900 is called the 'demographic transition'. At the beginning of this period the populations of European countries were characterized by high infant mortality rates and short life expectancy. But as wealth increased, people were able to afford better housing and better quality food and, for some, improved education, with the result that the rate of infant mortality dropped and life expectancy increased. Eventually people limited the size of their families as there was a greater chance that all the children would survive to adulthood and be able to care for their elderly parents. Population growth rates levelled out in these countries so that by 1980 the general trend was for low birth rates and low mortality rates. By the 1990s the birth rate in most of the industrialized countries fell below replacement levels. For example, the birth rate in the UK in 1993 was 1.9 children per woman of childbearing age, and in Italy the rate was 1.3 children.

The Third World and population growth

The pattern of population growth in Third World countries has been very different to that of the industrialized nations. Up until the 1960s the UK, France, Germany, the Netherlands, Belgium and Italy regarded their colonies as useful markets for the goods produced in the mother country, and also as useful sources of raw materials from which many of those goods were manufactured. The welfare of the native inhabitants was regarded as being of secondary importance, with the result that the incidence of indigenous morbidity[4] and mortality was high. This was aggravated by the fact that the colonizing powers brought with them such diseases as measles and venereal disease, which were endemic to their own countries but to which the native populations had little or no immunity. These combined factors resulted in a high birth rate in order to ensure that some children survived to adulthood.

When the colonies achieved their independence during the 1960s and 1970s, the new governments of these countries attempted to address the problem of disease, but the period post-independence was also characterized by major conflict, both international and inter-tribal, by long periods of drought, and by regular natural disasters such as flooding, tidal waves and earthquakes, and finally in the 1990s by a world recession. Upon gaining independence many Third World countries had borrowed money from the banks of the developed world and from the International Monetary Fund (IMF), so that by the 1980s they were paying more money in interest than in capital borrowed. With the reduction in international trade which characterized the 1990s, the ability of Third World countries to repay debts was also reduced. In 1980 Third World debt was US$971 billion, by 1985 it had increased to US$1250 billion, and by 1993 it was almost US$1800 billion. Because of this financial imbalance, Third World countries tend not to have the resources to spend on health services or improving the housing stock or on education, with the result that they continue to have high rates of infant mortality and consequently high levels of births.

1960s: annual increase in world population was 67 million.
1970s: annual increase in world population was 75 million.
1980s: annual increase in world population was 83 million.
1990s: annual increase in world population was 87 million.
The greatest increase in numbers is in developing countries.

World population growth rates

Human beings and their ancestors have inhabited this earth for approximately 2 million years. Figure 1.5 shows that population growth was at first very gradual, before increasing at a logarithmic rate from about 1750 onwards when the world population was estimated to be 720 million. This figure leapt to 900 million in 1800, 1.6 billion in 1900, 2.5 billion in 1950 and 5.7 billion in 1994. The United Nations has predicted that by 2050 this number will have increased to between 7.8 and 12.5 billion before growth rates level off. This reflects the pattern of population growth already apparent in industrialized countries, which as we have seen is in decline to below replacement level.[5] It should be emphasized that these predictions are based on the assumption that international trends in mortality

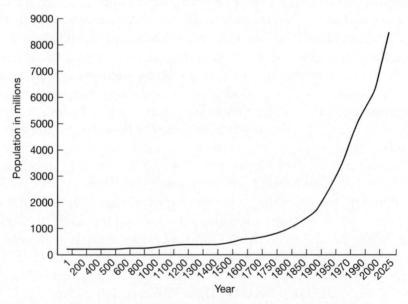

Figure 1.5 The logarithmic rate of growth of the world's population

Source: Alistair Gray and Philip Thayne, *World Health and Disease*, Open University Press (1994), p. 49.

rates will remain constant, but it is impossible to predict the future accurately. The advent of HIV and Aids now places a major question mark over the rate of population growth of many Third World countries, although there are differing opinions as to how the impact of these diseases will affect world population growth in the longer term.

The problem is, therefore, will there be enough food and water to sustain the 10 billion people projected to be alive in 2050?[6] In addition to this, these people will require space to live and work, and they will consume a massive range of resources including transport, energy and a whole range of consumables considered necessary for modern existence. Ninety-seven per cent of future population growth will occur in the Third World; will these resources be available to them? If so, will such a growth in population mean that the world's resources will be even further depleted?

The population of the UK

In 1972 the UK population was 56 million, by 1992 it was 58 million and it is predicted to grow to 61 million by 2012, and to reach a peak in 2030 of 62 million. This will be accompanied by an increase in the number of people living alone, leading to a 14 per cent increase in housing stock. If there are real increases in incomes as the Government projects, then there will be increased expenditure on housing, increased demands on goods and services and consequently upon renewable and non-renewable resources.

The problem for all government planners is to balance the demands of population growth and the change in its structure[7] and improvements in standards of living, with the reduction or minimization of consumption of natural resources, pollution and waste generation. This can only be achieved by a judicious combination of regulation and self-restraint on the part of the individual (through education).

World food production

Traditional checks on population growth have included famine, disease and war. Famine is the greatest check as it exacerbates or causes the effects of the other two. Even if it were possible to produce enough food for the 10 billion who are projected to be alive in 2050, this does not mean that it will be distributed equitably, and therefore famine will continue. Grain is used as a standard measure of food production as it supplies over half of the energy value of human food, and because it is widely used for animal feed in meat production. Between 1950 and 1983 the global production of grains increased by 3 per cent per annum, mainly due to the successes of the 'Green Revolution'.[8] This was greater than population growth rates which averaged 1.8 per cent per year, but many experts now argue that we have already achieved the maximum output that the earth's soil, water and crops can produce, and that in fact we have reached the 'carrying capacity' – that is, the maximum number of people that the world's resources can support. The peak year of production was in 1984, when grain production stood at 346 kg per head. Since then the yield rates have dropped to 341 kg in 1986 and 303 kg in 1993. This reduction in consumption per capita is equivalent to a steady rate of grain production of 1 per cent per annum; in 1984 each tonne of fertilizer yielded an extra 9 tonnes of grain whereas by 1989 this had fallen to 1.8 tonnes, a production figure which remains constant; the world's soil appears to have maximized its production levels. If the current rate of increase of global grain production – equivalent to 12 million tonnes per year – continues, then by 2020 the total world harvest will be 2.1 billion tonnes, which will need to feed a projected world population of 8.5 billion. This is equivalent to 247 kg per head. If this rate of increase continues, and if the world population does indeed increase to 10 billion, then in 2050 global grain production will have reduced to the equivalent to 244 kg per head. Given that current levels of world grain production are approximately 300 kg per head, and that it is only necessary to produce 200 kg per head to provide all the energy required for human existence, in theory there is no problem. However, even in 1998 it is estimated that 700 million people are malnourished, so if there is to be a more equitable distribution of food resources, there will need to be major changes in political will and international economic practices.

Another factor is that as countries improve their economic circumstances the amount of meat consumed per head increases. Current world meat production per capita is approximately 32 kg, and if this figure is to remain constant more grain will be required to produce animal protein. It requires 7 kg of grain to produce 1 kg of beef, 4 kg of grain to produce 1 kg of pork, 3 kg of grain to produce 1 kg of cheese, and 2 kg of grain to produce 1 kg of chicken. There are already major international imbalances between overall grain consumption per head as a result of differences in levels of meat consumption. At the bottom end of the scale is India whose current grain consumption is 200 kg per head as the majority of the population are vegetarians, and China which consumes 300 kg of grain per head. Italy, whose national diet is regarded by many authorities as being 'healthy', consumes 400 kg per head, and at the top of the scale the annual average per capita consumption of grain in the USA is 800 kg. So if there is to be a more equitable distribution of food resources, and in order to avoid major famine, disease, death and even war, there is a pressing need for many people to adopt a vegetarian diet.[9]

Agricultural land quality

Some experts estimate that the annual rate of increase of grain production will further slow to 0.5 per cent as increasingly intensive techniques of production exhaust both soil quality and water supplies. For instance, soil microbiology[10] has been seriously affected by the intensive and indiscriminate use of pesticides and monocultural[11] practices. This has resulted in a slowing down of the rate of increase of yields of wheat and rice in Pakistan, Nepal, Bangladesh and India. It is also argued that the extent to which land is made fit for production through irrigation is unsustainable; aquifers[12] are drained faster than they can be refilled, for example in the Ogallala aquifer in the US Grain Belt, and under the north China plain, and under the Punjab wheatfields, despite being fed by water which has drained from the snows of the Himalayas.

Currently 16 per cent of all agricultural land is irrigated. This produces 36 per cent of the world's grain. There is little scope to increase this as new sources of land, for example deserts, would be expensive to develop as it would be necessary to transport water very long distances, or alternatively it would require the construction of new dams which not only need major capital investment, but which would also divert water from other destinations. In addition, we have already seen that some current models of the effects of climate change as the result of global warming indicate that new areas of desert and new areas of flooded land will develop which will inevitably change the patterns of agricultural activity.

Furthermore, each year 0.5 per cent of the world's farmland – equivalent to 7 million hectares, or 24 billion tonnes – is permanently lost as a result of erosion. Erosion is caused by the action of winds and water which move topsoil from the land and deposit it in lakes, rivers and the sea. Although a natural process, erosion can be accelerated by overgrazing, the removal of natural windbreaks and soakaways for water, by deforestation and hedge removal, and by poor agricultural practices such as monoculture. Eventually this process contributes to the increase in the extent of deserts, or 'desertification', in lands which are semi-arid. The removal of tropical forests, which are major stores of water, and which also affect weather patterns, results in the reduction of rainfall in areas that already have a low rainfall. Approximately 6 million new hectares of desert are created each year. Countries affected include the USA, Australia, Brazil, Iran, India, China, Afghanistan and many African countries.

It is arguable, therefore, that a 'sustainable' population may well need to be even less than the numbers we have today, depending upon the 'carrying capacity' of the earth. Even if post-harvest losses, which currently stand at 1.3 per cent of total yield, are reduced, and if genetic engineering techniques assist in making crops resistant to pests, disease and drought, and if distribution is improved, this would still not solve the problem. It is impossible to predict whether the earth will have the capacity to feed the estimated 10 billion people in 2050 – and that is a medium estimate of population growth.

There are eighteen agricultural research centres which are funded by the Consultative Group on International Agricultural Research which includes the World Bank and the industrialized countries. These centres, which include the International Rice Research Institute (IRRI) in the Philippines and the Wheat and Maize Improvement Centre (CIMMYT) in Mexico, and which were involved in the development of the Green Revolution, are now less confident that it will be possible to create a new generation of plants that will provide enough food for 10 billion people. Moreover many experts currently consider that alternative food sources such as the sea or grazing land are already being exploited to their maximum.

Family planning

In 1984 the UN Population Conference in Mexico City concluded that the best way to reduce the rate of growth of the world's population was to improve economic growth in the poorest countries. Improved standards of living, it was argued, would trigger the 'demographic transition' experienced by the industrialized countries over the past 200 years, but this transition would be, and would need to be, far more rapid. As personal economic circumstances improve it was argued that people would perceive each additional unplanned child as a drain on family resources, and people would limit their family size by the increased use of contraception. Although the global rate of population growth had indeed reduced from 2.1 per cent in 1970 to 1.8 per cent in 1977, the rate of reduction has since slowed to 1.6 per cent per year so that by the time of the International Conference on Population and Development in Cairo in September 1994 it was realized that 'demographic transition' was a flawed model, and that a different approach would need to be made to increase the rate of use of contraception in the most rapidly increasing countries of the world.

In 1960 only 10 per cent of women of childbearing age worldwide were using contraception; today approximately 55 per cent do so. In the 1960s the average completed family size was 6.5 children; today it is 4.2. But if the target set by the International Conference on Population and Development to achieve worldwide replacement-level fertility rates by early next century is to be achieved, then contraceptive use must increase to 60 per cent of all women of childbearing age no later than by the year 2000. The experience of many countries has shown that this is possible. These countries have discovered that the best way to achieve economic development is to limit family size in order to escape from the 'poverty trap', and that wherever possible women will happily limit family size, even without the prerequisite of economic growth. For instance, despite being one of the poorest nations of the world, Bangladesh has quadrupled the use of contraceptives, and in Indonesia, a primarily Muslim country, 50 per cent of women use contraception. Other countries show different fertility patterns between localities; for instance the total population of India is currently 896 million and this is growing at the rate of approx. 17 million per year. Yet within India, in the state of Kerala, women average 1.8 children, whereas in Uttar Pradesh they average 5.1 children. India has set itself a target to reduce the national average to 2.1 children by 2010. Thailand has reduced the average family size from 6.5 in 1970 to 2.2 today; similar successes have been recorded in China, Sri Lanka, Cuba, Mexico and Colombia. Together these successes encompass every political, economic, religious and cultural philosophy.

It has been estimated that in the Third World every second birth is unplanned and every fourth birth is unwanted. The 1994 conference therefore set itself a twenty-year programme to realize four objectives in order to achieve significant reduction in global fertility rates. These were to:

1 reduce maternal, infant, and child mortality;
2 ensure improved standards of education, especially for girls;
3 provide universal access to 'reproductive health services' including family planning;
4 achieve equality between the genders.

In order to realize these objectives it was agreed that it was necessary to increase spending on healthcare and birth control in Eastern Europe and the Third World from $5 billion per annum to $17 billion by 2000, and to $21.7 billion by 2015. Should such levels of expenditure be achieved it was predicted that this could keep the growth down to 7.5 billion by 2050 instead of 10 billion. The industrialized countries agreed to increase their contribution from $800 million to $5.7 billion by the year 2000. The balance of funding was to be supplied by the Third World countries themselves. Of the $17 billion, $7 billion was specifically earmarked for 'reproductive healthcare' including family planning. This embraces a new philosophy whereby quality of care and real choice are emphasized rather than coercion. Women are to be encouraged to choose the method of contraception that is appropriate to their particular circumstances; this should improve the continuity of use of contraception and hence the success of the schemes.

The conference also predicted that after 2050 there is likely to be a downturn in world population levels. Fertility rates in many industrialized countries in Europe, the Caribbean, and China have already fallen below replacement levels. Should this be the case then the United Nations predicts that the world's population will stabilize at 8 billion by 2045, and then stabilize at a global fertility rate of 1.7 children per woman of childbearing age. Note that in order to achieve replacement levels it is necessary for every woman of childbearing age to have 2.1 children (the '.1' of a child is to allow for child mortality).

Only time will tell whether the predictions on population growth and its eventual downturn are correct, and it is heartening to see an international consensus that the potential rate of human population growth, if left unchecked, poses the potential for untold damage to the earth and its resources, and that the countries of the industrialized world have agreed to increase their contributions to population control in the Third World sevenfold; nevertheless only history will tell whether they will keep to this commitment in times of national and international economic difficulty.

The population of the world in 1999 reached 6 billion, 80 per cent of whom are located in the countries of the Third World. However, it is the actions of the 20 per cent of those who live in the industrialized world that have created major threats to the wellbeing of the global ecosystem, and which if left unchecked will continue to contribute incalculable damage to the world of the future. The 57.5 million extra people born in the Northern industrialized countries in the 1990s will consume far more of the earth's resources than the 900 million people born in the Third World. Jonathon Porritt[13] has argued that if the extra 2.6 million US citizens that are born each year continue to pump the current US per capita annual average of 20 tonnes of carbon dioxide into the atmosphere then US population growth alone will be responsible for an additional 52 million tonnes of CO_2 per year. In contrast, although the population of India grows by approx. 17 million each year, they will only add a total of 13 million tonnes of carbon dioxide to the atmosphere each year, and China with a similar annual population rate of growth of 17 million will only contribute a total of 37 million tonnes to the atmosphere. It is simple to see that the impact of the two largest countries of the world is less than that of the USA.

It is vital to understand that it is equally important to continue to persuade the industrialized countries to reduce their levels of consumption while also campaigning to improve the quality of life of those in the Third World by reducing their fertility levels, if the earth is not to exceed its carrying capacity and hence possess any chance of long-term sustainability.

The difference between the UN's largest projection of population size by 2050 of 12.5 billion, and its lowest projection of 7.8 billion is 4.7 billion people – only 1.3 billion less than are alive today. In Chapter 2 we will examine, albeit briefly, the extent to which those threats to the environment caused by such a volume of human beings are being met. It will not be hard for the reader to imagine the potential for damage to the fragile ecosystem posed by a world population of 12.5 billion, or even 10 billion.

QUESTIONS AND ISSUES FOR DISCUSSION

1 The average car in the UK travels 12,000 miles each year. If a car covering this mileage has an average petrol consumption of 35 miles per gallon, work out:
    (a) the number of tonnes of fuel that it consumes each year;
    (b) the volume of carbon dioxide that it will contribute to the atmosphere.

    For the purposes of this exercise, assume that:

    1 tonne = 100 kg;
    the petrol contains 80 per cent carbon;
    1 gallon = 5 litres;
    1 litre is equal to 0.8 kg;
    1 kilometre = five-eighths of a mile.

2 If you have a car, carry out the same exercise as in question 1 using your own car as an example.

3 If the average UK emissions of carbon dioxide are equivalent to only 2.6 per cent of total world emissions, is there any point in the UK attempting to reduce this volume?

4 'The problem for all government planners is to balance the demands of population growth and the change in its structure and improvements in standards of living, with the reduction or minimization of consumption of

natural resources, pollution and waste generation. This can only be achieved by a judicious combination of regulation and self-restraint on the part of the individual (through education)' (quoted from p. 21). Is it possible to educate people to reduce their consumption of energy, or to produce less waste? What is the position in other countries?

5 The Cairo Conference prioritized the education of girls as a necessary component in population stabilization. Discuss this issue. What benefits in terms of population stabilization could this achieve?

6 Why is 'gender equality' of prime importance if the targets listed on p. 25 are to be achieved?

7 What causes acid rain? What harm does it do to the environment and why is this seen as a problem?

8 What function does the ozone layer serve? What are the current concerns about it? What are the implications if the concerns of the scientific community turn out to be correct? What are the major causes of damage to the ozone layer? How can this damage be reduced? What commitments have Western governments made to limit the damage?[14]

9 In order to combat the effects of acid deposition, lakes have been limed, attempts have been made to breed acid-resistant fish and 'scrubbers' have been installed in the chimneys of power stations. Comment on these activities.

10 As it is not possible to accurately predict the future, scientists have to rely on computer models to assess the possible pace and impact of global warming. Some people have argued that there are too many uncertainties and that therefore we should not act on these gloomy predictions. Comment on this attitude.

Patterns of energy use in the industrialized world:

Oil	37 per cent
Coal	26 per cent
Gas	18 per cent
Other (hydro-electric, nuclear and biomass)	19 per cent

Patterns of energy use in the Third World:

Oil	18 per cent
Coal	24 per cent
Biomass	36 per cent
Other (hydro-electric, gas and nuclear)	22 per cent

Notes

1 Cited in a book review by Norman Myers, *Times Higher Education Supplement*, 2 September 1994, pp. 20–1.
2 In this instance, a 'sink' is a term used to mean a 'store'. See the section on the carbon cycle (pp. 7–8) for further details.
3 See Chapter 2 for a more extensive discussion of the effects of CFCs on the ozone layer and what steps are being taken to curtail their use.
4 Morbidity means the frequency of occurrence of illness.
5 Replacement levels are the levels of births in a population that will permit the population number to remain stable. This is usually taken to be 2.1 children per woman of childbearing age.
6 The figure of 10 billion is the medium projection by the UN and will be used for our purposes in this book.
7 All industrialized countries face the prospect of increased numbers of elderly people supported by reduced numbers of young people – an inverted 'population pyramid'.
8 The 'Green Revolution': new crop varieties were developed that required extensive quantities of water and fertilizer in order to provide extra yields; today water is a more scarce commodity.
9 The good news is that a number of studies have shown that not only do vegetarians live longer than people who eat meat, but that many of the nutrients present in fruit and vegetables can act as a protective factor against degenerative diseases, including cancers.
10 Soil microbiology: the presence in the soil of beneficial creatures including bacteria and worms. These play a major part in the breakdown of waste plant and animal matter and improve soil quality.
11 Monoculture: the same crop is produced on the same soil year in and year out. Nutrients are provided in the form of fertilizers.
12 Aquifer: a water store which is formed by the accumulation of water draining through the top layers of soil and porous rock to accumulate in natural underground caverns formed of non-porous material.
13 Cited in Paul Harrison, *The Third Revolution: Environment, Population, and a Sustainable World*, London: Tauris/WWF, 1992.
14 To assist you in answering this question see Chapter 3 on refrigeration.

Further reading

Daniel D. Chiras, *Environmental Science – Action for a Sustainable Future*, 4th edition, Redwood City, California: Benjamin Cummings Publishing Co., 1994.

Department of the Environment, *This Common Inheritance: UK Annual Report 1996*, London: HMSO, 1996.

Francis Graham-Smith (ed.), *Population – The Complex Reality: A Report of the Population Summit of the World's Scientific Academies*, London: The Royal Society, 1994.

Stanley P. Johnson, *World Population – Turning the Tide: Three Decades of Progress*, Graham and Trotman, 1994.

Kerstin Lindhal-Kiessling and Hans Landburg (eds), *Population: Economic Development and the Environment*, Oxford: Oxford University Press, 1994.

New Scientist. This excellent weekly magazine contains numerous articles on many of the issues covered in this chapter.

CHAPTER 2

National and international action

In order to protect the environment, the precautionary approach shall be widely applied by States according to their capabilities. Where there are threats of serious or irreversible damage, lack of full scientific certainty shall not be used as a reason for postponing cost effective measures to prevent environmental damage.

Principle 15 of the Rio Declaration[1]

OBJECTIVES

1 To identify the most significant international conventions and treaties which have addressed the issues outlined in Chapter 1.
2 To demonstrate an understanding of how those treaties to which the UK and EU are signatory have been incorporated into law.
3 To assess the efficacy of these treaties and conventions and/or their potential to address today's environmental issues.
4 To describe and evaluate the concept of 'sustainability'.

INTRODUCTION

In Chapter 1 we identified the main challenges to the environment that scientists regard as today's greatest threats. Although these threats and their potential to cause permanent damage to the earth's delicate ecosystem are alarming, in most cases enough evidence has now accumulated to indicate that this is not scaremongering on the part of scientists and environmentalists. As a consequence, in the past twenty years many governments have taken some action to reduce or minimize the environmental impact that their countries' activities make. This chapter will examine a number of major international conventions and treaties which have addressed these issues. In some instances the way in which the UK has implemented international agreements into national law, and any inherent weaknesses of such a system, are highlighted.

Much new terminology which has been incorporated into everyday vocabulary has been generated as the result of these international gatherings: such terms as 'sustainable development' and 'renewable resources', and, to a lesser extent, 'Agenda 21'. At the end of this chapter we will define and discuss the meaning of some of these terms.

INTERNATIONAL ACTION

The United Nations

The United Nations Environment Programme (UNEP) was established in 1973 as the environmental voice of the UN. Its main concerns are water, and the implementation of conventions on biodiversity, climate change, desertificaton and ozone. It also monitors issues to do with wildlife conservation and habitat, freshwater resources, ocean and coastal area preservation, health and chemical safety, biological diversity and technology, environmental law and ethics. The agency's programmes are mainly funded by voluntary contributions from UN member nations; in recent years its budget has dropped from US$20 million in 1994/95 to US$3.5 million for 1997/98. UNEP funds World Environment Day.

The Brundtland Report

In 1987 the World Commission on Environment and Development to the United Nations (UNCED) was established. This commission is well known primarily for publishing the Brundtland Report which defined sustainable development as 'development that meets the needs of the present without compromising the ability of future generations to meet their own needs'. This has been interpreted as meaning that each generation must rely on the use of renewable resources, and to reuse and recycle waste materials before considering taking 'virgin' resources from the earth which cannot be replaced. In this way we must adopt a way of life which passes on the earth's resources undiminished to the next generation. This encompasses the concepts of 'stewardship' of the earth, and living within its 'carrying capacity'.

The key objectives of sustainability include:

1 reviving economic growth so that it has a reduced impact on the environment by using less materials and energy;
2 meeting essential needs for jobs, food, energy, water and sanitation;
3 ensuring a sustainable level of population;
4 conserving and enhancing our natural resource base;
5 reorienting technology and managing risk;
6 merging ecological and economic considerations in decision-making.

The Montreal Protocol

The Montreal Protocol on substances that deplete the ozone layer was signed in 1987 in response to the evidence of damage to the ozone layer. The signatories agreed to reduce the production and consumption of chemicals harmful to ozone. These included CFCs, halons, carbon tetrachloride, '1,1,1 Trichloroethane', hydrobromofluorocarbons (HBFCs), hydrochlorofluorocarbons (HCFCs), and methyl bromide. It was agreed to limit CFC emissions by 2000 to 1990 levels, and CFC production was to cease by the end of 1995. The Netherlands committed itself to an extra saving of 5 per cent by 2005, and Germany an additional 20 per cent.

At a subsequent meeting in Copenhagen, Denmark, 70 nations agreed to phase out CFC production by 1996. Western countries agreed to phase out production earlier than developing countries, who do not have to do so until 2010. India, China and South Korea are major producers of halons.

CFCs were used in the manufacture of foam to insulate fridges and also in the coolant; they have contributed to 24 per cent of the increased greenhouse effect (global warming). HFCs are similar in chemical construction and function to CFCs but they have a global warming potential half that of CFCs. They do not damage the ozone layer to the same extent since they do not contain harmful chlorine gas. Nevertheless they remain a significant greenhouse gas. The damage they cause occurs when the foam degenerates and/or the coolant leaks, thereby contaminating the atmosphere.

Differing responses to the Montreal Protocol

In 1993 the United States published its global warming action plan, whereby HCFCs were only to be permitted where no alternatives existed. In contrast, the UK decided to work with voluntary agreements whereby HCFCs will be used where there is no possibility of emissions, and no safe alternatives.

'Caring for the Earth'

In 1991 the IUCN (World Conservation Union), UNEP (United Nations Environment Programme) and WWF (World Wide Fund for Nature) launched a joint programme, 'Caring for the Earth', which outlined a strategy for sustainable living. The strategy was developed in collaboration with a range of UN and non-UN organizations including FAO (the Food and Agriculture Organization), UNDP (UN Development Programme), UNESCO, UNFPA (UN

Population Fund), WHO, the UN Centre for Human Settlements, the Asian Development Bank, the International Labour Office, the World Bank, the World Meteorological Organization, the World Resources Institute, the Secretariat of the Organization of American States, the International Institute for Environment and Development, and the Istituto Superiore di Sanita. It is aimed at policy-makers who make environmental decisions, including governments, politicians, company executives, senior civil servants, leading citizens and 'other citizens in communities and settlements everywhere'. As the policy document states, 'Caring for the Earth is everyone's business.'

The policy addresses three major points:

1 Principles for sustainable living
   - Building a sustainable society
   - Respecting and caring for the community of life
   - Improving the quality of human life
   - Conserving the earth's vitality and diversity
   - Keeping within the earth's carrying capacity
   - Changing personal attitudes and practices
   - Enabling communities to care for their own environments
   - Providing a national framework for integrating development and conservation
   - Creating a global alliance
2 Additional actions for sustainable living
   - Energy
   - Business, industry and commerce
   - Human settlements
   - Farm and range lands
   - Forest lands
   - Fresh waters
   - Oceans and coastal areas
3 Implementation and follow-up
   - Implementing the strategy

Each section addresses in detail the issues for sustainability and makes suggestions as to how these can be taken into account by policy-makers.[2]

The Rio Earth Summit

As a result of the publication and dissemination of the Brundtland Report, over 50 countries, including the UK, had publicly supported it by the end of 1988 and the United Nations passed a resolution which called for a UN

Conference on Environment and Development (UNCED). This conference, the Earth Summit, was held in Rio de Janeiro, Brazil, in June 1992.

The Earth Summit was the first international conference to be attended by heads of state: over 120 world leaders attended, and 150 countries were represented. A number of agreements were reached which were to form the basis of future action. These included the 'Rio Declaration on Environment and Development' which set out 27 principles for the achievement of sustainable development.[3] These principles were then incorporated into 'Agenda 21'[4], an extensive list of measures aimed at governments, local authorities and NGOs (non-government organizations). Of particular significance is that Agenda 21 required local authorities to adopt a partnership approach in order to achieve progress at a local level by 1996.

Unfortunately, five years after the Rio conference, some would argue that international commitment to and awareness of the concept of sustainable development has changed, and maybe even weakened. The perception is that world leaders are more concerned with regional conflicts, the flurries in the world financial markets and unemployment. The concept of sustainable development is no longer on the main government agendas.

The World Population Conference, Cairo, Egypt, 1994

The concerns and agreements reached at this conference are discussed in the section on population in Chapter 1, pp. 24–6.

The Kyoto Conference, Japan, December 1997

At the Kyoto Conference the participants agreed certain targets to reduce their countries' emissions of greenhouse gases. The United Nations Framework Convention on Climate Change protocol, signed by 159 countries, also established the principle that nations could buy and sell 'emissions permits', and scheduled a climate conference to be held in Buenos Aires in November 1998 to agree the rules for this.

At Kyoto the European Union (EU) made a collective agreement to cut greenhouse gas emissions by 8 per cent from 1990 levels by 2012; however, national targets ranged from a 25 per cent reduction for Germany and Austria and a 10 per cent reduction for the UK to a 40 per cent increase for Portugal. France and Italy agreed to stabilize their emissions. There have since been discussions within the member states to renegotiate these targets.

It is interesting to note that the agreement on global warming excluded aircraft emissions as the negotiators disagreed on how to allocate national responsibility for emissions during international flights.

The USA did not ratify the Kyoto protocol until November 1998 due to the Republican majority in the Senate blocking it, and demanding a pre-condition that the developing nations also agree to reduce their emissions. The protocol gives the Ukraine and Russia a large emission allowance, and because their economies are in a state of collapse they are unlikely to fulfil these quotas. The Republican-dominated Senate agreed to ratify the protocol under the condition that the USA could 'purchase' this excess emission allowance.

Over and above this, the UK has set itself an even tougher target to reduce its carbon dioxide emissions by 20 per cent by 2010.

Buenos Aires, Argentina, November 1998

At this conference in Buenos Aires in 1998, 180 countries met to agree the finer details of the Kyoto protocol. There was much dissent, however, as the developing countries, especially Brazil, China, India and Mexico, argued that they could not afford to comply with the proposed cuts in emissions if they were to continue their programmes of industrial development. Indeed India, whose population is growing at the rate of approx. 17 million a year, needs to create 4 million new jobs each year just to keep up with this increase in numbers. The developing countries insisted that the developed countries should first reduce their emissions in accordance with the set timetables, before any discussions about the reductions of developing countries could take place. Currently developing countries are exempt from the Kyoto protocol's greenhouse gas emissions reduction requirements.

The conference also discussed the Clean Development Mechanism (CDM) which will allow industrialized nations to finance clean air projects in developing countries. One suggestion is for companies to invest in renewable energy projects, such as wind or solar power, in the developing world. This should result in reductions in emissions of greenhouse gases in those nations which do not have formal limits under the Kyoto protocol. The companies involved would receive certificates indicating the quantity of carbon dioxide the clean air projects have prevented from entering the atmosphere. These could eventually be sold to power companies in the industrialized world who need to emit more carbon dioxide than they are permitted under the present Kyoto agreement.

For example, it might cost a renewable energy project US$25 to prevent one tonne of carbon dioxide entering the atmosphere, but the certificates could be sold for $30 per tonne. It is envisaged that a scheme such as this would reduce the costs of implementing the Kyoto targets. It has also been estimated that the CDM could have an annual turnover of US$17 billion.[5]

Another initiative is to finance tree planting in Third World countries to make up for deforestation. Forests act as 'carbon sinks' and the loss of trees leads not only to the release of more carbon dioxide into the atmosphere but also to the loss of a valuable resource to contain it.

The CDM scheme is scheduled to begin in 2000 and on the surface it appears to be an excellent plan. But it has been criticized as being impossible to measure its effectiveness. For instance, how can the savings be substantiated? If a country announces that it has abandoned plans to build a coal-fired power station in favour of a wind farm, how do we know that it was serious about the first project in the first place, and that the announcement is not a plan to earn tradeable (and valuable) carbon credits? In the same way, how permanent does a forest have to be in order to earn credits? Would the credits have to be returned when the forest is felled? What about the impact of forest fires? What is the liability of purchasers of carbon credits if their project fails? These issues and other problems are to be discussed over the next few years.

ACTION BY THE EUROPEAN UNION

Since the 1970s there has been extensive activity on the part of the European Community/Union in the area of environmental protection; more than one hundred items of legislation have been enacted. The rationale behind this is that

- the wellbeing of the Union's citizens is affected by the state of their environment;
- as pollution of air and water has no national boundaries, regulation needs to be implemented at an EU level;
- in order to assure a common market in goods and services it is important to standardize regulations across the Union.

The Single European Act of 1986 consolidated the Community's environmental legislation; three articles (Articles 130r, 130s and 130t) establish the aims and objectives of environmental legislation: 'to preserve, protect and improve the quality of the environment, to contribute towards protecting human health, and to ensure a prudent and rational utilisation of natural resources' (Stanbrook and Hooper, 1995). The principle of EU environmental action is that it should be preventative, it should occur at the source, and the polluter should pay.

The EC Treaty requires that the Community's other policies, in particular the Common Agricultural Policy, take account of the need to protect the environment, in consideration with the latest scientific and technical data, the environmental condition of the various regions of the EU, the potential costs and benefits of action – or lack of action – to protect the environment, and the need to ensure the balanced economic and social development of all the regions. Member states are permitted to take more stringent action if they wish provided this is compatible with the EC Treaty.

If the EU is a signatory to an international Treaty then its provisions are implemented in the form of a Directive or Regulation which requires each member state to legislate accordingly, for example in the case of the Montreal Protocol. Responsibility for the environment comes under the Directorate-General XI (Environment, Consumer Protection and Nuclear Safety) which is divided into four Directorates: general and international affairs; environmental instruments; nuclear safety, civil protection and safety of industrial installations; and quality of the environment and natural resources.

The European Environment Agency

Council Regulation 1210/90 of 7 May 1990 established the European Environment Agency (EEA) and the European Environment Information and Observation Network (EEION). The EEA is an EU-wide body with membership also open to countries outside the Union. Its role is to monitor the state of the environment across the EU, with the objective of providing 'the Community and the Member States with the technical and scientific support to allow them to achieve the goals of environmental protection and improvement'. The EEA and the EEION

- provide the EU and member states with information;
- monitor the results of EU action regarding the environment;
- develop techniques of environmental modelling and forecasting;
- ensure the comparability of information provided by member states and the EU regarding the environment.

Priority will be given to

- air quality and atmospheric emissions;
- water quality, pollutants and water resources;
- the state of the soil and of vegetation;
- land use and resources.

Other Directives relevant to the subject matter of this book include those on waste management, including treatment; recycling; water and atmospheric pollution; noise and dangerous chemical substances; and packaging. All of these have at least an indirect impact on the business activities of the hospitality industry.

Since the Kyoto agreement, the EU has been examining the ways in which the transport industry, one of the major causes of greenhouse gas emissions, can be encouraged to reduce its contribution. After negotiations with leading car manufacturers a voluntary agreement was reached to cut carbon dioxide emissions from new cars by 25 per cent by 2008; this represents a reduction of 140 gm per kilometre. The EU's eventual target is 120 gm per kilometre. There are also EU plans to introduce a new car labelling scheme to indicate which models have low carbon dioxide emissions, and there is talk of introducing a Union-wide carbon tax on vehicles.

ACTION BY THE UK GOVERNMENT

Once a country has signed an international agreement the way in which it chooses to implement the agreement is its own choice. Factors that contribute to this include the political and cultural characteristics of the country and also the political doctrine of the government. A Conservative government was signatory to the Montreal Protocol, as well as to the Climate Change Convention, the Biodiversity Convention and Agenda 21. A distinctive characteristic of the Conservative Party is its belief in the virtue of market forces rather than regulation and government 'involvement'. Certainly in the 1990s the Government started a rolling programme of deregulation, arguing that the extent of petty regulation actually impeded the commercial world. Regulation was to be used only as a final resort. Instead, their policy was to employ a combination of 'economic instruments' (taxes) and voluntary agreements as powerful incentives to encourage both business and individuals to modify their behaviour.

> Economic instruments can work by encouraging efficiency, introducing innovation, providing flexibility, generating information about environmental damages and costs, and by providing additional public revenue.
>
> *Sustainable Development: The UK Strategy*, 1994

How can 'economic instruments' be used to encourage people and businesses to act in a more environmentally responsible manner? The Government suggested, in its policy document titled 'Sustainable Development', that it would consider imposing charges on emissions from industry, including water pollution, placing a levy on environmentally damaging products, on waste disposal (this was introduced in the November 1994 Budget) and also on the abstraction of water. Other options included the introduction of deposit refund schemes, the use of subsidies to encourage Green practices, the issuing of permits to industry allowing the pollution of the air or water, or the abstraction of water, and as a final recourse, the concept of 'legal liability'.

Each option would be considered on the grounds of its potential effectiveness in changing behaviour while at the same time ensuring that it would not take away a business's competitive edge. The market would then reflect the true cost of environmental damage.

An example of environmental taxation: carbon dioxide

In February 1994 the UK Government predicted that there would be an estimated annual increase in the emission of carbon (in the form of carbon dioxide) of 10 million tonnes. It forecast that an increase in petrol duties would reduce this by 2.5 million tonnes, and that an increase in VAT would lead to a reduction in energy use by central and local government of 1 million tonnes, efficiency improvements by business of 2.5 million tonnes, and also a reduction in domestic production of carbon dioxide by 4 million tonnes. This would stabilise the emissions at 1994 levels and leave room to reduce emissions still further by education and increased technological efficiency.

Even at the stage of discussing its options, and in the light of its overriding belief in reducing the burden of regulation on business and industry, the Conservative Government conceded that in the immediate term it might well be necessary to use a combination of regulation and fiscal incentives to bring about change in attitudes and actions.

When the Labour Party won the General Election in May 1997 it was on an election promise of, *inter alia*, environmental improvement. A new government department, Department of the Environment, Transport and the Regions, headed by the Deputy Prime Minister John Prescott, was created. The inclusion of such previously disparate government departments under one titular head indicated the importance of taking an integrated overview of environmental development; no longer were government departments to fight amongst themselves or to create conflicting policies in terms of the environment.

To date the Labour Government has issued consultation documents, discussion papers and White Papers but no serious legislation has been enacted. The Transport White Paper was finally published in summer 1998 after a number of delays, and there was disappointment that its provisions did not find a place in the Queen's Speech later that year.

In 1994 the Government published its response to the Rio Summit in its report 'Climate Change: The UK Programme'.[6] It included a discussion on the implications for the UK of climate change, biodiversity and sustainable forestry, and acknowledged that there was a need to change attitudes 'throughout the nation'.

In 1994, a Government Panel on Sustainable Development was appointed to identify problems and to monitor progress. All government ministries had access to it and its first report, published in 1995, made recommendations on the following issues:[7]

- environmental pricing and economic instruments
- depletion of fish stocks
- the depletion of the ozone layer
- technology transfer
- reform of the Common Agricultural Policy
- climate change.

The UK agreed at the Kyoto conference to produce 10 per cent of its electricity from renewable sources by 2010, and in summer 1998 a review of renewable energy policy took place. Table 2.1 indicates how recent advances in technology have made 'alternative' sources far more competitive, although massive investments would need to be made before wind and wave power could generate electricity on a large-scale basis.

Table 2.1 Current prices of alternative energy compared with conventional sources, 1998, in pence per kWh

Gas	2.5
Wave	2.6
Wind	3.0
Coal	4.0
Nuclear	4.5

Source: G. MacKerron, SPRU,[8] cited in *New Scientist*, 16 May 1998.

UK legislation

The Environmental Protection Act 1990

The Environmental Protection Act rationalized various legislation relating to the environment that had been introduced over the last hundred years. It strictly controls all emissions to air, land and water, and embodies the principles of 'Best Available Techniques Not Entailing Excessive Cost' (BATNEEC) and 'Integrated Pollution Control' (IPC). It places a 'duty of care' obligation on industry and local authorities, and gives a detailed list of all those activities which are subject to its regulation, and thus require permission to emit into the environment. This will only be given if the BATNEEC principle has been applied. The objective of IPC is to ensure that the 'Best Practicable Environmental Option' (BPEO) is chosen.

The regulatory authorities, usually the Local Authority, the Water Authority or the National Rivers Authority, have the power to impose enforcement notices on non-compliers, or even a prohibition notice if the pollutant is serious. There is also an allowance for prosecution, fines and/or imprisonment of the person or persons responsible.

Issues of direct relevance to the hospitality industry include the following:

- Landowners have a statutory duty to keep public land litter free.
- Anyone who causes litter faces a potential fine of up to £1000.
- There is a legal requirement that any commercial premises employing a private contractor to dispose of rubbish must ensure that it is disposed of in a 'healthy' manner and that contractors are registered with the Local Licensing Authority.
- There is usually a charge made for the disposal of commercial waste.
- There is a daily fine for every day any nuisance persists, e.g. atmospheric discharge from boilers or smells.
- An environmental health officer can serve a statutory nuisance order on an offender.

DEFINITIONS

Renewable resources

A term applied to resources that are limitless, such as the energy from the sun, wind and sea. Current examples include the generation of electricity by wind farms, which is growing at 13 per cent per annum worldwide, or by hydro-power in countries with a rainy and hilly environment. The use of solar panels to heat water, and of photovoltaic panels to directly produce electricity, are becoming more feasible as technology improves and prices drop. Other uses of renewable resources include the growing of wood for coppicing, which is then burnt to produce electricity, the active design of new buildings to harness passive solar energy, and the use of 'biogas' which is the product of the biological breakdown of human and animal waste for fuel.

Agenda 21

An action plan for the twenty-first century that was endorsed at UNCED in Rio in 1992.

'Pollutor pays' principle

This principle was adopted by OECD countries as long ago as 1972. It means that if a product or process is likely to damage the environment then it is the producer or user rather than society in general who should pay the costs of prevention, or the elimination of the nuisances it generates.

It is designed to encourage potential polluters to minimize or avoid the impact of their activities on the environment. If goods or services were to cost too high a price in the eyes of the consumer as a result of the imposition of environmental taxes or 'permits to pollute', then the poor sales figures would encourage the 'polluter' to address the root causes of the pollution.

Industry Case Study

The Danish town of Kalundborg was designed so that steam from the local power station directly heats a number of industrial buildings and homes. The smoke emissions from the power station are minimized as the ash in the smoke is retrieved for road building, and the calcium sulphate is used for plasterboard manufacture.

The petrol refinery is heated by the power station steam. The refinery supplies gas (a by-product of petrol refining) to the company which makes the plasterboard, and water (another by-product) to the power station for cooling. Yet another by-product, sulphur, is sold to a manufacturer of sulphuric acid. The local fish farm (also heated by steam from the power station) supplies sludge for agricultural fertilizers.

QUESTIONS AND ISSUES FOR DISCUSSION

1 What is the Montreal Protocol? What happened in Rio in June 1992? What is the Brundtland Report?

2 What is the concept of 'sustainability'? Is it achievable? Is it possible to create a 'sustainable' society?

3 What are the implications for the hospitality industry if legislation and consumer power militate in favour of Green issues?

4 A report by the OECD in 1991 argued that in order to reduce emissions of greenhouse gases by 20 per cent from their present level a carbon tax of

US$250 per tonne would be required in Europe, US$400 in the USA and US$700 in Eastern Europe (*OECD Economic Studies*, Spring 1991, no. 16). This would mean doubling petrol prices and quintupling the price of coal. Comment on this.

5 What political considerations would a government take into account when deciding whether to implement the options for encouraging both business and individuals to adopt more environmentally responsible actions? Can you find any examples of where the Government burnt its fingers in this respect in the mid-1990s?

6 Obtain a copy of the Transport White Paper published by the Government in 1998. What implications for the hospitality industry might this have if all the intentions were to be implemented?

7 At the Kyoto conference in Japan in 1997 the principle of 'emissions permits' was agreed. Comment on this.

Notes

1 Principle 15 of the Rio Declaration, United Nations Conference on the Environment, 1992.
2 *Caring for the Earth – A Strategy for Sustainable Living*, Gland, Switzerland: IUCN/UNEP/WWF, 1991.
3 The 'Rio Declaration on Environment and Development', 1992.
4 *Agenda 21 – Action Plan for the Next Century*, endorsed at UNCED, 1992.
5 Author not named, 'Green futures', *New Scientist*, 21 November 1998, p. 16.
6 Department of the Environment, *Climate Change: The UK Programme*, London: HMSO, 1994.
7 Department of the Environment, *British Government Panel on Sustainable Development: First Report*, January 1995.
8 Science Policy Research Unit, University of Sussex.

Further reading

Agenda 21 – Action Plan for the Next Century, endorsed at UNCED conference 1992.

Commission of the EC, *Towards Sustainability: A European Community Programme of Policy and Action in Relation to the Environment and Sustainable Development (The EC Fifth Environment Action Programme)*, Cm(92) 32/11 Final, 1992.

Department of the Environment, *The UK Environment*, London: HMSO, 1992.

Department of the Environment, *Making Markets Work for the Environment*, London: HMSO, 1993.

Department of the Environment, *Sustainable Development: The UK Strategy*, London: HMSO, 1994.

Department of the Environment, *Climate Change: The UK Programme*, London: HMSO, 1994.

The Rio Declaration on Environment and Development, 1992.

Stanbrook and Hooper, *A Business Guide to European Community Legislation*, 2nd edn., Chichester: Chancery Law Publishing, 1995.

The World Commission on Environment and Development, *Our Common Future* (the 'Brundtland Report'), Oxford: Oxford University Press, 1987.

Part 2
The hospitality industry

CHAPTER 3

Refrigeration

The large ecological issues – the greenhouse effect, the disappearing ozone layer, and sustainable utilisation of tropical forests – are tasks facing humankind as a whole. Our goal should now be to make the 1990s a decade of rapid social, economic, and environmental co-operation rather than confrontation.

Gro Harlem Brundtland [1]

OBJECTIVES

1 To identify those refrigerants that have global warming potential.
2 To identify the steps taken by the refrigeration industry to select alternative refrigerants which have a minimal environmental impact.
3 To outline steps so as to minimize energy use and cost when using refrigeration.

INTRODUCTION

In Chapter 1 we discussed the problem of the destruction of the ozone layer which is located in the stratosphere between 7 and 30 miles above the earth. Its major beneficial role is that it acts as a screen for ultraviolet light, which in excess can cause skin cancer, blindness and damage to crops. Ozone is an alternative form of oxygen. A number of refrigerants, the most notorious being CFCs (chlorofluorocarbons), but also HCFCs (hydrochlorofluoro-carbons), halons and bromines, destroy the ozone layer; collectively they are referred to as ODS (Ozone Depleting Substances). In addition those which contain chlorine are also contributors to global warming because they absorb infra-red radiation from the earth's surface which would nor-mally be lost into space. Unfortunately these gases tend to have a long life and the effects of their use today will last for many decades. This chapter will discuss the issues that challenge the manufacturers of refrigeration and air-conditioning equipment and consider the solutions which they have arrived at.

The hospitality industry would be lost without the wide availability of refrigeration that is in extensive use in all businesses. From sophisticated air-conditioning units, chilled counters and display units, deep freezers, fridges and minibars to ice-making machines, the industry is heavily dependent on these machines to provide the quality of product and service and also the safety that customers require.

A BRIEF LOOK AT REFRIGERATION CHEMISTRY

There are only eight elements which have the potential to be used as refrigerants: oxygen, carbon, nitrogen, hydrogen, chlorine, sulphur, bromine and fluorine. These have been used in a variety of chemical combinations to create a range of coolants. None of these are entirely satisfactory; some are toxic, some are inflammable, and others are unstable as refrigerants.

Nearly all modern systems are of the vapour-compression type. Each system is tightly sealed, and if no leakage occurs, the same refrigerant will remain for the life of the unit. The use of absorption refrigeration has declined to the point that it is largely limited to air-conditioning applications in large-size units.

THE REFRIGERANT DILEMMA

A number of refrigerants are currently in use, including CFCs, HFCs, ammonia and hydrocarbons. The refrigerant liquid circulates in a sealed system and removes heat from the food in the cavity; it then changes into a gas before once more condensing into a liquid. The circulation of the refrigerant keeps the unit at a predetermined temperature. As long as it is securely contained the refrigerant doesn't present a problem; it is only when it escapes that it poses a hazard. This normally occurs during routine service visits, or if the unit develops a leak, or when the cabinet and motor are scrapped. It has been estimated that probably as much as 40 per cent of all CFC emissions in the UK are due to these factors. However, emission monitoring equipment is now sensitive enough to detect leakages as low as 14 grams per year.

CFCs were first used in the 1930s and at that time they were regarded as a major breakthrough in the technology of refrigeration as they are extremely stable. This means that they do not transform themselves into other compounds by reacting with other chemicals in the environment. At that time scientists were unable to predict the impact these chemicals would have on the environment. By 1988 the world production of CFCs had reached a peak of 1250 tonnes; by 1993 this had declined to 510 tonnes as the result of ratification of the 1987 Montreal Protocol. However, the use of stored and recycled CFCs is still permitted for maintenance purposes, and as they have become more scarce a thriving international black market has grown up. This means that equipment can be used for as long as a refrigerant is obtainable, although older equipment is estimated to lose 8–15 per cent of its refrigerant annually compared to 2 per cent in newer models.

As a signatory to the Montreal Protocol the UK Government agreed to phase out the manufacture of CFCs and their use in new refrigeration by the end of 1995, a pledge which was incorporated into national legislation in Section 33 of the Environmental Protection Act, 1990. It has been estimated that more than 21,000 tonnes of CFCs are locked away in refrigeration in the UK alone. Stocks of CFC refrigerants will still be available for many years, as they will be recycled from old equipment, although the costs of servicing elderly equipment will become increasingly high as replacement (recycled) CFCs become more scarce. It will eventually be more practical to replace the refrigeration than to repair or service it, or to adapt it to run on CFC-free gases, especially if the energy efficiency rating of the equipment is also calculated; a new freezer or fridge can pay for itself in a couple of years on energy savings alone.[2] Another option, if the fridge cabinet is still in good condition, is to exchange the refrigeration unit for a unit designed to run on alternative coolants to CFCs; this would cost only 20 per cent of the cost of a totally new cabinet and motor.

It is the stable nature of CFCs that causes the problem. Because they do not react with other chemicals in the environment when released into the atmosphere, they reach the stratosphere unchanged, after a journey that can take as long as ten years. Once in the stratosphere they react with ultraviolet light which at that height is unscreened and therefore very concentrated, and the chlorine of which they are made up is released. The chlorine molecules join with oxygen molecules to form chlorine monoxide which then creates more chlorine. It has been estimated that one molecule of chlorine can destroy 100,000 molecules of oxygen in the ozone layer over a period of 100 years.[3]

Not only have CFCs been utilized as refrigerants, but because they are extremely good insulators they are also locked up in insulated polyurethane foam which is used to insulate the refrigerator cabinet. These are released as the foam degenerates, a process which can take decades. This means that abandoned refrigeration in landfill sites will continue to release CFCs into the atmosphere for an indefinite period.

There are many different types of CFCs, and they have different effects upon the ozone layer. Unfortunately the two CFCs that were most widely used by the manufacturers of refrigerators – the refrigerant CFC 12 and the insulation material CFC 11 – are highly damaging (see Table 3.1 for CFC 12 details).

Table 3.1 The potential damage to the ozone layer and contribution to global warming of a number of refrigerants in common use

Refrigerant	ODP	GWP	Life in the atmosphere, in years
CFC 12	1	8500	130
HCFC 22	0.055	1700	15
HFC 134a	0	1300	15
HFC 404A	0	3748	>48
Ammonia (known as R 717)	0	0	<1
CARE 10 (known as HC 600a)	0	<3	<1
CARE 30 (a blend of HC 600a and HC 290)	0	<3	<1
CARE 40 (known as HC 290)	0	<3	<1
CARE 50 (a blend of HC 290 and HC 170)	0	<3	<1
HFC 407C	0	1610	>33
HFC 410A	0	1890	>33

Key:
ODP: Ozone Depletion Potential (as defined in Council Regulation (EC) No. 303/94, R11 = 1).
GWP: Global Warming Potential (based on 100-year integration time horizon, defined in the Intergovernmental Panel for Climate Change (IPCC) Scientific Assessment, 1994, carbon dioxide = 1).

Signatories to the Montreal Protocol met in Copenhagen in November 1992 to review its provisions. As a result certain dates for phase outs of the use of CFCs were advanced and HCFCs were added to the list. In December 1992 EC ministers confirmed the reformulated timetable as follows:

CFCs
By 1 January 1994: 75 per cent cut from 1986 levels of production.
1 January 1996: total phase out.

HCFCs
1 January 1996: production capped.
1 January 2004: 35 per cent cut.
1 January 2010: 65 per cent cut.
1 January 2015: 90 per cent cut.
1 January 2020: 99.5 per cent cut.
1 January 2030: total phase out.

Table 3.1 shows that HCFCs do less damage than CFCs to the ozone layer but that they still contribute to global warming. HCFCs and HFCs are less damaging because the hydrogen that they contain contributes to their breakdown in the lower atmosphere, which means little or none reaches the ozone layer. Although the HFC R134a is an ozone-friendly refrigerant, it still has a global warming potential 1300 times more powerful than carbon dioxide, and should be recycled rather than released into the atmosphere.

Denmark plans to be HFC free by 2007, and Greenpeace is exerting huge pressure on countries to act similarly. HCFCs and HFCs should be regarded only as transient refrigerants.

HFC (hydrofluorocarbon): It doesn't contain chlorine and is therefore not a danger to the ozone layer. But it has high global warming potential.
CFC and HCFC (chlorofluorocarbon and hydrochlorofluorocarbon): Both contain chlorine and therefore damage the ozone layer and have global warming potential.

ALTERNATIVES TO CFCS

The new generation of environmentally-friendly refrigerators and freezers are based on different refrigeration systems to the old style, and require both new service methods and refrigerant gases.

The German company Bosch in 1994 became the first fridge manufacturer to completely phase out the use of CFCs and HCFCs. New domestic refrigeration has been designed to run on the hydrocarbons butane, propane or isobutane. Pentane and butane can replace CFCs as a hydrocarbon refrigerant, and pentane and isobutane can be used as foam insulation material as well.

In the UK Calor Gas has developed a range of hydrocarbon refrigerants (HCs) under the CARE label: CARE 10, 30, 40 and 50. These are designed to replace CFCs, HCFCs and HFCs. Hydrocarbons occur naturally. However, although they are very efficient refrigerants they are highly inflammable, although careful design of the refrigeration units ensures that they are safe. Systems which use HCs are 22 per cent more energy efficient than other refrigeration systems. Most importantly, hydrocarbons are chemically stable, non-toxic and non-corrosive, they do not damage the ozone layer and have an almost zero impact on global warming.

These refrigerants have been adopted by many manufacturers, and have been used successfully in some Swedish and German supermarkets. British users of HC units include Foster, LEC, Williams, Barkers, IMI, Unilever and the environmental chain store Out of this World. HCs are also used in air-conditioning units.

The Total Equivalent Warming Impact (TEWI) measures both the direct and the indirect contribution refrigerants have on the environment. The direct impact of hydrocarbons is negligible and their indirect effect – as

Industry Case Study

In 1998 Sainsbury's applied for planning permission to build a superstore on the Greenwich Peninsula, next to the site of the Millennium Dome and next to the Millennium Village. If built this would be the UK's first low-energy superstore, using hydrocarbon refrigerants throughout, natural ventilation, underfloor heating reclaimed from the refrigeration system, wind turbines and solar cells to power signs, with surplus energy being stored in batteries for venting and night-time requirements. The ceiling would let in daylight to allow natural lighting of the store; reinforced concrete walls and floors would act as a giant storage heater, absorbing heat in the day and releasing it at night.

energy consumption – gives savings of 15–22 per cent, which results in a reduction in the amount of carbon dioxide their refrigerators contribute to the environment.

British Gas has developed refrigerants based on ammonia and water. Ammonia is a poisonous gas, however, and its use is not permitted in confined spaces. Thus a refrigeration plant containing ammonia needs to be situated away from any occupied rooms and a secondary coolant, such as ethylene glycol, pumped through the chilling units. Trials using this system have taken place on a commercial basis in a Tesco supermarket in London.

In January 1993 the Foster Refrigerator Group, the largest UK manufacturer of commercial refrigeration, marketed over 90 fridges operating on the transitional refrigerant R 134a, and 140 medium to large models operating on the transitional refrigerant R 22. They have now adopted the refrigerant R 404a as the standard refrigerant in all their freezers, and R 134a in refrigerators; both refrigerants are HFCs. A polyurethane foam, R 142b, has been adopted as the blowing agent to replace CFC 11 for insulation purposes.

Whatever the chosen refrigerant, it is important that all equipment can conform with the following legal requirements for temperature control:

Dairy	1–4 °C
Wine	10–12 °C
Chilled storage	0–2 °C
Meat	0–2 °C

All refrigeration must be designed to cope with an ambient temperature of 43 °C (for tropical climates and very hot kitchens in the summer months).

This new generation of environmentally-friendly refrigeration units is not only better for the ozone layer, but the units have a much lower global warming potential, if any, and the motors are more energy efficient. Not only does this save on fuel bills, but the reduced demand for electricity means that there is less carbon fuel burnt (to generate the electricity) and consequently less greenhouse gases. This will lead to a reduction in the number of power stations. Indeed, energy inefficient equipment has a far greater impact on global warming than leakages of refrigerants. As noted before, the total combined effect of direct (leakages) and indirect (energy use) contributions to global warming is known as TEWI (Total Equivalent Warming Impact). It has been estimated that in new equipment the direct contribution of leaked refrigerants is only 2 per cent and the indirect contribution is 98 per cent.

Energy efficiency gains have also been made as the result of the substitution of aluminium for stainless steel in cabinet design; aluminium is an extremely efficient reflector of heat (second only to gold), and it is used on cabinet side walls and interiors. Defrosting systems use the energy generated by the refrigeration system to de-ice the evaporator within the cabinet, and then to vaporize the melted water. This replaces the heater elements of automatic defrosting systems in older models. In addition, the use of microchip technology in the control systems means they are far more sensitive to the operation of the fridge and can respond more quickly and hence more effectively to surrounding conditions.

The Greenfreeze fridge

In 1992 Greenpeace discovered that a team of East German scientists had developed a fridge using a coolant based on a mixture of butane and propane.

In 1993 the first Greenfreeze fridge rolled off the production line of an East German factory, with the aid of Greenpeace, and by 1998 over 25 million had been sold worldwide. The sales and development of the fridge won Greenpeace the United Nations Ozone Award. This is one of the few types of fridge that qualify for the EU 'Eco-label'.

THE DISPOSAL OF CFCS

The Environmental Protection Act 1990 makes the safe disposal or recovery of waste CFCs and other chemicals that deplete the ozone layer mandatory.[4] To aid in this, the Government gives grants to local authorities for the recycling of CFCs and has shown support for the Halon Users' National Consortium to establish a halon bank to encourage recycling once the production of halon ceases.

Industry Case Study

Forte have installed heat recovery units in a number of their larger refrigeration units. They are more efficient and easier to maintain, and waste energy is used to heat water. Although the initial capital costs are high, this is balanced by overall long-term savings. They will recoup their costs in five years.

REFRIGERATION AND ENERGY EFFICIENCY

Although the energy capacity of refrigeration in kitchens is usually only 2–3 per cent of the total energy capacity of a kitchen, as it is in continuous use it can cost a significant amount to operate. In a hot summer motors have to work harder to keep temperatures down; consequently they produce more heat which has to be extracted using even more electricity! As a result refrigeration motors can account for 30 per cent of electricity consumption in catering, and up to 80 per cent in food retailing and manufacturing.

A typical chest freezer rated at 550 W costs 95p a day to run, and a cabinet freezer rated at 820 W costs £1.41 per day. Based on this rate, to run a chest freezer costs £6.65 per week, or £26.60 per month, and a cabinet freezer £9.87 per week, or £ 39.48p per month.[5] To minimize running costs therefore:

- Fridges and freezers should be located in a cool place far from other sources of heat and with sufficient ventilation to ensure that any heat generated in the cooling process is removed.
- In larger operations the compressor should be located away from the refrigeration units themselves. It is possible to combine this with heat recovery systems where the 'waste' heat can be used to generate hot water.

- Cabinets should be kept full, but not over-packed. It costs as much to cool an empty or half full cabinet as a full one, and if a cabinet is overfull the cold air is unable to circulate and the correct temperature is never achieved, which will result in the deterioration of the food.
- Hot food should *never* be placed in a fridge or freezer. Apart from the danger in terms of food hygiene it will cost more to cool down the total contents of the warmed-up fridge than to rapidly cool just one dish.
- Staff should be trained to keep fridge and freezer doors tightly shut, and to open doors only when necessary and for a minimum period so that cold air is not lost. All door seals should be checked regularly to ensure that there is a tight seal. Frozen food should be defrosted in refrigerators. A rolling programme of defrosting and cleaning should be introduced and kept to.
- If a kitchen refit is planned then a wise caterer will ensure that all refrigeration required for storage is kept away from the hot environment of the kitchen and held in a cool room; any supplies that are required for the service period or day's preparation can be transferred to a smaller unit in the kitchen.
- It is time to reconsider the use of minibars in hotel bedrooms. Poor room design can mean that the unit is incorporated into a small inadequately ventilated space and this places a strain on the cooler motor which generates more heat, thus creating a vicious circle. Some hotels now have a pre-payment minibar in the lobby area of each floor to address this problem.
- Note that the cheaper models of refrigeration will in the long run be a more expensive investment as they will cost more to run.
- Although all refrigeration on the market is currently powered by electricity, it is possible to produce gas-fired CFC-free absorption chillers which would not only run silently but also run at a fraction of the cost.

AIR-CONDITIONING

Although air-conditioning is not widely used in the UK, it is a major user of refrigeration and energy in the hotter developed countries. Therefore the same principles in terms of choice of refrigerants, units, maintenance of equipment and use apply as to other forms of refrigeration. New technology has developed absorption chillers that are more energy efficient than older models. They are a preferred choice in systems where gas is cheaper than electricity, or where waste heat is available. HCs can also be used in air-conditioning units.

A good practice is to incorporate the provision of air-conditioning into a combined heat and power (CHP) plant, where the heat generated by the chilling unit is used by the CHP unit to produce electricity, energy for cooking and hot water.

CONCLUSION

The intelligent business will anticipate the eventual need to replace all its refrigeration equipment and will implement an ongoing replacement programme so that they are not faced with a massive capital charge all at once. This means ensuring that the oldest and most energy demanding equipment is replaced first with the latest technology.

If you have CFC refrigeration then it is inevitable that the value of your business will decrease, as CFCs, like asbestos, play no part in the future.

QUESTIONS AND ISSUES FOR DISCUSSION

1 Carry out an 'environmental audit' of the refrigeration of a hospitality operation with which you are familiar. Present your findings in the form of a chart showing:
   ● type of unit
   ● age
   ● power rating
   ● usage
   ● recommendations
   ● calculations based on your recommendations which show running costs of new equipment
   ● savings in the immediate term
   ● payback period to recover costs of investment

   Note that it may not be necessary to replace equipment.

2 Collect details of the EU Eco-labelling Scheme as it applies to refrigeration in the UK. Carry out an audit of some refrigeration equipment and calculate the score you would give it based on the above scheme.

3 Devise a staff training programme titled 'Our Refrigeration and the Environment'. Show how you would deliver this programme to a range of staff of mixed ability and responsibility in a busy pub/restaurant.

Notes

1 Gro Harlem Brundtland, in P. ReVelle and C. ReVelle, *The Global Environment*, London: Jones and Bartlett, 1992.
2 See Chapter 4.
3 'Food Safe Refrigeration: Must it cost the earth?' Information sheet produced by Foster Refrigerator Group of Companies, Oldmeadow Road, King's Lynn, Norfolk, PE30 4JU.
4 See above, this chapter, for these.
5 These are approximate costings.

Further reading

HCIMA, *Ozone Depleting Substances in Refrigeration Equipment*, HCIMA technical brief.

Energy management

The Government believes that improved energy management by consumers, and straightforward investments with a payback of up to three years, could achieve energy savings of around 20% of current energy consumption outside the transport sector, equivalent to CO_2 emissions of 24 million tonnes of carbon (MtC) assuming the 1990 fuel mix.

Sustainable Development – The UK Strategy[1]

OBJECTIVES

1 To describe the major energy cost areas in a hospitality operation.
2 To make recommendations for action in each cost area to reduce energy costs.
3 To devise a checklist in order to carry out an energy audit, and apply this to a chosen business or area within it.
4 To make recommendations for change based on the energy audit.
5 To identify short-, medium- and long-term strategies and savings.
6 To calculate the hourly running costs of a range of equipment.

INTRODUCTION

Although there are a number of ways in which energy can be generated without contributing to global warming, at the present time each one has a drawback. Although nuclear energy does not contribute to global warming, it poses its own problems in that its waste products need to be stored for thousands of years in safe conditions, and at the moment there is no guarantee that this is possible. As well, many people have reservations about the safety of nuclear power stations.[2]

Wind turbines are an environmentally-friendly way to generate electricity but they need to be sited in wild and windy locations, and there are objections to this on the grounds that they spoil the appearance of beauty spots. The technology of wind and wave power has developed so that it can produce energy at a rate which is highly competitive with conventional fossil-derived sources, but it will be some time before this can be developed on a commercial basis. The technology of photovoltaics – the harnessing of solar energy – is not yet at the stage where energy can be stored or even generated at an economical rate to sell to the national grid, although it is certainly an option for the future. However, photovoltaic panels can be installed on buildings where peak demand for electricity coincides with the time of brightest sunshine, so that it is not necessary to store solar-powered electricity. At the time of publication (1999) the cost of photovoltaic panels is the same as for marble or granite cladding, so this is a viable choice for some buildings.[3]

Renewable energy facts

The fastest growing global energy source in 1996 was wind, growing at a rate of 26 per cent.

The slowest growing energy source in 1996 was nuclear power, at a rate of 1 per cent.

Germany was the leading generator of wind energy power, followed by India.

Denmark is the world's leading supplier of wind turbines. Wind provides 5 per cent of Denmark's electrical generating capacity.

Renewable energy sources currently supply 2.5 per cent of the UK's energy, with plans to increase this to 4 per cent by 2003, and to 10 per cent by 2010.

The second fastest growing energy source is solar power; the manufacture of photovoltaic cells grew by 16 per cent in 1997.

Source: Worldwatch Institute.

In the light of these facts it follows that in the future all countries will continue to produce the majority of their electricity from non-renewable energy sources. This will mean continued pressure to reduce energy consumption by a combination of the development and use of more energy efficient appliances, and by the imposition of deterrents such as increased taxation of energy. This chapter will look at the ways in which the hospitality industry can reduce its use of energy.

It is impossible to give exactly precise figures about the total amount of energy consumed by the hospitality industry in the UK. This is because it is a diverse industry, a large proportion of which is devoted to servicing the needs of other industries such as the welfare and industrial sectors.

It should be noted that it is often the case in the 'cost sectors' that energy costs incurred during the provision of food are not separated out from the overall running of a business, although the requirement that all public

The hospitality industry

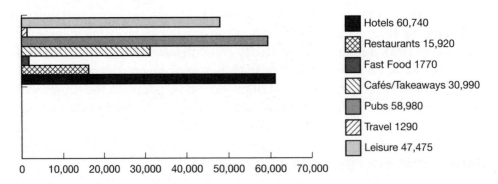

Hotels 60,740

Restaurants 15,920

Fast Food 1770

Cafés/Takeaways 30,990

Pubs 58,980

Travel 1290

Leisure 47,475

0   10,000   20,000   30,000   40,000   50,000   60,000   70,000

Figure 4.1 The hospitality and catering industry – number of outlets in the UK, 1996

Source: HCIMA Yearbook, 1998.

sector operations should be accountable means that increasingly management control systems to assess the true costs are being implemented.

The hospitality industry operates 365 days a year. In 1983 the Energy Efficiency Office estimated that the total consumption of energy by the UK catering industry was in excess of 21,600 kWh per annum. In 1983, 32.1 per cent of the energy was used in purely commercial catering establishments, 16.7 per cent in hotel restaurants and guest houses and 51.2 per cent in the welfare sector. In total the catering industry accounted for 1.3 per cent of all energy used in the UK in 1983. The consequent use of heat, light and power converted into an energy bill of £500 million in 1983.[4] Yet it has been estimated that at least 20 per cent of all energy used in the hospitality sector can be saved. This would have saved the industry £100 million in 1983, equivalent to 4,320 kWh.

The amount of energy consumed by any hospitality business is dependant upon a range of factors: the size and location of the building, the specifications to which it has been built, the heating and lighting systems that it employs, and the activities that take place inside it. When addressing energy efficiency it is important to determine the contribution each cost sector of an operation makes to overall energy costs. In the next section we will examine each of these factors in turn. If a building is new, then it is likely that more rigorous standards in terms of design and energy efficiency are incorporated into the construction than is the case with properties which have been standing for many years. The following section will examine the actions which can be taken in the case of older buildings and established businesses.

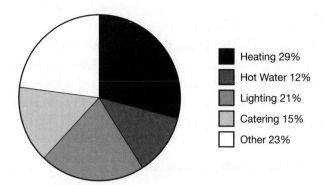

Figure 4.2 Use of energy by cost in hotels, 1983
Source: Energy Efficiency Office, 1983.

THE BUILDING

The first major cost centre is likely to be the building, which is the infrastructure of any business. In the case of a new business, the design and insulation standards of the building as a whole should already have been addressed, but they will need to be investigated when considering upgrading an existing business. This should then be followed by an investigation into the way in which the building temperature is currently controlled, and whether there are any environmental monitoring systems already installed.

Building regulations

There are at present government proposals to tighten up current building regulations in order to achieve a 25 per cent improvement in space and water heating.

The Government has estimated that if all plant that is replaced in British industry were to be replaced with energy efficient plant with a payback of 3–5 years, then this would mean a national saving of 10 per cent on the energy bill; this figure could rise on a longer-term basis.

The next step would be to subdivide the building into its component operational parts, such as the public areas, back of house, bedrooms, kitchens, dining rooms, lounges, meeting rooms and swimming pool area, and to carry out a detailed examination of the heating and insulation standards of each.

Location

The amount of energy a building uses is determined by its location. If it is in a very exposed area, for example on the seafront, and it has a broad frontage, more heat will be lost than if the building is located in a sheltered spot, for example in a town centre or in a warmer climate. A detached building will use more heat than if it is part of a row of buildings.

Design and insulation standards

The standard of insulation, the amount of glass frontage and the number of doors opening onto the exterior will also affect the energy efficiency of a building. Much heat is lost through large windows in dining areas, although it is possible to reduce some of this loss by the use of net curtains, blinds or canopies in order to reduce air movement.

Heat loss through the roof can be enormous: the installation of 100 mm thickness insulation will reduce loss by 50–70 per cent with a payback period of 1 to 2 years, and if 150 mm of insulation is installed the savings will be proportionately greater.

Temperature control mechanisms

When planning energy-saving strategies, it is important to consider what are the current energy requirements of the building, in order to calculate which will be the easiest and most cost effective measures to implement in the short term. It is a good idea to create a baseline from which to work so that the true extent of the savings can be seen over time.

Industry Case Study

The Grand Hotel in Brighton is one of the UK's most prestigious hotels. After the IRA bomb attack on the hotel in 1984 the hotel needed major refurbishment. The heating system that was finally chosen as the result of an energy audit included temperature control sensors and individual bedroom radiator controls. The average fuel bill before the new system was implemented was £200,000 per year. The payback period was only 14 months.

The hotel installed heat exchangers which used the heat created by the air-conditioning plant to heat the hotel swimming pool.

Lighting

The lighting requirements for kitchens and dining rooms can account for the consumption of as much as 15–25 per cent of the total energy bill. In terms of health and safety, levels of illumination in kitchens need to be 500 lux for efficient working, whereas in the restaurant it need only be 100–200 lux.[5] The calculation of lux is highly technical, and beyond the scope of this chapter. For our purposes we shall assume that the correct wattage of standard lighting has been installed to provide the optimum illumination. If a manager is unsure whether the levels of illumination are sufficient, s/he should call in a qualified electrician to assess the energy efficiency of the lighting.

Table 4.1 Required levels of illumination, in lux[6]

Food stores	150
Kitchen working area	500
Canteen, Cafeteria	200
Staff dining room	200
Restaurant	100
Cash desk	300
Lounge	400
Cellar	150
Servery	300
Staff changing room	150
Toilets	150

Source: The Food Hygiene (General) Regulations 1970.

In order to reduce energy costs incurred by lighting therefore, a business would simply need to replace standard lighting with low-energy lighting which provides the equivalent illumination.

Although standard fluorescent tubes can be up to four times more efficient than standard light bulbs, high frequency fluorescent tubes can save another 30 per cent of energy. In addition, 26 mm diameter fluorescent tubes use 8 per cent less electricity than 38 mm diameter ones, while providing the same levels of illumination.[7] High frequency lights also have a life expectancy of up to 50 per cent longer than conventional fluorescents.

One of the most recent lighting innovations is the high efficiency ('TL'5HE) fluorescent lamp which is more compact in size. It has a diameter of 16 mm, a 40 per cent reduction in size on the 26 mm lamps, and it provides an increased energy saving of 25 per cent. It does not fade as quickly as conventional fluorescents, has a 16,000-hour life and is designed to minimize installation costs. It also contains a reduced mercury content.

Life-cycle analyses show that at least 99 per cent of the contribution of lighting to pollution is caused by energy consumption during use.

Table 4.2 The relative levels of energy efficiency provided by a range of lighting

	38 mm standard fluorescent	26 mm fluorescent	high frequency fluorescent
Wattage	2 × 65 W	2 × 58 W	2 × 50 W
Control gear losses	2 × 12W = 24 W	2 × 12 W = 24 W	1 × 12 W = 12 W
Total consumption	154 W	140 W (saving 9 per cent)	112 W (saving 27 per cent)
Light output	9980 lumens	10,400 lumens	10,000 lumens

Source: Philips Lighting, Croydon, UK.

Although the initial purchase and installation costs of the high frequency fluorescent lights is greater, the reduced energy costs and longer potential life will rapidly pay for this.

Whenever comparisons are made between energy-saving devices and conventional systems it is important to include the initial costs of installation, purchase and change. For example, a 6 ft double fluorescent tube with a diffuser would cost approximately £52.50 to purchase and £15 to install in a kitchen. A simple equation to estimate the energy that can be saved is as follows:

(no. of bulbs currently in kitchen) × (wattage of each bulb) × (unit cost of electricity) = cost per hour to light the kitchen

Then,

(hourly cost of lighting kitchen) × (no. of hours lights on) = daily cost

Then calculate the weekly/monthly/annual cost of lighting the kitchen as required.

The same exercise should then be carried out for the number of fluorescent tubes necessary to provide the required illumination. Subtract the results of the second exercise from those of the first to indicate savings, and work out how long it would take to recover the costs of installation from any savings made, and then how great a saving would be made over a 5-year, and then a 10-year period.

Light bulbs

Compact fluorescent light (CFL) bulbs are more energy efficient than standard bulbs. They can save up to 75 per cent of energy compared with conventional lighting due to their much lower wattage, while at the same time providing similar levels of illumination. The initial investment of approximately £10 per bulb is large, but they last much longer (8000 hours) than a standard bulb (1000 hours). An attractive range of decorative styles has now been made available, although it should be noted that compact fluorescent lights cannot be used with a dimmer switch.

Compact fluorescent energy ratings

 9 W compact = 40 W conventional bulb
13 W compact = 60 W conventional bulb
18 W compact = 75 W conventional bulb
25 W compact = 100 W conventional bulb

Table 4.3 Comparison between illumination levels of standard bulbs and compact fluorescents

Compact fluorescent		Standard equivalent bulb	
Wattage	Lumens	Wattage	Lumens
9	450	40	420
13	650	60	710
18	900	75	940
25	1200	100	1360

To calculate the average savings per bulb, given that,

one unit of electricity = 1000 W (1kW)

and, for our purposes, one unit of electricity costs 7.21p, a 100 Wt bulb consumes 1 unit of electricity in 1000/100 = 10 hours

The hospitality industry

If the cost of 100 W tungsten-filament standard bulb is 60p, and
If it has an average life of 1000 hours:

   to run it for 10 hours costs 7.21p
   to run it for 100 hours costs £7.21p
   to run it for 1000 hours costs £72.10p

Add to this the cost of purchase of the bulb (60p).

Total cost of a 100 W tungsten-filament bulb is £7.81p.

Note that 8 per cent of the total cost is from the purchase of the bulb, and 92 per cent of the costs are for the energy.

Now compare this to the total costs of running a 25 W compact fluorescent bulb, which provides a similar amount of light as a 100 W conventional tungsten-filament bulb. (However, the compact fluorescents have an average life of 8000 hours.)

   Cost of purchase of lamp = 1200p
   Cost of changing the lamp = 100p
   = £13.

A 25 W lamp consumes a unit of electricity in 1000/25 = 40 hours.

   to run it for 40 hours costs £7.21p
   to run it for 100 hours costs £15.86p
   to run it for 1000 hours costs £158.60p
   to run it for 8000 hours costs £1264

Add the costs of installation and purchase (£13).

Total lifetime (8000 hours) cost of a CFL = £25.64p.

We have seen that the lifetime (1000 hours) cost of a tungsten-filament lamp is £7.81.
   Therefore the total costs to change and run eight tungsten-filament lamps would be £7.81 × 8 = £62.48p.

Total savings over 8000 hours of use of a CFL lamp would therefore be £36.84, or a staggering 59 per cent!
   If the savings made by one compact 25 W CFL that provides approximately the same illumination as one 100 W conventional bulb are 59 per cent, it is easy to see how great the savings would be if every 100 W bulb was replaced by a CFL.
   How long would it take to make these savings? That would depend on how long the lights were used each day. If, for instance, a restaurant light was kept on for six hours, six days a week, this would equal 36 hours per

week, or 1872 hours per year. This would approximate to almost two conventional bulbs per year (with an average life of 1000 hours each). The annual cost of purchase, installation (one change of lamp, say, £1) and running would be £7.81p × 2 (+£1) = £16.62p.

Compare this with the cost of running a CFL for 2000 hours (£25.64 ÷ 4) = £6.41p.

Annual savings therefore are £10.21p.

If it would take approximately 4.25 years to burn either lamp for 8000 hours, savings based on this example would work out at £43.39p per bulb.

A more sophisticated model of lighting costs is:

Initial capital investment

Cost of lighting equipment + costs of installation (labour and materials)

Plus

Operating Costs

Annual electrical energy costs + cost of replacement bulbs + cost of cleaning, maintenance and replacing spent bulbs.

This formula includes the costs incurred in the regular maintenance of lighting; it is important to keep the bulbs clean in order to achieve the best illumination.

Another factor to consider when choosing lighting is the effect of decorations; dark painted walls will not reflect as much light as light painted ones. It should also be remembered that the light output of all types of lamps will decrease gradually over time, while the energy consumption will remain constant. It is arguable that there will come a time when it is more cost effective to replace a bulb (or bulbs) before they are spent, rather than waste energy in fuelling inefficient lighting.

It is also important that all lights are able to be controlled individually rather than from a central control.

Figures 4.3 and 4.4 indicate the annual savings which can be achieved using more energy efficient lighting.

In public areas, conference rooms and bedrooms, the unnecessary use of lighting can be avoided by labelling individual switches, and by switching off lamps when they are not required. Sensor systems that automatically turn the lights on and off when the area is being used/not used are now being installed in many hotels. This system can also be used to turn off up to two-thirds of corridor lights during the night. Outside lights and signs can be operated by photocells that turn them on when natural light fades.

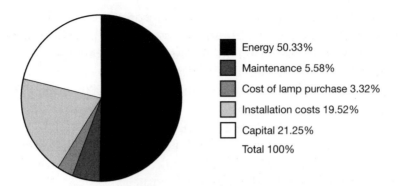

Energy 50.33%

Maintenance 5.58%

Cost of lamp purchase 3.32%

Installation costs 19.52%

Capital 21.25%

Total 100%

Figure 4.3 500 lux using twin 75 W battens plus diffusers
Source: Philips Comprehensive Handbook, 1986.

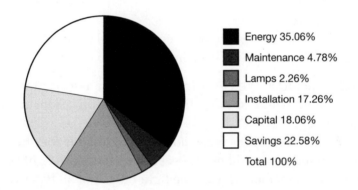

Energy 35.06%

Maintenance 4.78%

Lamps 2.26%

Installation 17.26%

Capital 18.06%

Savings 22.58%

Total 100%

Figure 4.4 500 lux using PSM 258 luminaires with TLD 58 W fluorescent lamp
Source: Philips Comprehensive Handbook, 1986.

Philips have marketed the TRIOS system, which is designed to adjust the levels of lighting in a room in conjunction with a light sensor according to levels of daylight entering the room. They can be fixed in offices and in larger rooms and can save up to 40 per cent in lighting costs. The TRIOS system can also work to automatically turn lights on and off by monitoring room use, and can be used in any room, corridor, sports hall or similar venue. Savings of up to 65 per cent have been recorded.

Exercise 1

Work out the total costs of lighting the restaurant or dining room of an establishment during its public opening hours, together with the additional costs of lighting while preparing for service and clearing up. What conclusions can you draw from your findings?

Exercise 2

Having worked out the current costs of lighting the restaurant, calculate the savings which could be made by the substitution of energy efficient bulbs and indicate how long it would take to make these savings.

Heating and ventilation

Heating and ventilation can account for 25–30 per cent of the total energy costs of a hospitality operation, depending on the type of heat source installed and the way in which it is used. It is a good idea to consider whether the heating system currently in use is appropriate for the business's current demands. A regular comparison of the costs of installing new systems fuelled by gas, oil and electricity is worth carrying out. The use of gas-burning condensing boilers can increase the efficiency of fuel consumption from 70 to 95 per cent. Although the initial cost of the boilers is greater than a standard one the large user will rapidly save the extra financial investment, as the average savings of fuel have been estimated to be as much as 20 per cent, giving a payback period of 4–5 years.[9]

Forte had a general policy guideline for the installation of energy efficient equipment which was a payback period of no more than three years.

It is important that the controllers and timers which operate boilers are correctly adjusted for the time of year and for the requirements of the business. Modern systems can be installed which will compensate for the cooling (or warming) effects of external air temperatures and wind speeds.

To save on heating costs, the following action can be taken:

- Extractor fans should be turned off when not needed.
- Filters, heating coils and grilles should be cleaned regularly to ensure that they work efficiently, and also to avoid the build-up of grease which is a fire hazard.
- Boilers, fans and all plant should be regularly serviced to ensure that they are working at maximum efficiency.
- Room thermostats and time controls for heating and air-conditioning systems should be installed. Fuel consumption for heating can be reduced by 15–40 per cent as the result of adjusting controls and thermostats according to weather conditions.
- In dining room areas double glazing, and the installation of draught lobbies at external entrances (if space allows) can make substantial savings on heat loss. External doors should be kept tightly shut, and the kitchen

extract ventilation system should be adjusted so that it does not draw excessive volumes of outside air into the restaurant. In addition, all doors and windows should be draught-proofed.

- It should be possible to isolate the heating controls of those rooms or parts of a building which are unoccupied at times.
- A large business should consider the installation of heat recovery systems and heat pump systems to recirculate waste heat (see below).

Combined heat and power systems

Small-scale combined heat and power systems (CHP) have been developed for hotels. A CHP is an on-site mini power station, usually fuelled by gas, which produces heat, hot water and electricity. When necessary this system is boosted from the mains. The system is most appropriate for businesses using 40 kilowatts of electricity or more per year, which have already undertaken a range of energy management projects. In some cases savings can be as great as 20 per cent, and in many cases the initial investment in CHP can be recouped in 2.5–4.5 years.

An added advantage is that these systems reduce carbon dioxide and sulphur emissions because they are based on gas; CHP increases the efficiency of the generation of electricity from primary fuels from 30–50 per cent to 80–90 per cent.

The UK Government has set a target to achieve 5000 megawatts of electricity to be generated by CHP by the year 2000 – each 1000 MW of CHP saves 1 million tonnes of carbon dioxide over conventional energy generation.

Industry Case Study

The Chewton Glen Hotel in Hampshire installed a 48 kW CHP unit in 1990 when the construction of a new leisure and conference centre and twelve bedrooms required the upgrading of the existing electricity provision. The system provides 20 per cent of the needs of the complex, and with projected annual savings of £10,620, paid for itself in four years.[10]

Air-conditioning

Although only the largest and most expensive hotels and restaurants in the UK have full air-conditioning installed, it is important to understand that these systems can make a very heavy demand on energy loadings and in some cases can increase the hotel's electricity bill by as much as 50 per cent. This is partly due to the use of more energy for heating which is required due to the rate of ventilation.

OPERATIONAL AREAS

Food production and service

On average 40 per cent of energy used in the hospitality industry is used in preparing, cooking and serving food. This varies from 25–30 per cent in operations with a limited menu to 50 per cent or more in traditional hotels or restaurants. Most of the energy is used by cooking equipment, and most of this energy is wasted as the result of poor use! Given such major energy costs for the production and service of food, it is necesssary to subdivide this process into separate procedures, and to examine each area in some depth.

Food preparation and service

In most kitchens cooking equipment accounts for 80–88 per cent of the energy used, and storage and preparation equipment only 2 per cent. The greater part of the energy used is in a concentrated period in the four to five hours preceding and during each meal service. Gas is used by 80 per cent of operations for cooking.

In 1983[11] the average energy costs per cooked meal were:
4p in snack bars
7p in coffee shops
18p in steakhouses
19p in traditional English restaurants
27p in 'high-class' restaurants
36p in hotel restaurants

In non-commercial catering (welfare and staff catering), the energy costs were between 9.5 pence and 10.8 pence per meal.

Gas appliances

Gas fryers: How they are used will affect total running costs, due to the action of the thermostat, but on average a fryer will operate on full power for 60–70 per cent of the time.

Bain-maries: It is interesting that in self-service cafeterias the serving equipment can use up to 9.4 per cent of the total energy consumption of the

Table 4.4 Typical energy ratings for equipment used in the preparation, cooking and serving of a meal

Combination steamers	9.4– 61 kW
Deep fryers (gas)	18.2– 52.1 kW
Convection ovens (gas)	14.4– 32.2 kW
Grills and griddles (gas)	5.3– 10.6 kW
Microwave ovens	900– 2100 W
Bratt pans (gas)	10.2–16.1 kW
Salamander (gas)	6.6 kW
Boiling table (6-burner gas)	27.25 kW
Solid top (6-burner gas)	7.33 kW
Boiling table and oven (gas)	38.3 kW

kitchen, just to keep the food hot, whereas in other restaurants bain-marie-style equipment normally uses only 2.4 per cent of the energy. Any savings on labour costs or through large-scale production methods will be reduced as a result of higher energy demands to keep food warm over a serving period of, for instance, two hours.

Strategies to reduce energy consumption in the preparation and cooking of food include:

- Preheating of ovens and friers: no more than 15 minutes is normally required.
- Use all equipment to its full capacity – menus and production schedules should be planned accordingly.
- All ovens should be turned off before, or immediately upon the end of cooking time.
- The use and installation of all kitchen equipment should be reviewed on a regular basis and all under-used equipment removed to avoid temptation.
- All cooking equipment should be cleaned regularly and maintained to remove any scale or corrosive parts which may affect heat transfer.
- All pots and pans should be of a size appropriate for the size of the burners to ensure good contact with, and maximum exposure to the source of heat.
- Staff should be trained to use lids and covers to retain heat, steam and fumes.
- Food should be kept hot for a minimal period of time, not only to save energy but also to maintain food in a good condition, and to minimize destruction of nutrients and, especially, food hygiene risks.

- The menu and cooking methods should be regularly reviewed to minimize energy use, and also when considering replacing equipment or refurbishing the kitchen.
- Deep fat fryers should be regularly cleaned and the oil filtered.
- It is often possible to use a toaster rather than a salamander.
- Double-sided grills not only cook food faster but they also produce less smoke.

Energy efficient equipment and strategies for its use

The EU has developed standards for energy efficiency for electrical equipment, starting with domestic refrigerators and freezers. These standards will eventually be applied to commercial equipment. However, the manufacturers of catering equipment already produce a good range of more energy efficient equipment:

Forced convection ovens reduce the amount of time required for cooking an item by up to one-third. They are most useful for batch cooking, and can take a full load as the shelves are spaced more closely together. Efficient air distribution ensures that there is an even temperature throughout.

Fan-assisted electric ovens claim to save between 10 per cent and 30 per cent energy compared with conventional ovens, and between 20 per cent and 40 per cent for fan-assisted gas ovens compared with conventional ovens. Heat loss into the kitchen is also reduced by 50 per cent and flue loss in gas ovens is reduced by the same amount due to the reduced volume of air required for complete combustion.

Microprocessor ovens are fitted with a temperature probe which is inserted into the centre of a dish or joint of meat, and will automatically turn off the oven when the pre-set required temperature is achieved.

Induction hobs can save up to 50 per cent of energy compared with conventional electric hobs. These are electric hobs which require no preheating, have an instant response, and which only heat the base of the pan when in contact with the hob, and cease immediately the pan is removed. In addition, the temperature controls can be regulated by degree which provides the user with similar levels of control as that provided by gas. This leads to minimal heating costs and a more comfortable working temperature in the kitchen. Portable models are also available for service trolleys, small counters etc. The payback period can be as little as two years.

The initial cost of investment in new kitchen equipment is high, but the pay-off can be considerable in terms of lower running and maintenance costs. It makes sense to regularly do some basic calculations to compare the difference between merely replacing an old item of equipment with a newer version of the same, and the purchase of an initially more expensive item of equipment which has much lower running costs and which would have a good pay-off period.

Multi-energy tunnels

Very high-volume kitchens use multi-energy cooking tunnels. These combine four types of energy: steam, microwave, forced convection and infra-red, a combination which provides optimum cooking quality and shorter cooking times up to five times less than conventional methods. These can deal with 1500 to 5000 meals per day. They are completely automatic and fully pro-grammable using either manual or computer-controlled systems.

Equipment use within the kitchen

It has been estimated that up to 30 per cent of all energy used in the kitchen is wasted as the result of equipment being turned on far in advance of its need to be used, and being left on even though it is no longer needed. Using graph paper or a spreadsheet it is possible to create an interesting chart to show this inappropriate use, and to use it for staff training in changing long-established work patterns. Table 4.5 shows a typical example.

A spreadsheet like this one can also be used to indicate the current esti-mated energy costs of running the business. The true costs will depend upon a number of factors, including the age of the equipment, its location and the use to which they are put. For instance, the energy rating of any item of equipment indicates the costs when used continuously on full volume for one hour, although in reality allowances must be made for thermostatic control and quiet periods of use.

If it is possible to install submeters for the gas and electricity supply to the kitchen, it would easily be possible to calculate the average current fuel costs per cover. This can then be compared with future savings.

Dishwashing and hot water

These two things together can use between 0.8 to 1.2 kWh per meal, which can account for as much as between 1.5 to 7.5 per cent of total energy use. There can be tremendous wastage due to under-utilization of a machine

Table 4.5 An example of a spreadsheet showing usage of a range of equipment

Equipment	Time turned on	Start time	Finish time	Time turned off	Hours used	Wattage (kW)	Cost per kW (pence)	Running cost per hour (pence)	Daily running cost (pence)
Gas deep fryer 1 (double)	9 a.m.	12 noon	3 p.m.	5 p.m.	8	26.4	1.477	38.9928	311.9424
Gas deep fryer 2 (single)	11.30 a.m.	12.30 p.m.	2.30 p.m.	5 p.m.	5.5	13.2	1.477	19.4964	107.2302
Salamander	11.30 a.m.	12.20 p.m.	2 p.m.	4 p.m.	4.5	6.6	1.477	9.7482	43.8669
Gas range	9 a.m.	10.30 a.m.	2.30 p.m.	4 p.m.	7	38.3	1.477	56.5691	395.9837
Water boiler	9 a.m.	12.10 p.m.	4 p.m.	6 p.m.	9	2.75	7.21	19.8275	178.4475
Freezer 1	24-hour usage				24	0.82	7.21	5.9122	141.8928
Freezer 2	24-hour usage				24	0.854	7.21	6.15734	147.77616
Refrigerated display unit	24-hour usage				24	0.55	7.21	3.9655	95.172
Meat fridge	24-hour usage				24	0.35	7.21	2.5235	60.564
Dairy fridge	24-hour usage				24	0.35	7.21	2.5235	60.564
Gravity-feed slicer		11 a.m.	12 noon		1	0.25	7.21	1.8025	1.8025
Mixer		10 a.m.	11 a.m.		1	0.35	7.21	2.5235	2.5235
Cash register		11.30 a.m.	4 p.m.	6 p.m.	6.5	0.45	7.21	3.2445	21.08925
Restaurant lights		11.30 a.m.	5 p.m.	6 p.m.	6.5	0.9	7.21	6.489	42.1785
Kitchen lights	9 a.m.			6 p.m.	9	0.49	7.21	3.5329	31.7961
Combination oven (gas)	10 a.m.	11 a.m.	12.30 p.m.	3 p.m.	5	22.6	1.477	33.3802	166.901
Griddle (gas)	11 a.m.	12 noon	3.15 p.m.	4 p.m.	5	10.6	1.477	15.6562	78.281
Microwave		12 noon	3 p.m.		0.5	1.7	7.21	12.257	6.1285
Dishwasher cold-fill	11 a.m.	1 p.m.	4.30 p.m.	6 p.m.	7	9.8	7.21	70.658	494.606
Total energy costs								315.25984	2388.74601

that is switched on well before the first items of dirty crockery are produced from the restaurant, regularly used for half or incomplete loads, and left on well after it is needed. The following list indicates a range of strategies an energy conscious manager would employ to make the most economical use of washing-up facilities, including a dishwasher.

Train all users to

1 Correctly stack the trays to improve cleaning and drainage.
2 Regularly clean sprays and nozzles.
3 Regularly maintain thermostats, heating elements and controls.
4 Check that the water softeners are working correctly.

Make regular checks to ensure that

1 Both hot and cold water pipes, tanks and cylinders are well insulated (and moisture-proof).
2 Equipment is regularly serviced and any leaking taps are rapidly repaired.
3 Thermostats are at the recommended setting. (But do not reduce the temperature of hot water below 55°C, which is necessary to avoid the risk of Legionnaires Disease.)
4 Taps are fully turned off after use, and that any leaking washers are repaired.

Install

1 Spray taps for handwashing facilities.
2 Mixer or spray taps for other sinks as appropriate.

A recent development is the tunnel dishwasher which is economical in its use of water, detergent and heat. Its electronic controls make it more reliable, and correctly positioned high-pressure water jets boost the initial removal of debris before the wash cycle. It is also fitted with a double rinse system whereby water used in the final rinse of previous dishes is recycled and used in the next cycle for the initial rinsing of detergents from the wash cycle. The water is then reprocessed by a pump and injected onto plates for the pre-wash. Their savings of water can be as much as one-third.

Exercise 3

Work out the running costs of some of the following items of equipment:

A deep fat fryer, dishwasher, microwave oven, gas cooker, electric cooker, refrigerator, freezer, *bain-marie*, mixer, food processor, meat slicer, a gas boiler, an electric space heater, a beer cooling unit, and a soft drinks display cabinet.

Where would you find the information regarding the costs of running the equipment?

Calculate your answer as 'x' pence per hour, then the cost per day and then the cost for a six-day week. If possible, make your calculations using a spreadsheet.

Long-term objectives

Businesses regularly change their menus and operating procedures in response to changing market requirements. But few businesses examine their menus dish by dish and calculate how much energy is required to produce each dish. They work on a gross profit safety margin in the expectation that all costs of production will be well covered. They should be asking such questions as: is it necessary to run the fryer all day just to serve a limited number of deep-fried items? Is it necessary to run the ice cream conservator in the winter if just a small number of ices are sold? Is it possible to substitute a fruit bowl instead? Is the salamander required any more? Is it possible to brown dishes/keep them hot/cook toast in any other way? Are there grilled items on the menu?

For each item of equipment, a manager should list the uses to which it is put, and ask him/herself a number of questions:

1 Is it currently being put to good use?
2 Should it be scrapped?
3 Is it possible to introduce other menu items or modify the menu so that its current use can be supplemented to make its running more cost effective?
4 Should it be replaced with a model which is more fuel efficient?
5 If so, how long will it take to recover the costs of the investment?

Hotel bedrooms

Some American hotel chains have installed occupancy detection devices that switch heating, ventilation, lighting and air-conditioning to energy conservation mode when rooms are unoccupied. This is increasingly being implemented by some of the larger UK hotel chains.

Another system increasingly in use is the key or key card system that activates the power supply when the room is unlocked and turns it off when the room is left locked up.

The Scandic Sjolyst Hotel in Oslo has installed a system whereby the temperature in each room is monitored and then transmitted to the management offices by a TV signal system. In this way it is possible to monitor and control unnecessary energy use. There are plans to install this system in all Scandic hotels.

The zoning of floors or blocks ensures that they can be isolated for letting, and therefore heating purposes, and this obviously assists in the whole range of service provision. Note that it is important to beware of problems caused by condensation if all the rooms on a floor are left unheated for a long period of time; it is better to leave them at a minimal temperature.

If a business is concerned about the percentage of energy used in its bedrooms, then it is possible to install electricity submeters which are read at weekly intervals so that a pattern of use can be established and the energy consumption per occupied room and per guest can be calculated.

The International Hotels Environment Initiative (IHEI)[12] has established a benchmark for energy use per occupied guest room per year:

Energy efficiency rating	Good	Fair	Poor
Electricity (kWh)	<1825	1825–2550	>2550

Most hotel bedrooms are now fitted with TV and radio, and many have hairdryers, a minibar and a range of lighting and air-conditioning. These appliances can significantly contribute to energy consumption.

AN EXAMPLE OF ELECTRICITY RATES[13]

In 1994, businesses which used more than 100kW of electricity at peak periods were able to take advantage of the Government's deregulatory programme for the electricity industries, and from 1998 all customers, whether industrial, retail or domestic, were also able to purchase electricity from the supplier of their choice.[14] Second-tier suppliers – licensed by the Government – purchase electricity from the national grid and sell it to the consumer at a competitive price.

The introduction of the competitive market into the electricity supply business has led to a range of options for small businesses to choose from. For instance, SEEBOARD offers the choice of the following tariffs:

Standard business tariff. For those companies whose electricity use at night is small and who do not use electricity as their main source of heating. Standing charge for each separate supply, a daily charge of £4.31 (inclusive of VAT). Unit charge is 8.39p (inclusive of VAT).

Economy 7 business tariff. This provides seven hours of cheaper electricity at night, and is suitable for businesses with electric storage heaters and where water is heated overnight by electric immersion heaters. Standing charge, a daily charge of 6.96p (inclusive of VAT). Night unit charge, for each unit supplied during a period totalling seven hours between 10.30 p.m. and 8 a.m. (predetermined by the company) is 3.13p (inclusive of VAT). Day unit charge for each unit supplied at other times is 8.39p (inclusive of VAT).

Evening/weekend and night business tariff. This is designed for businesses who use most of their electricity regularly during the evening, weekend and night. Standing charge, daily 8.24p (inclusive of VAT). Night unit charge for each unit supplied between 11.30 p.m. and 6.30 a.m. is 3.13p (inclusive of VAT). Peak unit charge for each unit supplied between 6.30 a.m. and 7.00 p.m., Mondays to Fridays inclusive, is 10.60p (inclusive of VAT). Evening/weekend unit charge for each unit supplied at other times, 4.95p (inclusive of VAT).

Note: a unit of electricity is one kilowatt-hour (kWh).

Industry Case Study

Hospitality businesses who have taken advantage of the deregulated electricity market include McDonald's, who contracted with Eastern Electricity to supply all 500 of its restaurants in England and Wales, in the expectation of reducing its £18 million annual electricity bill by £1.8 million.

Eastern Electricity also won the contract to supply 104 Forte sites, including their hotels and Welcome Break service stations, after the success of a pilot project at the Grosvenor House and Cumberland hotels in central London.

As the complexity of supply systems increases, computer software has been developed to aid the consumer in understanding patterns of use and costs. One such system is Appraise 100+ developed by Eastern Electricity.

Gas can also be supplied to large users at a discount by independent licensed operators providing a reduction of as much as 15 per cent on standard bills. However, it is not possible to provide an illustration of commercial gas tariffs as the industry is now so competitive that each supplier will only quote a price based on historical records of consumption, together with projected use, and the information is, of course, commercially sensitive. However, Table 4. 6 indicates the prices charged in 1994 before competition was introduced.

Table 4.6 An example of gas rates, 1994

Tier	Standard credit tariff, standing charge 10.1p per day kWh consumed p.a.	Commodity charge (per kWh)
1	0 – 146,536	1.477p
2	146,536 – 293,071	1.409p
3	293,071 – 439,607	1.375p
4	439,607 – 732,678	1.341p

Source: Segas

It is important to distinguish between energy efficiency and responsible energy management, and merely being able to purchase energy at a cheaper price. In the case of energy efficiency, a positive contribution will have been made to the minimization of global warming and pollution, whereas in the case of responsible energy management, although reduction of costs is good business practice, the actual volume of energy used may well remain the same. In practice most businesses will aim to combine both types of objectives. Indeed, if government policy to meet the targets established at Rio, Kyoto and Buenos Aires is realized in terms of increased taxes, then the wise manager will be more concerned with the former.

PLANNING ENERGY-SAVING STRATEGIES

It is important to distinguish between savings which can be made in the short, medium and long term. Immediate savings can be made with little or no capital investment by ensuring that lights and heating are turned off when not in use, and that thermostats are set to the required temperature.

Medium- and long-term savings can be made by considering investment in energy-saving devices and activities, and by considering how long it will take to recoup the cost and to make financial savings.

A large company might consider appointing an energy manager to monitor the use of energy in the business. He or she should regularly reappraise the situation with regard to energy-saving techniques and should be allocated a departmental budget, and have sufficient authority to carry out his/her tasks. The energy manager should report directly to senior management. S/he should be a good communicator, and should be able to run training courses for all levels of staff in energy management.

A smaller company might include responsibility for energy management as only part of the responsibilities of an assistant manager. No matter how the responsibility is devolved, it is most important that staff receive feed-back on the success of the energy-saving schemes if motivation and momentum is to be kept up.

In the medium term an energy manager might make savings by taking the following action:

1 Replacing light fittings with energy efficient light bulbs.
2 Fitting all radiators with individual thermostats.
3 Installing insulation in the roof.
4 Ensuring that all wall cavities are insulated.
5 Ensuring that all external doors are fitted with a closing device.
6 Implementing an ongoing programme of staff training in energy management.

Long-term action might include investing any savings made in the short and medium term into capital intensive systems, to include, *inter alia*:

● A computer-controlled air-conditioning system
● The installation of double glazing
● The installation of an energy efficient kitchen
● The purchase of energy efficient CFC-free refrigeration
● The purchase of fuel efficient transport, to be used only when essential, and to carry a maximum load – preferably both ways.

Industry Case Studies

In 1992 the oil-fired boiler system at the London Hilton in Park Lane was converted to gas to save £25,000 per year (at 1992 prices).

The standard of insulation of the cookers installed at the London Hilton in Park Lane is good enough for cooking to take place for eight hours with minimal use of power; only 2 °C is lost per hour.

In addition, there is a centralized computer system which controls the operation of the air-conditioning and electrical loads.

During the 1980s Trusthouse Forte (the Forte company's former name) implemented energy-saving schemes and incentives into some of its properties. In 1983 they introduced their first combined heat and power system (CHP) unit which was a joint venture with the Department of Energy. It was based on eight Fiat 127 motors running side by

▶

side to produce 38 kW per hour. In the first year, despite teething problems, there was a saving of £18,000 in fuel bills. The unit provided all the heat and hot water for the hotel, and after two years the experiment was deemed a great success.

In 1990 John Forte, the Environmental Services Director of the company, investigated how much the company had saved on fuel bills as a result of these operations. Taking a sample from the properties that were involved in the scheme, and basing the figures on the actual figures for energy consumption in 1980, he worked out that the fuel bill for these properties, which was £35 million, would have been £110 million if no conservation programmes had been implemented. This was a staggering saving of 68 per cent in just one part of the company.

The company decided that it had three options for energy saving:

1 No-cost savings based on a system of target establishment and monitoring, and good housekeeping.
2 Low-cost savings involving minor investment and target-setting and good housekeeping.
3 Capital investment – although this had to be accompanied by no more than a three-year payback period, due mainly to the fact of the rapid speed of technological change.

An energy conservation working group made up of chief in-house engineers and chaired by John Forte was established, and met on a monthly basis. All unit general managers were set energy-saving targets in agreement with their line managers, and an Energy Efficiency Working Group, chaired by the General Manager, was set up in each unit in order to carry out an energy audit, to identify potential savings, and to devise a plan in order to achieve these without compromising the safety of staff or customers. The incentive for the manager was that his or her bonus would partly depend on achievement of these targets.

When the company decided to replace existing heating systems with more efficient systems they sought a three- to four-year recovery period of their costs, although the systems would be expected to have a far longer life and also to require minimal maintenance.

The company decided that 60 per cent of lighting in all their restaurants could be converted to energy-saving equipment; the 40 per cent balance was lighting that was used to create the theme or the ambience of the restaurant. This could only be changed when a redesign or refit was required; this would usually be on a five-year rolling programme.

In 1995 Forte hotels estimated that if tungsten light bulbs were to be exchanged for low-energy bulbs throughout its 20 million hotel bedrooms worldwide, two-thirds of the energy presently used would be saved, and over the 5–10-year lifetime of the bulb, 100 million tonnes of carbon dioxide would be saved. It was also estimated that the re-cycling of one glass bottle from one of its bars would save enough energy to fuel a 60 W lightbulb for 4 hours!

Between 1988 and 1995 Inter-Continental Hotels reduced their worldwide energy costs by US$16.5 million, a saving of 27 per cent. This was achieved without compromising the comfort levels of guests, and saved the earth 54.6 tonnes of carbon dioxide emissions and 27.3 tonnes of nitrogen oxide emissions.

The Inter-Continental in London has made annual savings in energy use since 1980, in total these amount to US$270, 000. In addition, the Ritz Inter-Continental Lisboa has halved its energy bills between 1987 and 1995; and the Yokohama Grand Inter-Continental Hotel in Japan has reduced its fuel bills by 24 per cent in three years, despite increasing occupancy from 56 to 71 per cent.

CONCLUSION

This chapter has shown how substantial savings can be made in any organization, both immediately and in the long term; some of these will demand an investment of capital, but many merely demand a re-evaluation of working methods and attitudes. The saving of energy is the easiest contribution that any business can make towards considering the environment, and will be the first cost centre to show results. To tackle this area as the first step in the 'greening' of a hospitality operation will enable a manager to motivate their staff, and to reinforce the message as well as to gain a good grounding in the adoption of environmental management systems before undertaking an environmental audit.

QUESTIONS AND ISSUES FOR DISCUSSION

1 Devise an energy checklist for the restaurant or kitchen of a catering outlet with which you are familiar.

2 Carry out an energy checklist and make recommendations for the implementation of energy-saving practices and the installation of equipment which would result in energy saving in
   (a) the immediate term;
   (b) the medium term; and
   (c) the long term.

   In the case of the immediate and medium term, show calculations to prove that there would be savings, and in the case of the long term estimate what the probable long-term savings might be.

3 Approach a local hospitality business and offer to carry out an energy consultancy free of charge. Proceed as in exercises 1 and 2 above, and present your recommendations to the management professionally word processed and bound, as if it were a real-life consultancy.

4 Write an energy policy statement for a hospitality operation with which you are familiar. Identify and/or describe the company, and write a 1000-word rationale for your policy document.

5 Carry out a study of when equipment is turned on in a restaurant kitchen, when it is used, and when it is turned off. Express this in the form of a bar chart.

6 Monitor electricity, gas and other fuel use for a restaurant with which you are familiar for a day, and then for a full working week. From this work out the crude cost of energy per meal produced and/or per cover served. What conclusions do you draw from this? What recommendations can you make?

7 Choose a restaurant or a kitchen, and make recommendations for improvements in decor and lighting which would improve the general ambience and also result in energy savings in the longer term. Show any calculations and provide a written rationale for your decisions.

8 Explain why it is important to train all staff in energy management techniques if an energy-saving campaign is to be successful. What incentives and rewards would you instigate to aid the programme?

9 Devise a job description for the post of energy manager in a large city centre hotel of luxury grade, which has a large proportion of guests from abroad.

10 What are the three major energy costs in a hotel? How can these costs be reduced?

11 Some people would argue that energy saving and the reduction of acid rain pollution and global warming is not the responsibility of the hospitality industry but rather that of government. Is this a fair comment?

12 Issue for debate

In Chapter 1 we discussed how fossil fuels are a finite source of energy, and that there is currently extensive research to discover alternative, safe and renewable sources of energy. The Government has a target to produce 3 per cent of total electricity from renewable resources by the year 2000. Wind power has been suggested as one solution, and there are a number of 'wind farms' running experimentally throughout the world, including the west coast of the USA, in Denmark and in Wales. Recently there was considerable opposition to an application for planning permission to erect a wind farm in the Pennines, between Hebden Bridge and Haworth (Yorkshire). This is regarded as a beauty spot, and many people consider that the windmills will spoil the natural beauty of the area.

Do you agree with this argument? If so, do you think that this is a reasonable cost to society? Would you mind if a wind farm was established in a beauty spot close to your home? Is this an example of 'NIMBY' (not in my backyard) syndrome?

Figure 4.5 A wind farm in the West Country

Useful conversions
1 therm = 29.3 kWh
1000 kWh = 1 MWh
1,000,000 kWh = 1 GWh (Gigawatt-hour)
1,000 MWh = 1 GWh
1 kWh = 3.6 MJ (Megajoules)
1 MWh = 3.6 Gj (Gigajoules)
1 Gcal = 1,000,000 kcal
1 therm = 100,000 BTU
1 kcal = 3.97 BTU
29.3071 kW = 1 therm (natural gas)

A formula has been developed to convert the consumption of fuels to emissions of carbon dioxide, in kilograms of carbon dioxide produced per kWh of fuel used.[15] This is as follows:

gas   0.21
oil   0.29
electricity   0.72

Notes

1 Department of the Environment, *Sustainable Development – The UK Strategy*, London: HMSO, 1994.
2 In 1986 a nuclear reactor at Chernobyl in the Ukraine, at that time part of the USSR, exploded; three people were killed, 500 were severely injured and thousands were evacuated. Nuclear fallout spread across Europe and contaminated grazing land in North Wales, the Midlands and the Lake District.
3 A 40 kW photovoltaic panel system has been installed on the south face of a building at the University of Northumbria in Newcastle-upon-Tyne.
4 This is the latest available data on pure catering use.
5 Food Hygiene (General) Regulations 1970.
6 Lux refers to the Système International (SI) unit of illumination, equal to one lumen per square metre received on a surface. A lumen is an SI unit of luminous flux, which is used to describe the quantity of light emitted by a source or received by a surface. For example, a 100 W conventional bulb emits 1200 lumens.
7 They fit into the same fittings and thus don't require an adaptor.
8 All data from Philips Lighting, Croydon, Surrey, UK.
9 Energy Efficiency Office, *Condensing Boilers*, General Information Leaflet 3, January 1992.
10 Energy Efficiency Office; for more information see 'New Practice – Final Profile CHP in a medium-sized hotel', *Energy Efficiency Office Best Practice Programme*, no. 30, 1991.

11 Regrettably the most recent specialist catering costs available. Energy Efficiency Office, 1983.
12 IHEI Handbook 1993.
13 SEEBOARD business rates, 1998. Note that terms will differ depending on the supplier and whether the supply is for business or domestic use.
14 In practice the opportunities will be phased in, according to postal codes, to ensure an even spread across the country. Your local OFFER (the Office of Electricity Regulation) office can provide further information. Head Office: telephone: 0121 456 2100.
15 Energy Efficiency Office, *Energy Efficiency in Hotels*, Guide 36, Energy Efficiency Office, Best Practice Programme, 1993.

Useful addresses and further information

BRECSU, Building Research Establishment, Garston, Watford, WD2 7JR.
Energy Efficiency Enquiries Bureau, ETSU, Harwell, Oxfordshire OX11 0RA.
The Energy Efficiency Office, *Energy Efficiency in Hotels*, Guide 36, Energy Efficiency Office, 1993.

CHAPTER 5

Water

OBJECTIVES

1 To demonstrate the importance of the water cycle for life on earth.
2 To discuss patterns of rainfall and water usage in the UK.
3 To discuss the effects of climate change on rainfall distribution.
4 To describe the process of an audit of water use.
5 To discuss the importance of a high standard of water quality.

INTRODUCTION

Of all the water used by the hospitality industry, only 5 per cent is used for eating and drinking; the vast majority of it is used either for cleaning or for the preparation of food. Cleaning processes which include bathing and showering, laundries, dishwashers, and the actual cleaning up process itself, consume the greatest proportion of water. How much water does the average hotel resident use? General estimates are that guests use only 10 per cent of the total bedroom water use, and that the rest is used by the chambermaids during cleaning.

This chapter will examine current use of water by the hospitality industry in the UK, and consider whether there is excessive wastage. It will examine the costs of water to the industry, the effectiveness of metering, and the potential for savings both of water and money. We will also undertake an equipment survey to identify the costs of high and low water usage and possibilities for recycling. But let us first examine a few of the environmental considerations. Why is water such a precious commodity?

THE WATER CYCLE

Figure 1.3 in Chapter 1 (p. 11) is a very rudimentary sketch of how the water on the planet is recycled. This cycle is dependant upon the processes of evaporation and precipitation, and is driven by solar energy. The heat of the sun causes water to evaporate from both land and sea, and from the leaves of plants (a process known as transpiration); the warm air carrying the water vapour slowly rises and as it does so it cools. Warmer air has a greater ability to hold water than colder air, so as the rising air cools it is able to hold less water vapour; the water vapour condenses and forms clouds, mist or fog. Rain forms when the water vapour collects, or condenses, around tiny particles in the atmosphere: these can be dust from industry, or traffic, or salt above the sea. If the surrounding air is below freezing these droplets will form snow. Clouds are blown towards the land, and as they approach mountain ranges they rise, cooling even more and precipitating their contents onto the land. The rain runs off into streams, rivers and lakes and can eventually run to the sea; other rain percolates through the subsoil to boost the water table. Although almost half a million cubic kilometres of water are evaporated from the seas each year, only 14,000 cubic kilometres become available for use.

What are the uses of water? It is the habitat of an extensive range of plants and animals, fish and insects. It is essential for agriculture, industry is dependent on water for many of its processes, and it is used for the transport of industrial goods. Humans are dependent on a clean and regular supply for drinking, and it is also used for sewage processing. There is also an extensive use of water for recreation. Unfortunately it is indiscriminately used for the dumping of waste of all kinds and can be a major source of disease. Consequently there is substantial potential for conflicts of interest in the use of water.

Of the total amount of water found on earth, 97 per cent is distributed in the oceans and only 3 per cent exists as freshwater. Of the freshwater resources 99 per cent is found as ice at the North and South Poles, and in aquifers which are too deep for the water they contain to be accessible. Thus only 0.003 per cent of the total water on earth is available for humans to use. The water cycle diagram (Figure 1.3) shows how this freshwater is constantly recycled. It has been estimated that on a worldwide basis enough rain falls on the earth to flood the land to a depth of 86 cm (33 inches). This is sufficient to meet our needs many times over; however the problem is the distribution of this rainfall. Whereas tropical rainforests have copious volumes of rain, desert areas can suffer severe drought (less than 25 cm a year).

To add to this problem many parts of the industrialized world place excessive demands on the available water supplies. Worldwide, of the total rainfall only 9 per cent is withdrawn for human use; 90 per cent of this is used for agriculture, 7 per cent for industry, and the balance for domestic use. Obviously the distribution depends upon the country and its relative levels of industrialization and urbanization.

EXCESSIVE DEMAND FOR WATER

Excessive demand for water can lead to a range of problems including:

subsidence as the water table drops – this can make properties and roads collapse;

salination of the soil – again due to lowering of the water table – as salt water is drawn into coastal regions;

drying out of inland lakes and reservoirs;

rivers running dry as more water is drawn off; it is feasible for countries to draw off 10–20 per cent from rivers, and many industrialized countries draw off as much as 30 per cent, but in times of shortage high withdrawals can result in river levels being reduced dramatically.

Droughts occur when there is a 70 per cent reduction in rainfall for twenty-one consecutive days. This results in a drop in the water table, the destruction of flora and fauna, the loss of crops, and severe drops in the levels of lakes, reservoirs, streams and rivers.

Where is the water supply in the UK drawn from? In 1991 approximately 34.5 megalitres a day were abstracted by the water authorities; 51 per cent of this was for public supplies, and 47.6 per cent was taken by industry for private use. Of the supplies used by the public, 70 per cent is drawn from rivers, and 30 per cent from groundwater boreholes; only 4.4 per cent of rainfall directly enters the public water supply.

The south and east of England are particularly dependent on groundwater supplies. Since 1980 demand for domestic water supplies has increased substantially while that for industrial use has declined, as many of the traditional industries which used water, such as steel and coal, have closed down.

Rainfall patterns and population distribution in the UK mean that whereas in the Northumbria water supply area there is a 94 per cent surplus of water resources over demand, in the Thames region there is only a 4 per cent surplus, and in the Southern region only 3 per cent (1990 figures). The average rainfall in the south-east and East Anglia is 610 mm (24 inches); in Wales it is twice this. There are also yearly variations in rainfall.

Hence although the overall rainfall pattern in the UK is theoretically in excess of demand, the ability to supply those parts of the country where demand is greatest and supply the least can be problematical. At the same time, water consumption in the UK over the past thirty years has increased by 70 per cent, to a daily per capita average of 140 litres; this is still considerably less than that of most Western European countries, and of the USA.

The popular tourist location of Jersey has to desalinate its water supply in the height of the summer in order to meet demand. Not only is this expensive, but it is an energy intensive process.

THE EFFECTS OF CLIMATE CHANGE

Climatologists use very complex computer models to work out whether there is a world pattern of temperature increases that could indicate global warming. In the late 1980s and early 1990s the patterns of drought and flood and unseasonally warm winters have not been outside of similar recorded patterns, but the variables in the computer models are so diverse and complex that the results of different studies are rather mixed. Some models predict that the earth's average temperature will increase by 0.5 °C in the next 100 years, whereas others can provide no such evidence. However there is a greater consensus in favour of there being a very strong possibility of this happening. Models of the effects of global warming on rainfall patterns predict increased rainfall, increased patterns of evaporation as the result of drought, longer growing periods for agriculture, and more storms and flooding. It is likely that those areas of the UK that are already vulnerable to water shortages would experience extreme pressure on their resources.

There have been fluctuations in average temperatures and volumes of rainfall in the UK over the past 1000 years. Minor variations in temperature should not be regarded as confirmation of global warming. For example the south and east of England had well below average patterns of rainfall during the winters of 1988–92, whereas the winter of 1994/95 had higher than average rainfall, but all the extremes of temperature, rainfall and drought are well within previously recorded data.

We have established that prolonged drought would seriously affect the availability of water supplies, particularly in the south of England, and the water companies will increasingly be taking measures to restrict use, or to make realistic charges for water use. To this end it is important for the water authorities to be able to predict potential change as it can take up to ten years to develop new resources.

For instance, Table 5.1 shows the predicted increase in demand for public water supplies in 2021 over demand in 1990.

Table 5.1 The predicted increase in demand for public water supplies in 2021 over demand in 1990

Region (by company name)	Change in demand (%)	Surplus resources (%)
Anglian	42	–4
Northumbrian	20	62
Northwest	–10	24
Severn Trent	9	13
Southern	23	0
Southwest	39	11
Thames	26	1
Welsh	8	25
Wessex	45	0
Yorkshire	11	15

Source: National Rivers Authority (NRA), *Report in Sustainable Development*, no. 5143.

Table 5.1 shows the mismatches between water availability and demand currently and in the future. The south and east of England which has the lowest rainfall is expected to have the greatest increase in demand over the next 20–30 years. Factors which will affect demand include demographic patterns, average consumption of water per head, losses from both the mains system and individual premises, and the intensity of economic activity.

MEETING INCREASED DEMAND

What options are there for the water authorities in order to meet the projected increased demand for water in the UK in the next thirty years? It is possible to build new reservoirs, to increase the number of boreholes, to increase abstraction rates from rivers, and also to pipe water from areas of plenty to those of scarcity. However there are a number of financial and environmental drawbacks to all these proposals. Not only is the building of a dam an expensive and major civil engineering project, but it also has a significant impact on the environment and on the landscape. Dams destroy the local environment, habitats, property and farmland. They also impede the flow of river water to the sea causing shortages further downstream which can cause problems in the aquatic environment both for the freshwater and coastal species. The construction of dams consumes vast quantities of energy and aggregates. In addition, new water sources would create an increased demand for energy for pumping and treatment. Building new dams therefore does not solve the problem; demand will continue to expand to meet the supply and eventually there will be a need for yet another new dam.

The sinking of increased numbers of boreholes means that the water table will be reduced even lower, which will mean that poor quality water will be extracted, and also that the rivers which ground water feeds will have their flow even more drastically restricted. Increased withdrawal from rivers has similar effects on the flora and fauna habitat. The piping of water across the country also means costly civil engineering, and problems can also arise as the result of mixing waters of different chemical compositions.

The easiest, least expensive and most environmentally-friendly option is to manage current resources more carefully. The answer is to curb or restrict demand, which will involve a number of measures to manage demand. A Government Consultation Paper, entitled 'Using Water Wisely', published in 1992, argued that fiscal incentives and water metering would be the best options. This means that charges for water would be imposed on that sector which in the vast majority of cases do not pay for water on a usage basis but pay as a flat charge for the volume used – the domestic consumer. Metering trials of domestic properties in some parts of the UK indicate that the installation of meters does indeed reduce demand, and that there are potential average savings of 11 per cent, and as much as 20 per cent at peak times. The Labour Government has decided, however, that it will not introduce the compulsory installation of meters into existing properties, although all new homes will be metered.

We should not forget that commercial properties have always paid for their water on a metered basis.

It is estimated that up to 25 per cent of water that enters the mains system is lost through leakages. In the 1990s £2000 million was allocated to the repair of mains to reduce these significant losses. Leaks in the pipes belonging to water consumers are legally their responsibility, and metering trials have shown that if water lost through leakages is charged for then the customer will be more likely to mend the leakages.

Sustainable water supplies:

- Conservation of water sources and supplies
- Recycle wherever possible
- Restore lost sources
- Population control
- Reduce irrigation losses
- Charge the true cost of water
- Improve codes of building practice
- Stop mains leakages
- Use 'grey' water for irrigation
- Prevent or minimize the loss of vegetation

DRINKING WATER QUALITY

All water that goes into the public supply in the UK is produced to the standard required for food preparation and drinking. The regulatory authority is the Drinking Water Inspectorate (DWI). In 1989 regulations were made to implement the EC Drinking Water Directive which laid out very detailed standards for the quality of water intended for drinking from public supplies, and in 1992 for water from private supplies. In 1992 a report by the DWI indicated that in England and Wales 98.7 per cent of all the tests on water showed that it complied with standards laid down by the EC Drinking Water Directive. The figures were 98.4 per cent in Scotland and 99 per cent in Northern Ireland. The water companies have since this date implemented programmes to improve these standards even further.

The main potential pollutants of drinking water are lead, nitrates, pesticides and the parasite cryptosporidium. Although there are minuscule traces of lead in drinking water when it leaves the treatment works, most lead in water supplies is the result of water passing through old lead pipes, where the lead dissolves into the water, or as the result of being stored in lead cisterns. This is the case in old buildings which have not been refurbished. Lead can affect intellectual performance particularly in infants and children. The current EC and UK maximum permitted concentrations are 50 micrograms per litre, although the World Health Organization (WHO) have revised their guidelines to 10 micrograms per litre.

The EC limit for nitrates in drinking water is 50 milligrams per litre. Water contaminated in excess of this is likely to be drawn from areas where there is intensive farming, such as the Midlands and East Anglia;[1] the potential problem is methaemoglobinaemia, or blue baby syndrome, whereby babies are unable to bind enough oxygen to their haemoglobin. This is potentially fatal, although the last recorded death in the UK was in East Anglia in the 1950s. In addition, there are unresolved fears that high levels of consumption of nitrates in the diet can lead to cancer of the stomach and oesophagus; levels in excess of 50 mg per litre found in drinking water can make a significant contribution to the total individual consumption of nitrates.

Pesticide contamination is also due to intensive farming practices. The EC ceiling is 0.1 micrograms per litre, but the WHO regulations are more stringent, giving standards for 34 specific, commonly used pesticides. The WHO recommendations are based on modern toxicity tests in conjunction with estimates of the medical risks involved; this is the standard which the UK will eventually achieve.

Cryptosporidium is an animal parasite, again commonly present in agricultural areas. It is believed to run into water sources from farmland or sewage discharges, and finds its way into water supplies. The major problem with this organism is that it is resistant to chlorine, which is used to protect drinking water supplies from pathogenic bacteria. This parasite can cause diarrhoea; 'travellers' diarrhoea' is often caused by cryptosporidium.

WATER AND THE HOSPITALITY INDUSTRY

We have already seen that industrial and commercial users of water have been charged on a metered basis for many years. The catering industry in the UK uses 1.3 per cent of all water used in the UK. This section will examine in turn each area of a catering or hospitality business and will assess where water is used and to what extent savings can be made. It should be stressed, however, that water is essential for hygiene and safety and that if its use is restricted too radically there is potential for significant problems. Water is essential for cleaning; the question we need to ask is 'are excessive quantities of water being used and if so is it possible to reduce this usage without compromising health and safety?'

Food preparation

On average only 2–10 per cent of total water used in the industry is used for food preparation, eating and drinking. There are a number of actions that can be taken to minimize the waste of water in this area.

- Staff should be trained to defrost food by placing it in the fridge overnight, or in the microwave, rather than placing it under running cold water.
- Vegetables and fruits should be washed in a basin or bowl of water rather than under the running tap.
- The 'refreshing' of vegetables under cold running water should be discouraged; either place them in a basin of iced water, and drain as soon as they are cold enough, or else reconsider the cooking and preparation methods. For instance, if large quantities of vegetables are cooked and refreshed in anticipation of use, they will need to be reheated, which involves extra time and energy usage, whereas the use of a pressure steamer will ensure the rapid, nutritious production of a product which will look its best when needed.
- Install flow controllers on taps.
- Use cold water rather than hot wherever possible.
- Ensure all staff are trained in the conservation of water practices.

Toilets

Twenty-five per cent of the public water supply is used for flushing toilets and urinals; in hotels it can be as much as 30 per cent. Most cisterns in the UK use 9 litres (2 gallons), although new toilet and cistern systems installed since 1989 may use no more than 7.5 litres (under new water by-laws). However, research has shown that careful design can permit satisfactory flushing using as little as 5 litres.

Placing a brick in the toilet cistern is not a good idea. The volume of water necessary to clear a toilet pan is related to the design of the pan, so by restricting this volume it might require two flushes thereby using extra water! Such a measure can also cause the cistern to malfunction.

From January 1993 the installation of dual flush systems (other than as a straight replacement for existing ones), which deliver flushes of either 5 or 9 litres, was prohibited as there is evidence that mishandling can cause even more water to be used.

Urinals are normally fitted with automatic flushing systems; the frequency of flushing depends on the rate at which the cistern refills. There are also by-laws which require any system installed after 1988 to be switched off when the urinals are not in use, for instance overnight or at weekends. They often use a time switch or devices that respond to movement. However, it is estimated that 90 per cent of systems are not on a time switch and that the settings may be incorrect so that there is no differentiation between weekends and weekdays. More recently, passive infra-red (PIR) sensors have been used to trigger flushing. There have been reports of savings of 300 to 500 litres per bowl per day, even in systems already fitted with controls. But it has also been found that in some areas this reduction in the frequency of flushing has led to an increase in scale build-up, requiring an increase in maintenance to avoid odours, blockages and floods.

Industry Case Study

Sloane House, a Forte hotel in Aylesbury, was consuming 3600 m³ of water a year in each men's urinal due to the urinals activating automatically every two minutes. A PIR system was installed that activated flushing after each use, and the volume of water used in the building was reduced to 251 m³. This resulted in a 93 per cent reduction in costs, equivalent to £3200 per urinal.

Another system in use utilizes mineral oil as a barrier to prevent odours returning into the toilet area; this is used in conjunction with a waterless system. Another water-free system, devised by a British company, uses a small paper disc impregnated with a substance which eliminates odours from the urinal. Conversion to this system costs in the region of £30 per urinal bowl, and the cost of the disc is 50p, so the installation will quickly pay for itself.

As the majority of urinals are installed in properties which have their water metered, the installation of a proper control system would pay for itself very quickly.

Sewage disposal

Sewage in the UK is normally disposed of via a mains system which transports the waste material to a treatment centre where it is rendered harmless. The cost of sewage disposal is calculated on the volume of total water supplied less 5 per cent for that taken off the premises. This means that substantial savings in water use will be replicated in savings in sewage charges.

The average toilet uses 7.5 litres of water per flush; if vacuum toilets (similar to those used in aircrafts) were to be substituted (as Forte did at its M11 service station at Birchanger Green), this can then be reduced to 1.5 litres per flush. The capital installation costs for Forte meant an extra £40,000, but the payback over time in terms of reduced water charges (all paid for by a meter), and in sewage charges, was calculated to be two years.

In the 1990s Forte paid approximately £7 million annually in water and sewage costs.

There is tremendous scope when considering new building projects to incorporate an on-site sewage treatment plant. This could be installed either in the grounds or the basement, and the treated water can be used to run off into reed beds and for irrigation of the grounds, or even into a pond where it can be drawn on for toilets or irrigation. As the plants are cheap to run and maintain, the initial investment will rapidly be recovered in sewage costs savings. An additional investment in a small UV sanitizing system will return the water to potable standards, so that the project could become virtually self-sufficient in water and sewage disposal.

'Grey' water

It is possible to achieve a 60 per cent reduction in water use by recycling 'grey' water – water from baths and showers, and rainwater. Recent research shows that it makes economic sense in hotels and guest houses to use grey water for toilets, despite the extra costs involved in installing two separate plumbing systems.

If the chemical content of waste water is environmentally benign then it is also possible to recycle waste water for the irrigation of gardens, and if chlorinated it can be diverted for laundry use or other forms of cleaning.

Baths and showers

Twenty per cent of water in the UK is used for personal washing, and is mainly drawn from the hot water tank. Much of this is wasted due to the long pipe run between tank and tap. Often cold water is added to hot to ensure a comfortable temperature; this, of course, is a waste of energy.

There are 5.3 billion sleeper nights each year worldwide. If each guest takes a shower once a 'sleeper night' this will use 160 billion gallons of water a year! The installation of low-flow showerheads that limit the water flow to 12 litres per minute would reduce this consumption dramatically, at no inconvenience to the customer. Baths on average use 80 litres (17.5 gallons) of water, whereas the typical shower uses only 30 litres (6.5 gallons), although power showers and multi-showers use rather more.

Industry Case Studies

The installation of water-efficient showerheads in a luxury hotel in Jamaica in 1992 has reduced water consumption by 500,000 gallons a month.

The Wallard Inter-Continental Hotel in Washington, DC has reported annual savings of US$17,000 in water charges after a similar installation, and there have been no adverse customer comments.

It should be noted that some water-efficient showerheads rely on the addition of air to the water flow to produce an effective spray. This aerosol effect can provide the microclimate for the growth of bacteria which can be inhaled. It is therefore vital that these showerheads are regularly descaled and disinfected or replaced.

Taps

There is a vast range of 'quick action' taps that require only a quarter turn to operate. Some are fitted with 'flow regulators' that can be fitted to basins and these will quickly pay for themselves. The installation of aerators to taps will reduce the flow to 5–6 litres per minute.

Washing machines and dishwashers

There are no figures available for the volume of water that is used by washing machines in the service sector, but they account for 12 per cent of water use in the domestic sector. Obviously there is significant usage if we consider the volume of laundry and washing-up generated by hotels.

Both washing machines and dishwashers are heavy users of water, despite restrictions on the volume of water that they may draw. It has been estimated that the laundry of a 500-room hotel uses approximately 20 million litres of water per year, and that 13 fl.oz (400 ml) of water are used per glass washed-up.

It should be noted, however, that if less water is used in dishwashing then a greater amount of detergent and sanitizer needs to be used to achieve the same standard of hygiene; the costs to the environment change yet remain significant.

It should go without saying that good staff training will include advising them to operate dishwashers only when they are full, and also not to turn them on until there is equipment to wash.

Industry Case Study

The Hanover Inter-Continental Hotel installed a new dishwasher to replace an outdated model. Water consumption was reduced by 80 per cent, from 1800 litres per hour to 360 litres. This system paid for itself in 2.7 years.

In order to reduce the load on the laundry, many hotel companies throughout the world offer their guests the option of reusing their towels for as long as they desire during their stay. They are asked to place the old towel in the bath if they want a replacement. Not only does this save on water, but it also saves on energy and chemicals.

Other examples of good laundry practice include:

- Only operate the washing machines and driers when they have full loads.
- Install a water (and heat) recovery system from washing and dry cleaning machines.
- Check that the washing machines operate with the correct water levels during individual cycles.

General considerations

One major consideration in the responsible use of water is to train all staff in the monitoring of wastage, particularly in the instance of *dripping taps*; several thousand gallons of water a year can be wasted in this way, even if they are slow leaks. It is also essential to monitor all equipment for water leaks – washing machines, dishwashers, coffee machines, and so on. For a company on a water meter, leaks can prove very expensive.

Many companies have discovered that thorough staff training is vital in ensuring that water is treated as a valuable commodity; if staff do not see the point of careful use then they will not support a conservation programme.

Landscape and grounds maintenance

A tremendous amount of waste can occur through the inappropriate watering of grounds, for instance, when an irrigation system distributes water to places where it is not required, or because it is operated on a basic time switch principle which takes no heed of current weather conditions.

Industry Case Studies

The Abu Dhabi Corniche Hilton International trained its staff in water conservation techniques. Whereas previously the housekeepers would flush the toilets four times during cleaning, this has been reduced to one flush per clean.

The Ritz Inter-Continental Hotel Lisbon reduced water consumption by 74 per cent in eight years. It introduced flow regulators to all shower-heads and water taps, fitted garden irrigation systems with automatic timers, installed submeters into all departments, set goals for water reductions, improved the maintenance programme so that it detected and repaired leaks immediately, and made staff training a priority.

Le Grand Hotel Inter-Continental in Paris managed to reduce its water consumption by 44 per cent between 1992 and 1995.

The Al Bustan Palace Inter-Continental Muscat (Oman) recycles 450–600 cubic metres of water every day from the hotel's sewage treatment facility (which also serves the local village of 1500 residents). The water is used to irrigate the local area. Oman has only 1 mm of rain in July and 28 mm in the wettest month of the year.

We have seen how it can be possible to use 'grey' water, or water diverted from in-house sewage plants, for irrigation. It is also possible to install moisture sensors in grounds which trigger the irrigation system only when needed.

Other ways in which to minimize the demand for water include the planting of drought-resistant flora, or native species of plant which have adapted to the climate patterns; the use of thick beds of mulch to minimize evaporation; and to accept that a 'perfect' lawn is not the standard to which the modern, caring and environmentally-friendly business aspires. Consider the development of wildlife areas and reseed the lawn area with traditional hedgerow flowers. Ensure the area is not cut down until the flowers have bloomed and allowed the seeds to fall for next year's growth. Tell the guests about your environmental objectives. You will be surprised at the extra range of insects, butterflies and birds that you will attract, to the benefit of your environment.

In line with such ecologically-sound principles, the use of pesticides and fertilizers should be either minimized or avoided. The success of the Henry Doubleday Research Association display grounds in Coventry and Kent is one excellent example of organic gardening.

Table 5.2 Benchmarks for daily water consumption by department (submetered), in litres per guest

Department	Good	Fair	Poor
Guest rooms	<250	250–330	>330
Kitchens (litres per cover)	<35	35–45	>45
Laundry without recovery	<25	25–30	>30
Laundry with recovery	<15	15–20	>20

Source: IHEI, 1993.

Table 5.3 Benchmarks for daily water consumption by hotel, in litres per guest

Type of hotel	Good	Fair	Poor	Very poor
Large with laundry, kitchens, air-conditioning, pool	<600	600–770	770–880	>880
Medium-sized (50–150 rooms)	<440	440–500	500–600	>600
Small (4–50 rooms), no laundry, limited air-conditioning	<330	330–380	380–440	>440

Source: IHEI, 1993.

You can make a virtue of your environmental commitment by advertising the manner in which the grounds are cultivated, and showing that the 'perfect' manicured garden and lawn can be replaced by an environment far more attractive and beneficial to wildlife.

Finally, establish cleaning rotas and procedures for all outside areas to minimize the use of water and chemicals, and cover swimming pools when not in use, as most water is lost from pools through evaporation.

CONDUCTING A WATER AUDIT

Before any financial savings can be made the sensible manager will carry out an audit of the amount of water that the business is currently using, and compare this with previous years. The most straightforward method to do this is to look at the metered water and sewage bills. If possible, it would be wise to install internal usage meters on equipment such as dishwashers, or in areas such as the laundry, which are major water users. A typical example of water use in a large international hotel can be seen in Table 5.4.

Table 5.4 Example of water usage in a large international hotel, by percentage

Kitchens	21
High ventilation air-conditioning	1
Guest rooms	37
Pool	2
Public toilets	17
Steamroom	4
Laundry	12
Coldrooms	7

Source: IHEI, *Green Hotelier*, no. 1, 1993.

Compare your business's water usage figures with the figures in Tables 5.2 and 5.3 (p. 104) which show the industry standards.

DETERGENTS

The hospitality industry is an intensive and extensive user of detergent; this is because whiteness and brightness are associated with cleanliness (the result of aggressive promotions by detergent companies). Detergents are designed to work with water and end up in waste systems, and therefore the amount of detergent that is used should be considered. However, we must remember that it is essential to maintain a balance between environmental considerations and the need for high standards of hygiene in the industry. When we assess the environmental performance of the use of detergents we need to consider the following: biodegradability, tensoactivity, toxicity and dermatological issues.

The speed at which detergents biodegrade depends on the temperature of the water. OECD guidelines state that 80 per cent of the total product must biodegrade within 28 days at a constant temperature of 25 °C. The permanent reduction of water tension is a major pollutant and a key cause of destruction of aquatic life. The toxicity of these detergents is often the result of overperformance; optical brighteners give an impression of whiteness but can also cause dermatological problems. World Health Organization data indicate that in the West damage to the skin caused by detergents has increased fivefold in the past 20 years. This is attributed to the harsh chemicals that are used by detergent companies in a highly competitive market.

There have been a number of spurious claims made by the advertising industry to do with detergents, the most glaring one being that a product is 'phosphate free' – yet phosphates have never been a component of washing-up liquid!

Let us now compare the declared environmental performance of two companies which supply the hospitality industry with a range of cleaning products, Ecover and Diversey.

Diversey Ltd

> Diversey Ltd's business, cleaning and sanitising, has a high profile in today's environment conscious world. In any food producing business there can be no compromising with standards but this does not mean that environmental considerations do not apply. Formulation of an environmental policy is a necessary first step to realising environmental obligations but then comes the difficult part of putting it into practice.
>
> Dick Lowe, Technical Director, Diversey Ltd[2]

Diversey Ltd markets a range of concentrated products for use by the hospitality industry, covering such areas as kitchen hygiene, room service and the cleansing of dispensing equipment. Concentrates use less packaging, consume fewer resources in their manufacture and in the manufacture of their packaging, consume less delivery fuel and have reduced waste disposal requirements. Diversey also claims that it introduced the first biodegradable rinse aid to the UK market.

EC requirements for Eco-labelling include a full life-cycle analysis.

Diversey is working towards BS 7750 (see Chapter 12, pp. 218–20) for its environmental management systems, and it claims that it has a rolling programme of chemical reduction and minimization, yet the company provides no details of the content of its products/list of ingredients. Diversey has instituted both an environmental audit programme and an environmental operating committee to respond to customer and employee concerns.

The Ecover group

Established in 1980, Ecover built the world's first 'ecological' factory and first water purification scheme based on wind and solar energy. Ecover claims that its products are manufactured without phosphates, enzymes, optical and chemical bleaches, petroleum-based detergents, synthetic colourings and perfumes. In addition it claims that all products are made from natural raw materials, and are not tested on animals. Ecover also designs its detergents so that 99.7 per cent of the product biodegrades within eleven days at a constant temperature of 10 °C, although their eventual target is 99.9 per cent biodegradability in four hours at 5 °C. Ecover will custom-make detergents according to the water quality of individual customers. For example, a pilot project using Ecover products was carried out for the SAS Hotel chain. Ecover also undertake contract research for Diversey and Rentokil.

Industry Case Study

In 1995 Scandic Hotels installed a dispenser system which reduced the use of washing-up liquid and cleaning chemicals by more than 25 per cent. It also worked with Ecolab to develop a computer program which can compare the consumption of certain chemicals at different hotels. The hotels use liquid soaps and shampoos based on vegetable matter that quickly biodegrade. They are dispensed in a system which halves the amount normally used – to 19 ml per guest per night.

CONCLUSION

This chapter has shown the importance of water in the UK and the differing patterns of rainfall. It has also examined those systems in the hospitality industry which make the greatest demands on the water supplies and has provided guidelines to minimize loss. Despite extensive media debate about the 'fairness' of charging the domestic customer for the actual volume of water that s/he consumes, we should not forget that the average charge in the UK is £1 per person per week. Given the volume of water that we use for daily living this is incredibly cheap. We tend not to value water because we feel that it is 'free', or that it should be. If global warming does take hold, and all the terrible predictions of its effects do occur, then we could be the last generation in the UK to take water for granted. Which is the more essential to life, water or electricity? Yet we don't complain as much about the cost of electricity.

QUESTIONS AND ISSUES FOR DISCUSSION

1 Choose a catering establishment and carry out an audit of water.
   (a) Calculate the average volume of water used over a month. Identify areas of the operation and equipment with the greatest use.
   (b) Make recommendations for change if appropriate.
   (c) Make short-, medium- and long-term projections for savings both for the business and for the environment.

2 Discuss the importance of a high standard of water quality.

3 'Water is a precious commodity not to be wasted.' Debate this issue.

4 On a large blank map of the UK, draw a diagram of the water cycle as it works in the UK. Identify areas of greatest precipitation and evaporation, irrigated areas, areas of potentially high nitrate levels in the groundwater and boreholes, indicate lakes and dams which are used for water storage and indicate which conurbations they serve, and highlight those parts of the UK which make the highest demands on the water supplies.

5 You have been appointed project manager to oversee the building of a new brasserie. Its location is on the seafront of a popular but exclusive resort on the south-west coast of England and you have been asked to liaise with the architect. The costs of both water and sewage are very high in this area, so you have been asked to ensure that the very best/latest equipment and systems are installed to minimize water usage without endangering health or food safety. The brasserie will seat 100 people indoors, with potential for 20 covers outside when the weather permits. The menu design, choice and style of equipment, and decor are for you to decide. Present your choices and decisions in the form of a report to the architect, providing a rationale in each case to support your decision. Include costings as appropriate.

6 Are green cleaners as effective as conventional cleaning products? What exercise might you carry out to establish which is the more effective? If you have access to laboratories, you might extend your work by also undertaking a microbiological analysis.

Notes

1 Recordings of nitrate concentrations in drinking water in some parts of the Midlands and East Anglia have been as high as 80 mg per litre in the 1980s.
2 Diversey Ltd, *Diversey and the Environment, 1993–4*, Report published by Diversey Ltd, 1995.

CHAPTER 6

Green technology in the hospitality industry

OBJECTIVES

1 To critically evaluate equipment currently used by the hospitality industry, with reference to its environmental performance.
2 To describe and assess a number of new technological innovations that can assist a business to conform to more demanding environmental legislation, i.e. energy efficiency, waste, etc.
3 To undertake a number of comparisons of costs between conventional equipment and equipment which could minimize effects on the environment while also maintaining quality and efficiency

INTRODUCTION

In Part 1 we discussed the range of concerns shared by scientists and governments about the ways in which modern industrial economies are creating environmental problems, not only for the current generation, but also for future generations. We have also examined a variety of ways in which governments encourage individuals and businesses to adopt more responsible working practices, including regulation and the use of financial incentives and deterrents in accordance with the 'pollutor pays' principle. This chapter will examine some of the ways in which manufacturers of equipment designed for use in the hospitality industry have responded to these initiatives, and to the opportunities presented by a more environmentally aware society. We will also assess how newer innovations and technology can assist businesses to achieve environmental targets. It is better to prevent pollution at source, or to minimize the effects of activities on the environment at source, rather than having to take the extra time and trouble to reduce the effects that the pollution created. Invariably this approach is cheaper and easier, especially if financial costs are also included in any assessment.

COOKING EQUIPMENT

Combination steamers

These are available in a range of sizes and are especially suitable for the cooking of larger volumes of food, although they can of course process small quantities (uneconomically). They can be gas or electrically powered, and are able to steam, bake, braise, poach, grill and roast foods; these functions can be carried out either separately or in combination. They are also able to regenerate previously cooked frozen or chilled foods and to prove bakery items. Although an expensive investment, these ovens more than pay for themselves as a result of their versatility and their economical size. Energy savings as high as 60 per cent compared to traditional cooking methods and equipment are claimed for some of these appliances due to their rapid heating up times and excellent insulation properties.

As the name implies, combination steamers use a combination of steam and dry convection heating, and can be programmed to work in a variety of ways. The smallest oven costs approximately £4000 (1998 prices) and prices can go up to £11,000 for larger models. However, it is their versatility that makes the high price worth paying. Such expenditure can easily be exceeded by the more orthodox combined purchases of a conventional oven, a grill or salamander, perhaps a steamer, together with the additional running and maintenance costs of these separate pieces of equipment. Combination steamers, although large, can also represent significant savings in space. Let us consider the variety of uses of the 'Combi' steamer.

Roasting
Potential savings using combination mode include a 20 per cent reduction in shrinkage in joints if they are steamed before being roasted. This should produce a greater yield from the joint and hence increased profits. In addition, steaming means that it is not necessary to baste the meat with fat in order to ensure that it does not dry out, as the steam has substituted for the fat, yet the meat remains moist and succulent when served. Nutritionally this can mean as much as 95 per cent savings on the fat content of meat dishes.

Vegetables

If used in steam-only mode there can be a 25 per cent saving in the cooking time of vegetables, resulting in less loss of nutritional quality and improved cooked appearance.

Baking

When the ovens are in convection mode not only can the cooking temperature be reduced by 25°C, but the cooking time is also reduced by 10 per cent for most products which means considerable savings in time and energy costs. Cooking in these ovens is very even so they can be used to maximum capacity without any worrying about temperature zones.

Delicate dishes

The range of programmes and sensors which maintain the correct level of humidity and temperature means that food can be cooked in individual dishes ready for service at table, or *en papillote*, and very delicate items such as fish, mousses, royale dishes and crème caramels can be gently steamed at temperatures as low as 30 °C; this results in dishes of excellent quality.

Grilling

Grilled meats and vegetables require no turning, which can result in tremendous savings in labour and time, yet they are evenly cooked both top and bottom.

Combination steamers are designed either to work with a separate steam-generating unit standing alongside, which will inject steam into the oven cavity as required, or to work without a boiler, where in this instance controlled jets of cold water are sprayed directly on to the oven's heating elements or gas heat exchanger to be instantly turned into steam. This latter method is claimed to be more energy efficient as there is no necessity to pre-heat a boiler, and the makers claim a 25–30 per cent saving in water use. However, there can be problems with scaling inside the oven cavity in hard water areas which can result in unsightly discoloration. This can be countered by the fitting of a water conditioning unit.

Combination microwave and convection ovens

These ovens, the first type of combination oven, were developed in the 1980s. They are more suited for cooking smaller volumes of food, or for use in an operation which has limited space. Like the combination steamers,

Table 6.1 Comparison between the costs of running conventional cooking equipment and methods and combination steamers and combination microwave

	Traditional	*Combination*
Connected load	9.4 kW	9.4 kW
Usage	8 hours daily	8 hours daily
	300 days per year	300 days per year
	= 19,176 kWh @ 2256	= 19,176 kWh @ 2256
	8.39p/unit	
	= £1893	
		typical savings up to 25% (564 kwh)
		= £1420
		typical savings at 40% (902 kwh)
		= £1136

they are able to carry out a range of cooking processes, including defrosting, grilling, roasting, baking, and regeneration. Because the cooking time of dishes is substantially reduced there is less shrinkage, and flavour, nutritional quality and appearance are again much improved in comparison with many conventional methods of cooking. To illustrate the versatility and savings on time and energy that can be achieved, one manufacturer[1] claims that it is possible to roast a 15 lb turkey in 45 minutes, or a four-bone rack of lamb in four minutes, to bake four jacket potatoes in eight minutes to provide a result identical to that obtained from conventional baking (i.e. crisp skin on the outside), to roast ten portions of potatoes in fifteen minutes, to roast an individual beef Wellington in five minutes, and to bake pies, pasties and sausage rolls from frozen in just nine minutes. In other words, there can be a saving of up to 80 per cent in cooking time.

The manufacturers claim that the powerful microwave settings ensure that the heating process is efficient and even, and the convection option allows browning and crisping. Grilling is also possible. Again, these ovens have sophisticated sensor systems and a range of optional programmes, and it is claimed they are simple to operate. Smaller than the combination steamers, their cost ranges from £600 to upwards of £2000.

A fat-free chip production unit

A machine has been developed in Germany, and is now available in the UK, which can turn pre-blanched frozen or fresh chips into a high-quality product identical, and even superior to, the deep-fried version. A little larger than a table-top deep fat fryer, the 'RoFry' contains a perforated 'tumbler' basket which rotates the chips in a convection-style oven. It can be pre-programmed, and can produce up to 2 kg of chips in four minutes. It then can either keep them on 'hold' or automatically unload the chips into a storage tray for immediate service.

Not only are there tremendous nutritional advantages to this system, but it does away with the need for oil which means there is no greasy steam, and thus no need for ventilation and ducting. And, of course, there are no time consuming and unpleasant tasks to perform such as cleaning out the deep fryer or filtering the oil.

The RoFry has three cooking cycles: first it senses the weight, the temperature and the moisture content of the chips, then it 'makes use of the natural moisture content of the chip to stop it drying out', and finally it drives out the moisture to crisp and brown the product. This process ensures a consistent crisp and well-coloured product with a very low fat content which is identical to products produced conventionally.

However, costing approximately £5000 – including installation – this machine compares unfavourably with a standard table-top fryer.

Ware washers

This term includes both glass washers and dishwashers. Caterers are today seeking minimal use of energy, water and chemicals at maximum efficiency. If a machine is not constantly reheating replacement water in its tank then heating costs are reduced. Machines come in a range of sizes from the small compact model for the smaller operation, to the very large conveyor system for businesses with a substantial turnover of glasses and crockery. The small compact models have a running cycle of one to four minutes while the larger systems are designed to be used as a continuous flow which is very heavy on power.

When comparing costs of disposables and reusables it is important to take into account the cost of manufacture of the dishwasher, its running costs, costs to the environment of the chemicals used, etc. for a true comparison.

Most modern machines have a hot or cold fill option for economy: wash temperature is 55°C; rinse temperature is 85°C. On new machines most cycles are run so that the water tank refills only every four cycles: the rinse water is used for the pre-rinse and wash operations in the following cycle, so that the only fresh water that is used is in the rinse cycle. If the water is pre-softened then this also reduces the need to use as much detergent. New machines are also normally built with heater and storage tanks; when investigating efficiency it is important to consider water consumption per cycle, i.e. 8 litres, 13 litres, etc., depending on the size. Modern machines are also double-skinned and highly insulated to reduce both loss of heat and noise.

PURCHASING POLICIES: PRODUCTS AND MATERIALS

The following list is a summary of some of the factors that should be taken into consideration when investing in new equipment or processes. Although perhaps idealistic, it does serve to indicate the depth to which it is possible to work if necessary.

1 Raw materials from which the machinery or other product is manufactured: have they been acquired from sustainable or renewable sources?
2 Manufacturing processes when the machinery or other products were manufactured. Did these create pollution or waste? Was energy use minimized? Was the staff working environment of a good standard?
3 The product. Can it be easily maintained? Will it require products or processes which are in themselves environmentally damaging?
4 Does the use of the product or machine generate high levels of waste or pollution?
5 Can the product or machine be recycled or reused, and/or disposed of safely?
6 If the product is made from wood (especially from tropical hardwoods), is this from a sustainable source, i.e. properly managed forests?
7 Packaging: is it excessive?
8 Cleaning materials: are they biodegradable and/or phosphate free? Is there too much packaging?

CONCLUSION

We have seen that there is a range of equipment which the wise manager will choose not only for its environmental benefits but also because it will save in energy costs. In addition, the installation of such equipment will dictate the range of dishes on the menu, and also the methods of production. Less frying for instance will result in a cleaner kitchen and restaurant, a more pleasant working environment for the staff, and less risk of fire or other accidents. Today's more sophisticated customers are more aware of eating healthily, and a menu which offers 'healthier' dishes and methods of preparation will have a competitive advantage over more 'traditional' offerings. It makes sense to invest in the environment!

QUESTIONS AND ISSUES FOR DISCUSSION

1 The manufacturers of combination microwave ovens claim that it is possible to cook an individual beef Wellington in five minutes in one of their ovens. The power ratings of one such oven are as follows:

Microwave	1.2 kW
Convection	2.5 kW
Grill	2.8 kW
Radiant heat	2.8 kW
Total loading	5.1 kW

Work out the total cost of preparing the beef Wellington in
   (a) the combination oven;
   (b) a conventional oven. (You may need to refer to a cookery book for recommended cooking times, and you will need to find out the power rating of the oven you would use.)

Calculate the difference in
   (a) time
   (b) fuel costs
   (c) energy used.

What conclusions can you draw from your findings?

2 You are the head chef in a popular restaurant that has 120 covers and which is situated close to a popular tourist attraction. You have been asked to provide a traditional lunch for a group of American tourists who are visiting the UK for the first time. Your kitchen is equipped with a large combi-steamer with six racks. Its total energy rating is 9.6 kW (both its steam and convection outputs are rated at 9 kW, and the motor control unit at 0.6 kW). The menu they have requested is as follows:
   Roast beef, Yorkshire pudding
   Roast potatoes and roast parsnips
   Carrots and peas
   Home-made apple pie
   Coffee

Cost: £5.95 per head (inclusive).

The hospitality industry

The combi-steamer's manual gives the following guidelines:[2]

20 kg of potatoes steam in 25–30 minutes.

10 kg of broccoli steam in 15–20 minutes.

90 pieces of salmon darnes will steam gently in 5–8 minutes.

72 fillet steaks will grill to medium-rare on the convection mode in 7 minutes.

70 chicken drumsticks will bake in convection mode in 20 minutes.

90 portions of fruit pie will bake in 45 minutes.

30 kg joint will roast in 85–100 minutes by combi-steaming.

(i) Using recipe books, devise a food order for this party.

(ii) Show how your order for the beef might differ if you were to use a conventional oven for roasting the meat. What reduction in costs does this represent, and what percentage of extra profit on the total bill?

(iii) In the form of a timetable, describe how you would prepare the meal for service using conventional equipment.

(iv) Explain why you have chosen this method of working and show an alternative method using the combi-steamer.

(v) What other benefits to the restaurant can you identify by the use of a combi-steamer?

(vi) If the menu price were to be increased to £7.95 per head (exclusive of VAT) what difference would this make to your answer?

3 A busy hospital provides 2000 meals every day. It calculates that it purchases an average of 850 kg of meat for roasting each week. Calculate:

(a) the savings in fuel, time and money to be made by roasting the meat in a combi-steamer as opposed to a conventional oven.

(b) the extra number of portions that can be served as a result of cooking in a combi-steamer, given a portion size of 60g of meat purchased.

4 A restaurant has 50 covers. It estimates that it serves each day 50 lunches and 100 evening meals. Its weekly food purchases include:

20 kg rib of beef

10 kg leg of lamb

10 kg roasting chickens

20 kg green vegetables

50 kg potatoes

(a) Calculate the savings the restaurant will make by cooking this produce in a combi-steamer rather than in a conventional oven and range.

(b) Calculate the savings the restaurant will make by cooking this produce in a combination microwave rather than in a conventional oven.

(c) In each case calculate the savings in time, energy, and money, and suggest the number of extra portions this would produce.

Which type of oven is most appropriate for this restaurant? Give reasons for your answer.

Note: assume that sales of menu items are roast meats and equal portions of jacket, roast and boiled potatoes, and that the green vegetables featured are broccoli, peas and spinach.

5 You have been asked to redesign a kitchen and choose equipment for a catering business. Basing your project on a real catering business, investigate whether the cost of purchasing a combination-steamer oven is justified, or whether it would be better to purchase a range of conventional equipment. Describe what factors you would need to take into account, and show how you would come to a decision. Present your findings in the form of a report to the manager of the business.

Guidance notes: factors might include initial purchase and installation costs; running costs; depreciation over 3–5 years; maintenance costs; style of menu; number and turnover of customers; style of operation; number and skills of staff.

Notes

1 Bradshaw Microwaves, 173 Kenn Rd, Clevedon, North Somerset, BS21 6LH.
2 Adapted from publicity material from Rational UK Ltd, Unit 4, Titan Court, Laporteway, Portenway Business Park, Luton, Beds LU4 8EF.

CHAPTER 7

The product

Think global, act local

'Agenda 21', endorsed at the UNCED conference, 1992

OBJECTIVES

1 To explain how a business might change the image of its product to one which is more environmentally-friendly.
2 To consider how to carry out a project to 'green' a given product or operation.

INTRODUCTION

How is it possible to 'green' a hotel or a restaurant? The theme throughout this book has been about the examination of current activities and how these should be reviewed from an environmental standpoint. It has also been argued that if it makes financial sense then it is prudent to implement these measures. What are the products of a hotel and/or a restaurant? Is it possible to 'green' the menu, or the bedrooms, or the banqueting suites for instance? Let us examine a few of these areas and see if it is possible.

FOOD AND BEVERAGE SALES

Many people's idea of environmentally-friendly food is either vegetarian or organic. Although both these styles of food are found in environmentally-aware businesses, they are not incompatible with menus that include meat dishes. This section will examine these three categories of food provision.

ANIMAL WELFARE

Issues to do with animal welfare and the production of meat have in recent years become very topical. In 1994 the cross-channel ferry companies banned the transport of live animals on their ferries which were intended for slaughter in Europe. The Northern members of the European Community found themselves in disagreement with the Southern countries over the issue of the number of hours it was permissible to transport animals before they should stop for rest, water and food.[1] Compassion in World Farming,[2] a pressure group which works for the improvement of conditions for all livestock, has a rapidly growing membership in the UK, particularly among the young and the middle classes. It successfully orchestrated a high-profile national campaign of protests in late 1994 and the early months of 1995 against the export of live calves to Europe for rearing in crates (a practice which is banned in the UK).

This kind of publicity has heightened public awareness of the ways in which meat is produced and how animals are treated. This will no doubt have an impact on patterns of sales of meat and also on the demand for certain dishes featured on menus.

In July 1994 the RSPCA launched its 'Freedom Food' scheme.[3] The meat from animals that are reared in accordance with certain agreed standards can be labelled with a 'Freedom Food' logo (Fig.7.1). The objective of the scheme is to provide the consumer with an easily identifiable choice of meat produced from animals which have been reared and slaughtered according to the RSPCA's welfare standards. The scheme was initially applied to the production of pork, bacon and eggs, and it was marketed through supermarkets. The RSPCA's standards are based on five basic freedoms which they consider all animals should enjoy:

Freedom from fear and distress.
Freedom from pain, injury and disease.
Freedom from hunger and thirst.
Freedom from discomfort.
Freedom to express normal behaviour.

The RSPCA has established an independent company called 'Freedom Food Ltd'; its employees inspect the farms and the transport and premises of hauliers and abattoirs who wish to take part in the scheme. The scheme makes provision for spot checks.

The Freedom Food scheme imposes rigorous standards: for example, hens must have enough room to forage, a perch to roost on and a quiet nesting area in which to lay their eggs. This means that battery eggs cannot display the Freedom Food logo. Pigs must have room to root about, to explore, and must not be tethered. No animal is allowed to be transported for more than eight hours. The scheme operates so that it is possible to trace the product from the farm to the abattoir and back again.

Figure 7.1 The RSPCA Freedom Food logo

The RSPCA has carried out extensive market research which indicates that the consumer is prepared to pay extra for products which carry this logo; the fact that the scheme was rapidly extended so that by 1998 it included among other things beef, milk, lamb and turkeys shows that there is a lively market for such produce. For example, non-caged eggs make up 65 per cent of sales in Waitrose supermarkets, and 52 per cent in Safeway supermarkets. Marks and Spencer in 1988 made the decision to sell only 'non-caged' eggs.[4]

The major supermarket chains, including Tesco, the Co-op, Somerfield, Waitrose, Safeway, Asda and Iceland, have all been supporters of the Freedom Food scheme. At the same time other major supermarket chains have marketed meat bearing their own 'welfare' labels. For example, Sainsbury's' 'traditional beef', which on average is priced at 30p per pound more than regular beef, accounted for 30 per cent of the company's total beef sales at the start of 1995. The situation was similar with pork. The company's free range eggs sell at a premium of 25 per cent more than the intensively produced eggs and account for 25–30 per cent of sales. The demand for free range eggs continues to increase.

The British public, renowned for their concern over animal welfare issues, have clearly shown that they are prepared to pay more for meat which has been produced in a more humane way. Increasing numbers of customers are shunning the use of 'exotic' ingredients or those produced in a controversial manner such as frog's legs, veal, turtle (farmed or wild), *foie gras, confit d'oie* or *confit de canard* (by-products of *foie gras* production). Paradoxically, during this same period the market has seen the successful introduction of such 'exotic' foods as kangaroo and ostrich meat.

FREEDOM FOOD IN THE HOSPITALITY SECTOR

In November 1998 the Restaurant Association launched a campaign to encourage British restaurants to purchase free range eggs in preference to battery eggs. In association with the RSPCA and Compassion in World Farming (CIWF), restaurants which sign up to the scheme will be able to display a logo both on their menus and entrances. Like the producers, members will be regularly checked, and will need to renew their membership annually. It will be interesting to monitor the success of this venture and to see whether it can be extended to include the full range of animal products.

ORGANIC PRODUCE

Organic fruit and vegetables are sold at a premium price in the large supermarkets, but there are a number of restaurants which also use only organic produce in their menus. If the produce is bought directly from the market there is little difference in price between chemical-free produce and non-organic produce. The more exotic fruits and vegetables are imported, but there are increasing numbers of organic producers in the UK. Guaranteed organic produce carries the Soil Association symbol (Fig. 7.2).

Figure 7.2 The Soil Association symbol

Symbol-holders must undergo a long process of conversion from conventional to organic methods of production which takes seven years to rid the soil of residual chemicals. They are then inspected on an annual basis to ensure that the quality of their production methods remains at the very high standards set.

The definition of organic

Produce which has been grown without the aid of artificial fertilizers, pesticides or fungicides, normally in a system where practices such as crop rotation, use of natural soil improvers (including animal and green manure), and biological pest control are applied. The term also includes animals reared for human consumption which are fed on organic produce, and which have not been exposed to any growth-promoting drugs.

There is no noticeable difference in nutritional quality between produce which has been produced conventionally and that produced organically, but there can be a noticeable difference in flavour as often different varieties of vegetables are selected for growing, chosen because they possess more resistance to pests and diseases. These might not provide such a high yield, and they may not be so perfect in appearance, but they do make up for all this in flavour!

VEGETARIAN DISHES

A study published in the British Medical Journal[5] found that vegetarians and people who consume a very low level of meat tend to live longer than those who eat a large quantity of meat. The researchers gave no explanations for this finding, but the results of a number of studies suggest that meat consumption is associated with higher levels of fat consumption, especially saturated fat. Excessive consumption of saturated fats is associated with an increased risk of heart disease and some cancers. Other studies have suggested that the antioxidant vitamins, A, C and E – found in fruit and vegetables – are protective factors against the development of heart disease and cancers if eaten in adequate amounts. Other research suggests that it is phytochemicals which perform the protective role. This kind of publicity, coupled with the continuous increase in the numbers of vegetarians, especially among young people, indicates that increasing numbers of customers will be looking for a range of vegetarian options on their menus. Customers requesting vegetarian dishes were at one time offered either an omelette or a plate of boiled vegetables; today there are an increasing number of restaurants which offer inspired vegetarian dishes, and interest is so great that the Vegetarian Society runs a number of courses for professionals who would like to specialize in this area, or who would like to improve their knowledge of vegetarian cuisine.[6]

ORGANIC BEVERAGES

There are a number of producers of organic wines and beers. The beverages are produced using ingredients that are grown under strict organic agricultural standards. During the process of vinification no artificial ingredients, chemicals or finings of animal origin are used. Although these wines and beers cost more, they are of an equal standard to those produced on a more commercial and conventional basis.

Industry Case Study

In the autumn of 1994 the Little Chef restaurant chain launched a 'healthy eating' winter menu. It featured eleven dishes with an emphasis on chicken, fish, vegetarian dishes and salad.

FAST FOOD AND POLLUTION

There are 30,000 fast food restaurants in the Los Angeles area. It has been estimated that these release nineteen tonnes of volatile organic compounds (VOCs) each day into the air; this is equal to the volume of VOCs released by the oil refineries in the same area. In addition, they release 13.7 tonnes of smoke particles (PM10s) every day, which is nine times more than is released by the buses in the city. These particles reflect sunlight away from the earth's surface, thus contributing to the normally hazy atmosphere of LA. They also contribute to respiratory problems and are believed to be possible carcinogens (this is because the favoured method of cooking burgers is to chargrill them, whereby the melted fat drips from the meat onto the flames where it is burnt at a very high temperature). Also during this process organic molecules which play a part in the formation of ozone at ground level are formed.

The University of California at Riverside has set up a scientific project to establish the volume of particulates produced by cooking different types of meat, such as chicken, burgers and fish patties, and also to investigate the most satisfactory alternative cooking methods, and whether there are any items of equipment which could be installed to reduce the volume of emissions. Ironically frying does not cause the same generation of particulates as the cooking temperature is far lower than when chargrilling; however, the end product is different, and of course we are advised not to fry food in the interests of our health.

HEALTH AND ETHICAL ISSUES

In November 1994 the long-awaited COMA Report was published, entitled *Nutritional Aspects of Cardiovascular Disease.*[7] Its recommendations were greeted with concern by some sectors of the industry, but in fact they make sound common sense and certainly justify the inclusion of healthy dishes on the menu, and indeed the use of healthy ingredients and cooking methods in recipes at all times. There are some who argue that the caterer should take an ethical stance and that s/he has a duty of care towards the health of his/her customer, in the same way as s/he has a duty of care towards other aspects of the safety of the customer, for example ensuring that the food is safe to eat and free from toxins and pathogens.

The main recommendations of the COMA Report:

1 The consumption of total fats in the diet should contribute no more than 35 per cent of total daily energy.

2 The consumption of saturated fats and trans-fatty acids should be kept as low as possible.

3 The consumption of starchy foods (complex carbohydrates) and fruit and vegetables should increase.

4 Salt consumption should be reduced from 9 grams to 6 grams per day.

5 Potassium consumption should be increased.

The report's recommendations were set out more extensively than here, and it also translated these recommendations into practical suggestions. This was because there are many people who are confused by terminology such as 'saturated' and 'trans-fatty'. Unfortunately the press implied that the Government was dictating to people what they should eat and acting like a 'nanny state' which caused a lot of ill feeling and misunderstanding. In fact its attempt to clarify complex information was a sensible step; indeed the recommendations were no different to those made by a number of other previous government reports.

How can these recommendations be incorporated into a menu? The caterer who works from an ethical stance will ensure that the choice of cooking methods and ingredients conforms to the Department of Health guidelines. This does not mean that the range and choice of menu items need be restricted; rather, quite the opposite!

Ingredients
- Minimize the use of butter and hard fats.
- Choose polyunsaturated and monounsaturated oils in which to cook – these are normally pure vegetable oils (but avoid 'blended' oils as some of these can have dubious origins which can include saturated fats).
- Offer a good selection of fresh or frozen red and green vegetables.
- Ensure that boiled potatoes as well as chips are offered.
- Reduce the amount of salt used in cooking.
- Reduce the range of pre-prepared foods that are offered – these can often be high in salt and fats.
- Don't pour melted butter or margarine over vegetables before serving.
- Offer oily fish dishes on the menu – salmon is a popular menu item and the price is extremely competitive.
- Purchase low-fat, high-quality meats.
- Offer a range of pulses on the menu.

Cooking methods
- Consider reducing the number of fried items on offer.
- Grill rather than fry foods.
- Boil or steam vegetables.
- Offer stir-fry dishes (using a minimum of fat).
- Roast meat on a trivet and throw away the fat.

Equipment
- Get rid of the deep fat frier and the frying pan.
- Purchase a good grill.
- Consider the purchase of combination cookers.

In Chapter 6 we discussed new types of equipment and technology that are more sustainable in their use. We also looked at the advent of a machine, the RoFry, that can cook pre-blanched chips without the further addition of oil or the need to deep fry.[8] The Potato Marketing Board estimates that in the UK 42 per cent of potatoes consumed in the home, and 69 per cent of potatoes consumed away from home, are in the form of chips. If we then consider that during 1992/93 everyone in the UK consumed 106.2 kg (233.64 lbs, or $10\frac{1}{4}$ oz daily) of potatoes each,[9] this means that a significant proportion of many people's daily fat allowance is derived from chips. Given the state of many deep fat fryers, and the types of fat which are used – often of poor nutritional quality as well as being of poor frying quality – it is certain that if the RoFry lives up to its claims, it can make a significant contribution to people's health. The quality of the RoFry chip is identical to the best quality deep-fried product, but the output is consistent and it contains only as much fat as the blanched product. Reputable producers of frozen, pre-blanched chips use premium oils, so it is possible that the chipped potato of the future could become a more acceptable and regular part of a 'healthy' diet. Unfortunately the RoFry is quite expensive at the moment and it is likely to be bought only by caterers with a special requirement.

THE BUILDING

Occasionally a company is fortunate enough to have the opportunity to build completely new premises. One example is Birchanger Green, the Forte-built motorway service station on the M11.[10] At other times, there is the opportunity to incorporate a range of environmental considerations when premises are being refurbished. This section will briefly discuss issues that can be taken into consideration when designing, or redesigning, a work space. There will always be a range of limitations about what is possible; these range from design aesthetics to the actual investment costs. There are a number of companies that specialize in environmental consultancies to the catering industry, offering specialized advice on an individual basis.

Most buildings have a long life, so decisions taken by planners and designers today will affect the users of a new building well into the next century. Their design and location will affect energy use patterns; buildings should be designed so that they make the greatest use of natural sources of light and heat, i.e. south-facing with extensive windows, and even a glass roof. Examples of purpose-built structures incorporating a range of environmental considerations include the London Wildlife Centre and the extension to the Horniman Museum in Dulwich.

The process of building construction and use contribute up to 50 per cent of the UK's carbon dioxide emissions. Hence increasingly there will be fiscal incentives to improve the energy efficiency of all buildings. This will involve government advice, increased levies on the use of fuel, the use of energy efficient technology, and the refinement of building regulations policy to ensure the incorporation of increased levels of energy efficiency.

There are a number of government supported advice schemes which currently operate to encourage energy efficiency. The Building Research Establishment has developed a scheme titled the Building Research Establishment Environmental Assessment Method (BREEAM) which assesses the energy efficiency of both new and existing buildings, whether offices, domestic homes, supermarkets or industrial buildings. Assessment under this scheme enables designers to make adjustments at the construction stage to new buildings, and in the case of existing buildings there are two assessments: to the fabric and services, and also to the operation and management of the building. The BREEAM scheme predicts the quantity of carbon dioxide that a building will produce as a result of its current energy use patterns, and indicates how this could be reduced. The BREEAM scheme for new buildings also assesses the ecological value of the site, and gives credit for the amenity value of the site and advises on methods whereby ecological damage can be minimized.

The Energy Efficiency Office, part of the Department of Trade and Industry, has published a range of guidance notes under its Best Practice scheme in which it recommends how different industry sectors can incorporate the best available technology and systems to improve their energy consumption patterns.

Construction using sustainable and recycled resources is desirable. In Chapter 11, we discuss the volume of new aggregates used each year in the UK, 30 per cent of which is used by the construction industry. Yet there is considerable potential to reuse material from older buildings which have been demolished or refurbished. Indeed, the 1997 Budget penalized the dumping of hardcore in a move to encourage recycling.

Timber which has been produced in a managed and sustainable system is an excellent building material. It is cheap to produce, absorbs carbon dioxide, and has good strength and insulation properties. There is now a process whereby recycled newspaper can be treated so that it can be used as an insulation material; it has full BBA[11] approval and in terms of thermal efficiency is very competitive. The reuse of bricks, roof tiles and slates should be encouraged, just as doors, fireplaces and other internal fittings have been incorporated as design features for many years.

One company which pays particular attention to environmental issues when building and renovating is the Scandic Hotels chain. One-quarter of its hotel rooms in Scandanavia are designated 'eco rooms'. Natural materials are used wherever possible – for example, wooden floors, wool or cotton textiles – and plastic and metal fittings are kept to a minimum. These rooms are designed to have a longer lifetime than standard hotel rooms and as a consequence are more cost effective; an added bonus is that they are very acceptable to guests.

In September 1997 the Scandic Hotel Sjolyst opened in Oslo, Norway. This is a purpose-built environmental building which has attracted a great deal of public interest.

Industry Case Studies

The Considerate Hoteliers scheme was launched by Westminster Council in London in 1993, and includes 47 individual hotels and chains. There is an annual award scheme in the five separate categories of recycling, appearance, hygiene, communication and 'greening'.

The Hard Rock Cafe's founder, Peter Morton, sits on the Board of the Earth Communications Office (ECO). The proceeds from the company's recycling initiatives are donated to the World Wide Fund for Nature, and the Rainforest Action Network.

Forte have run a 'Community Chest' scheme for a number of years which funds a number of environmental projects that cost between £200 and £2000.

Sheraton ITT Corporation, based in Boston, between 1989 and 1994 under its 'Going Green' scheme raised $130,000 for a variety of conservation projects in the African and Pacific Ocean regions. Money was raised by adding an optional dollar to every guest's bill.

BEDROOMS

One of the most important products that a hotel sells is its rooms, and the business is judged by their quality. It is now common practice for many hotels to offer customers the choice of smoking or non-smoking rooms, an initiative which has proved very popular. The practice of supplying individually-wrapped bathroom toiletries and replacing these every day, even if the occupant of the room remains the same, is being reconsidered. This practice is terribly wasteful, even if the soap is saved and sold for re-cycling. Some hotels are experimenting with the provision of wall-mounted dispensers which offer substantial savings both for the environment and for the business.

Is it necessary to provide clean towels every day when the same customer is in occupation? Some hotels now display a notice informing customers that the towels will not be replaced unless they are heavily soiled, or if the customer requests an exchange. Again, there has been no adverse customer reaction to this scheme; the company saves substantially on laundry costs, and the greater environmental benefits come from a reduction in the volume of detergents and water used.

In Chapter 5 we saw that one of the most substantial users of water is the housekeeping department. Chambermaids use extensive amounts of water when cleaning a hotel bathroom; in comparison, it has been esti-mated that the average hotel resident uses only 10 per cent of the total water used.

Industry Case Study

Chambermaids working for Trusthouse Forte used to be issued with disposable plastic spray bottles containing liquid polish, disinfectant and other cleaning materials. When the bottle was empty it was thrown away and replaced with a brand new one. In this way, nearly 1 million plastic bottles were used each year. Forte decided to purchase the cleaning materials in bulk and the chambermaids were issued with refillable plastic spray bottles. The bulk ingredients were carefully mixed with water under computer control, and not only did the com-pany save on the costs of cleaning agents but there were fewer plastic bottles to bury in landfill sites. The scheme continues today under the new ownership.

SUPPLIER MANAGEMENT

There should be a working partnership between a business and its suppliers. Large companies have the advantage in that they have greater purchasing power, but many suppliers in the catering industry now claim to be environ-mentally-aware, so they should to a certain extent accommodate the smaller business. Trading conditions are highly competitive, so if one supplier proves inflexible then there are plenty more to approach. The following is a short list of some of the specifications that an environmentally-conscious purchaser is likely to dictate. This list is by no means definitive.

Wood
Avoid purchasing anything made from wood including furniture, doors and window frames unless it is guaranteed that they come from a reputable, managed source. This is of equal importance whether the wood is a tropical hardwood, or originates from plantations. The Soil Association has a labelling scheme for woods from sustainable sources which are also managed to promote biodiversity.

Packaging waste
Avoid purchasing any product that in your opinion is excessively packaged, or which is packed in materials whose disposal would create an undue environmental burden. If necessary negotiate a contract whereby the supplier agrees to collect the packaging so that the supplier bears the cost of disposal. In Germany this legal requirement resulted in substantial reductions in the volume of packaging waste in the early 1990s, and the EU Packaging Waste Directive will mean that all member countries will have to make similar provisions.

Food
Draw up purchasing specifications which minimize the volume of food waste that is brought onto the premises. In addition, ensure that the purchases are of the best possible quality, both nutritionally and from a safety point of view. If appropriate purchase organically produced foods bearing the Soil Association or Freedom Foods logos. Consider the purchase of ready-prepared vegetables.

Minimize the use of portion packs. These plastic containers are wasteful and expensive and encourage customers to use more than one.

Office equipment
Consider if the product can be recycled. If using photocopiers, check whether they produce ozone.

Laundry
Purchase unbleached cotton bed linen, but do explain to the customer why the sheets are not pure white.

TRADING POLICY

The company that implements environmental performance standards will do so for one of two reasons: either it is because those who are in a position to determine policy fervently believe in the importance of being 'Green', or else it is because their primary motivation is to comply with legislation and because they understand that it can increase profitability. In both cases the end product has the same result, but in the former, the company that has an environmental conscience is more likely to encompass other forward-thinking initatives. For instance, it may consider such issues as ensuring good employment practices (an issue which the hospitality industry certainly does need to address), providing good value for money, genuinely treating the customer as a 'guest', or ensuring that all bills from suppliers are settled within a short time.

FALSE CLAIMS

The following terms have all been subject to misuse by cynical marketing ploys, and have resulted in a far more sceptical attitude towards 'green claims' on the part of the consumer.

Biodegradable
Earth-friendly
Environmentally-friendly
Green
Natural
Organic
Recyclable
Recycled

CONCLUSION

We have examined a number of areas where it is possible to improve the environmental image of the product promoted by the hospitality business, but what *you* decide to include in your business, or to announce to your customers, is *your* decision. Will calling your business 'environmentally-friendly' mean that you gain or lose customers?

It is possible that if you declare your policies you will lay yourself open to criticism, as has been the case with McDonald's and even the Body Shop. After all, it is always easy to criticize and there is always room for improvement. This is why some hospitality companies have decided to implement environmental policies quietly, in order to avoid inviting criticism from the more radical conservation groups. This is understandable. However, if you give the overall impression of a caring business with a carefully thought out philosophy, and implement it in a non-didactic way, then on the whole the customers will respond positively to the objectives.

QUESTIONS AND ISSUES FOR DISCUSSION

1 Using a local catering establishment of your choice as an example, list six or more different initiatives that might improve its record on environmental issues, all of which must be visible to the customer. Show what is currently happening and explain why such action will be beneficial to (a) the business, and (b) the environment.

2 Examine some instances of 'green' claims and discuss whether they are correct or whether this is an abuse of the environmental movement. Use reasoned argument and data to support your case.

3 You have just opened your first catering business, a wine bar heavily dependent on casual staff. You have studied a course in business ethics at university and see this as your opportunity to show that a hospitality operation can be run along ethical lines as far as HRM issues are concerned. What issues would you consider and how might you put this policy into practice? What problems might you be creating for yourself?

4 You are the purchasing manager for a small company which is planning to build a suite of wooden holiday chalets in a beauty spot. They are anxious to promote their environmental awareness as a marketing tool. Discuss the factors that you would take into account when making decisions about purchasing. Illustrate your answer with examples.

5 A suggestion has been made that unbleached linen should be purchased. Explain why the omission of bleaching from the manufacture of linen is beneficial to the environment, and discuss how this point could be made to the customer, accustomed as s/he is to highly-bleached and starched linen.

6 The 'What's New' column in the *Caterer and Hotelkeeper*[12] reports that: 'The continuing mania for healthy eating is driving demand for lighter fish crumb coatings which processors say bring something new to proven popular lines.' The article proceeds to describe a new breadcrumbed product produced by

Youngs Seafoods which contains no artificial flavourings, colourings or preservatives. Discuss the following points:

(a) Should a leading industry trade journal adopt such an antagonistic view towards new trends in eating which are in response to government health guidelines?

(b) Is Youngs Seafoods taking a more pragmatic approach in response to market forces?

Notes

1 In October 1994.

2 Compassion in World Farming, Charles House, 5a Charles St, Petersfield, Hants.

3 Freedom Food Ltd, The Manor House, The Causeway, Horsham, West Sussex, RH12 1HG.

4 Non-caged eggs includes both free range and barn eggs. Only free range eggs are part of the Freedom Food scheme, although barn eggs do provide an improved quality of life for hens than cage-produced eggs.

5 Timothy J. A. Key *et al.*, 'Dietary Habits and Mortality in 11,000 Vegetarian and Health Conscious People', *British Medical Journal*, no. 313, 1996, pp. 775–9.

6 The Vegetarian Society, Parkdale, Durham Rd, Altrincham, Cheshire, WA14 4QG.

7 Department of Health, COMA Report on Nutritional Aspects of Cardiovascular Disease. Dept of Health Report on Health and Social Subjects, no. 46, London: HMSO, 1994.

8 See Chapter 6 for further details of the RoFry machine.

9 The Potato Marketing Board, *Potato Statistics in Great Britain, 1989–1993*.

10 Now part of the Granada Company.

11 The British Board of Agrément.

12 *Caterer and Hotelkeeper*, 26 January–1 February 1995, p. 87.

Further reading

Tom Woolley *et al.*, *The Green Building Handbook*, E. & F.N. Spon, 1997.

CHAPTER 8

Packaging and disposable products

Pizza boxes, burger boxes, baked potato boxes, fish and chip boxes, burger and chip boxes, full meal boxes, chip trays, paper cups, polystyrene cups, carrier bags (paper or polythene, with or without handles) straws (standard, jumbo or flexi), salt and pepper sachets, sauces of every kind, plastic knives, forks, dessert spoons, teaspoons, forks, snacknifes, sandwich wrappings, foil containers of every size, together with lids – are just some of the potential waste generated by the fast food industry! We could add to this list the disposable packaging used by the ready-meals industry: plastic vending cups, serviettes, food frills, food sticks, cutlet frills, pie collars, cocktail sticks, paper and plastic plates and bowls, disposable glasses, beer tumblers, cling film, tinfoil, banqueting rolls, foil platters, dishes and trays, with clear lids if required, doileys, dish and tray papers, placemats, microwave trays, freezer bags, trifle cases, sandwich flags and labels, portion pots, and lids, disposable ashtrays, bin liners, J cloths, paper refuse sacks, disposable visitors' coats, plastic aprons, chefs' hats, trilbys, single cup sachets of tea, coffee and chocolate for hotel bedrooms . . .

OBJECTIVES

1 To assess the environmental performance of a range of disposable products and packaging materials used in the hospitality industry.
2 To discuss the problems of identifying the most environmentally-friendly choice in the use of equipment, especially the debate about the use of disposables and reusables.

INTRODUCTION

This chapter underlines the complexities of the paradigm of sustainability. On the one hand the use of extensive packaging, or of disposable containers and cutlery, guarantees safety, hygiene and convenience, but on the other hand it can be a major source of litter, can create major disposal problems, and can also place a significant ecological burden on the biosphere in the course of its production and disposal. We will examine the strengths and weaknesses of these problems, and will show that there are choices that the caterer can make in order to minimize the use of packaging and disposables, but that there will always be occasions when these products will play a useful and essential role in meeting operating requirements.

ADVANTAGES AND DISADVANTAGES OF DISPOSABLE PACKAGING AND TABLEWARE

Before we go any further it is important to assess the advantages and disadvantages of the use of disposables and packaging. The major argument in support of the use of these products is hygiene. There have been a number of studies which show that the bacterial count on disposable crockery and cutlery, which are designed to be used once only, is far lower than that to be found on similar items which have been washed in dishwashers and stored in the kitchen area.[1] This is despite the fact that a dishwasher should wash and rinse at temperatures designed to sanitize the hardware. The explanation for this is that invariably there are a number of problems which can occur, including poor maintenance of the machine which means that it is not always functioning to the best of its ability, inadequate water temperature, and recontamination of the hardware during storage and handling. How many times have you seen 'clean' plates stored in grubby wash-up areas, or the 'polishing' of glassware, cutlery and plates taking place with a dirty cloth, often by an individual with dubious standards of personal hygiene? In contrast disposables designed for food use are manufactured to a very high microbiological standard, are stored in hygienic wrapping and are handled minimally.

Another argument in favour of disposables is that the need to wash up, or to employ staff to wash up, dry and stack cutlery and crockery is obviated, and, of course, that a massive investment in stock is also avoided. If disposables are used then the cost is normally included in the selling price of the meal. Not only does this reduce staffing levels, but also capital investment and time are saved!

There is therefore a very strong argument in favour of the use of disposable tableware in a range of situations, from outdoor catering and self-service provision, to use for those who are immunologically vulnerable, as in hospitals and similar institutions. As the scientific understanding of the mechanisms whereby humans can become ill as the result of food-borne disease increases, it is recognized that listeria monocytogenes, salmonella, campylobacter and many viruses, including the norwalk virus, need to be present in only *very low* quantities in order for there to be an infective dose. Figure 8.1 shows the apparently relentless increase in cases of food poisoning in the UK over recent years, and the signs are that this will increase

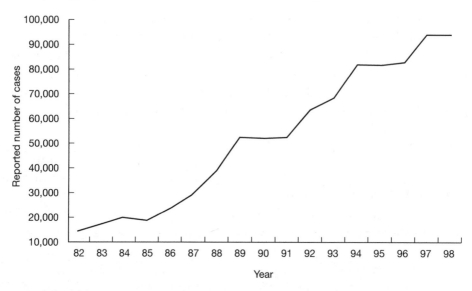

Figure 8.1 The rise in reported cases of food poisoning in the UK, 1980–98
Source: Public Health Laboratory Service.

despite the provisions of the Food Safety Act 1990 and increased public awareness of the causes of food poisoning.

Figure 8.1 suggests that it would therefore be sensible to use cling film to cover products during preparation, or during storage in fridges, in preference to a cloth or paper. This is because cling film is designed to be used once only and it normally gives a better seal round the container.[2] For the same reasons disposable wipes are superior to dishcloths no matter how well the latter are washed, and paper towels are more hygienic than rollers. In all cases the chain of infection can be broken.

PACKAGING

Unnecessary packaging is probably the largest single cause of the accumulation of waste on any premises, whether in the home or in business. Packaging is not only used as a hygienic method of protection, but also as a way of distinguishing one manufacturer's product from that of another, and maybe to add value to the product so that it can be sold at a premium price. There can be several layers of packaging, including paper, foil and plastic, and different types of plastics. The mixed nature of such packaging means that none of the packaging can be recycled as it would be impossible to separate it efficiently. To add insult to injury the additional costs of packaging are passed on to the customer who often has to pay for the costs of its disposal as well.

One method of dealing with packaging waste is to compact it, but the business responsible for disposing of it may still be charged for it by weight rather than by volume. Charges will also vary according to the type of waste, current charges for landfill (increased to £10 per tonne in April 1999), the number of collections, and ease or difficulty of gaining access to the waste. This issue of waste disposal is dealt with in greater detail in Chapter 9 on 'Waste Management'.[3]

Although the best option is to minimize packaging waste, it will never be possible to dispense with it entirely because of the need to ensure that food is stored, prepared and served in a safe and hygienic condition.

Sources of packaging waste

What are the major sources of packaging waste in the industry? What springs to mind are the portion control packs of milk and cream, margarine and butter, sugar, sauces, salt and pepper. Let us take the example of milk and cream tots. They are designed to provide convenience to the caterer. The standard 14 ml portion is supposed to contain an adequate volume of milk or cream to add to one cup of tea or coffee. But how many times does the customer help him/herself to a second portion, or even three? Have all these been costed into the selling price of that beverage? If not costed then the gross profit margins will be hit quite steeply. The only advantage is that the use of these containers is a hygienic and controlled way of providing milk or cream. Yet Pergals still remain a convenient and hygienic method of storing and dispensing milk; both 3 and 5 gallon machines are available depending upon requirements. Forte reverted to the use of Pergals and saved 29 million plastic pots – worth £400,000.

Industry Case Study

Trusthouse Forte used to purchase portions of sugar in sachets. These were supplied as 144 sachets to each inner section, and there were four inner boxes to each carton, all of which was overwrapped with plastic. By agreeing with their supplier to dispense with the inner cartons and that all 12 gross (12×12) would be supplied in one single case, the company was able to negotiate a reduction in price and saved £30,000 in the first year alone! Added to this were the environmental benefits.

The company took the same action with mini jams and preserves, saving 34,000 cardboard outers – a saving of £6000 per annum.

Cardboard is also a major source of packaging waste. Cases containing soft and alcoholic drinks, and cans of food, large or small, can either be entirely made of cardboard, or comprise a supporting base of cardboard surrounded by shrink-wrapped plastic. Once the goods are unpacked for storage, the empty boxes are normally flattened for storage but will still create bulk and will incur costs of disposal. Plastic, again, can also be bulky.

What is packaging made of?

Food packaging usually comes in a variety of guises, including paper, glass, cardboard, light steel, aluminium and a range of plastics. The early 1980s saw a massive increase in the use of plastics, as they were cheap, light and acceptable to the consumer. However, it was quickly realized that used in such vast quantities (and varieties) the plastics were not biodegradable and were taking up considerable space in scarce landfill sites. Towards the end of the 1980s consumer and environmental groups combined to question the need for the volume of packaging used; it was particularly the case that in the retail areas, products appeared to be packaged in an unnecessary amount of layers.

Environmentalists argue that although these products are light, attractive, cheap and highly serviceable, the true social and environmental costs of their production are highly complex and possibly incalculable. For instance, paper is a traditional packaging material, and certainly a number of manufacturers have returned to using paper on the grounds that it is biodegradable and less bulky. Hospitality companies use paper serviettes, tablecloths, bags and paper towels. Pure white is associated with hygiene and efficiency. Yet 'whiteness' is only achieved by the use of strong bleaches; natural paper pulp is cream coloured, and pulp composed of re-cycled paper is grey. Later in this chapter there is an analysis of the true environmental impacts of paper manufacture.

A great percentage of packaging is made of plastic as it is an ideal material in terms of hygiene and appearance, and its malleability means that it is very versatile. In addition, it is highly convenient to use, relatively cheap, easy to store and the price of the packaging to the manufacturer or producer can normally be included in the price of the product and passed on to the customer.

Another argument in favour of packaging is that it reduces food wastage – sealed packs of fresh produce often contain inert gases such as carbon dioxide or nitrogen, which exclude the oxygen which many bacteria require in order to thrive. Used in conjunction with temperature control the shelf-life of the product is extended. This saves the consumer money and time, although ultimately all food waste is biodegradable. For instance, the World Health Organization estimates that between 30–50 per cent of food produced in the world is wasted due to inadequate storage and packaging, whereas in industrialized countries this figure is only 3 per cent.

As we will see in the next chapter, where we discuss the problems of what can be done about the waste which the industry (and society in general) generates, the greatest problem is what happens to the packaging after use. We have seen that most packaging materials in common use today are plastics which are made from non-renewable resources, usually as by-products of petrochemicals, and that they do not biodegrade easily, if at all. They thus contribute to the bulk of waste in landfill sites and future generations will be left with the problem of how to dispose of them safely. In addition, there are environmental costs of production which also require examination. These include damage to the environment when extracting the raw materials, when transporting them to the refineries, and during the refining process. There can be significant leakages from pipelines and oil tankers which damage either the land or the marine environment – currently there are serious concerns about the damage caused by substantial and extensive leakages in the Russian Arctic tundra. And at the refinery stage there can also be significant emissions of waste products into the atmosphere during the process of refining the crude oil.

Packaging outside the UK

The Germans have probably the strictest environmental laws in Europe, and it is anticipated that their experience of regulating the disposal of packaging waste will become part of national laws of other EU members once the EU Packaging Directive has been issued. In Germany the producer is responsible for the disposal of his/her product, which means that the seller of goods which contain packaging must be prepared to accept the used packaging back for reuse or disposal. In addition, the German Federal Constitutional Court has permitted local authorities to impose a local tax on disposable products to cover their disposal, and also in order to discourage their use as they are seen as a major source of waste. For instance, Kassel has imposed a tax of DM .40 on all disposable products used in the catering and hospitality industry.

Denmark, too, has imposed a similar system of taxation of food service disposables which it is claimed has resulted in a significant reduction in the volume used.

In the USA the most environmentally proactive states are California and Oregon. The US packaging industry has formed a strong lobby group to counter the effects of potential environmental legislation which they perceive as being hostile to their industry. They also distribute videos and educational materials to schools and colleges in order to make the point that in the USA only 1.75 per cent of all waste generated is from food-service disposables.

WHAT ARE PLASTICS?

Each year in the UK 2.6 million tonnes of plastic are used, 36 per cent of which is used as packaging. In 1985 the world production of plastic was 74.5 million tonnes, and production doubles every twelve years.

Plastic is made of polymers from petrochemicals (from the oil industry) and constitute 4 per cent of its total production. Other raw materials used include natural gas, coal and salt. There are 100,000 polymers but the major categories used in the plastics industries are the following:

Thermoplastics are materials which soften when heated and harden upon cooling. Eighty per cent of plastics are in this category.

Thermosetting plastics are hardened in the process of manufacture and cannot be resoftened. They are used when rigidity is essential, for example for melamine table tops.

Plastics from each of the above categories are given individual characteristics by the use of chemical additives:

High-density Polyethylene
Bottles which contain household chemicals, bottle tops.

Low-density Polyethylene
Bags, sacks, bin-liners, squeezy bottles.

Polyvinyl chloride (PVC)
Blister packs, food trays, bottles.

Polystyrene
Egg cartons, yoghurt pots, vending cups.

Polyethylene Terephthalate (PET)
Carbonated drink bottles.

Polypropylene
Margarine tubs, crisp packets, cling film.

Recycling

It is not possible to mix plastics for recycling as they lose their original strength and flexibility, and they therefore need to be carefully sorted before recycling.

The British Disposable Products Association claims that the production of polyethylene, polystyrene and polypropylene presents no danger to human health or the environment when properly handled. They maintain that no plasticizers are used in their manufacture and that products which contain these chemicals can be incinerated under controlled conditions. Most of them can also be cleaned and recycled, and reprocessed with no great loss of strength. The volume of recycling is restricted only by the availability of the collected product, a ready market and economics.

Table 8.1 End uses of plastics production (as percentages)

Packaging:	35
Building:	24
Electrical:	10
Transport:	6
Furniture:	5
Toys and leisure:	4
Housewares:	3
Agriculture:	2
Mechanical engineering:	2
Clothing and footware:	1
Medical products:	1
Other uses:	7

Source: Plastics Recycling, Warmer factsheet, 1994.

It has been estimated that 1.1 million tonnes of plastic packaging are used in the UK each year. In the EU plastic packaging and containers make up 70 per cent of all municipal waste. In addition it is estimated that 5 million plastic containers are thrown overboard from ships each year worldwide.

Some suggested solutions to the problem of the excessive use of plastic packaging

1 **Banning**. One extreme view argues that the use of plastic for packaging should be banned outright.
2 **Degradability** should be built in to the products so that they are photo-degradable (by light), biodegradable (by bacteria) or chemically degradable. This is technically possible as this characteristic is already

used in the manufacture of sutures in medicine, and in capsules that dissolve in the body to release medication. However, the costs of production of degradables are very high, and there are the additional problems of being able to assess the shelf-life of a plastic which might start to disintegrate and damage the product it is designed to protect! It is also unknown what are the long-term effects of leaving biodegradable plastics in the soil. And there is always the temptation for increased littering.

However, ICI's agricultural division have developed a totally biodegradable plastic which leaves no residues. It is made from bacteria which produce a natural polymer called poly-3-hydroxybutyrate (PHB). The bacteria are grown on glucose substrates and they produce the PHB. Currently the polymer is very brittle but this should be resolved by further research. A major disincentive to research and develop alternative sources of packaging is the relatively cheap price of oil, which means that it is cheaper to produce plastics from oil than from the sugar necessary to rear the bacteria; oil prices at the end of 1998 were less than US$10 a barrel, an all-time low.

3 **Legislation**. The EU Packaging Directive requires member states to draw up legislation to reduce the volume of household waste which contains beverage bottles and to encourage and support recycling schemes.

'MULTI-JOURNEY PACKAGING'

In the 1970s and 1980s many companies in the food industries adopted a policy of using disposable packaging, including trays and delivery boxes, in order to ensure the highest standards of hygiene. This meant that bread and other bakery goods, meat, fruit and vegetables were delivered to the purchaser in large cardboard trays or boxes which would be disposed of by the purchaser. However, the costs of this packaging were also passed on to the purchaser who then had a double charge: first the 'purchase' of the tray that carried the goods, and then the costs of storage and disposal. The environmental costs of production of the trays were not even part of the equation.

In a new trading climate in the early 1990s, Forte decided to re-examine this practice. They undertook a study which compared the relative costs of continuing as before, and of changing to a system whereby the supplier provided good quality, reusable, returnable plastic trays. In one of their flight catering units they worked out a system whereby the trays were washed and returned to the companies which supplied bakery goods and meat. The savings achieved by the reuse of trays were passed on to the customer (Forte) in terms of reduced cost goods, and the company also made large savings on waste disposal costs. In the first year the flight catering unit saved £27,000 on meat and £30,000 on bakery goods.

DISPOSABLES

The list at the beginning of this chapter indicates the extent to which disposable products have been adopted by the industry. At one time their use was considered to be the best method to save tying up capital in laundry items such as tablecloths, and in hardware such as glassware, crockery and cutlery. Over time both the range and styles developed in sophistication and acceptability to compete with the very best of more traditional products. Today, however, we look far more closely at whether the use of disposables does in fact save a company money, and even if it does, not only should we be asking whether the use of disposables is appropriate for the function in question, but also whether its use is justifiable on environmental grounds.

The first disposable drinking cups were used in New York in 1908; they were designed to be used with the cold drinks dispensers which were starting to be installed in offices across the USA. Prior to this glasses were supplied with the dispensers, and the disposable cups were introduced in response to a perceived need for increased hygiene and convenience.

REUSABLES OR DISPOSABLES?

The debate concerning reuseables and disposables is a complex one. Let us examine the issues from a range of viewpoints, starting with durability and acceptability, and then proceed to examine the comparative environmental burdens which the production of paper, traditionally perceived as a 'Greener' product, and expanded polystyrene impose.

'Would you like your beer served in a real glass or a plastic glass, Sir?'
An independent research group at Surrey University carried out a project to assess the relative merits of glass versus plastic vessels, and found that plastic drinking vessels were tougher and more cost effective even in the busiest of bars – in this case the University Student Union bar. The project team

tested drinking vessels made of four different materials for breakage, durability and customer acceptability. The materials were polystyrene, SAN (styrene acronitril – a mixture of 80 per cent polystyrene and 20 per cent acrylic), polycarbonate and glass. Polycarbonate performed the best, followed in joint second place by SAN and polystyrene, and in third place came glass. Each type of vessel underwent three tests: they were subjected to 300 washing cycles in a commercial dishwasher, then breakage trials to test durability, and they were also subjected to everyday use in the student union bar. The results were as follows:

Polycarbonate
1 One hundred washes: showed little change other than a slight roughening of the rim in 30 per cent of the sample.
2 Dropped on hard flooring five times: it retained perfect appearance.
3 After 15 days in the student union bar, 40 per cent remained in excellent condition.

Polystyrene
1 One hundred washes: 10 per cent had developed a rough appearance and texture.
2 Dropped on hard flooring five times: 40 per cent split after being dropped twice.
3 After 15 days in bar 60 per cent were undamaged and looked good.

SAN
1 One hundred washes: 60 per cent had slight roughening.
2 Dropped on hard flooring five times: no breakages.
3 After 15 days in bar all in good condition.

Glass
1 One hundred washes: good results.
2 Dropped on hard flooring: all broke.
3 After 15 days in bar 20 per cent were broken.

If the purchase costs of the various drinking vessels are comparable and the customer is happy, then plastic drinking vessels are clearly the winner on the grounds of cost and safety. However, both broken glass and plastics can be recycled, so the environmental burden of plastics will be less than that of glass if the only variable is that they have a longer life; but the overall environmental impact needs to be considered. It is important to compare the total costs of glass and plastics manufacture – both in financial production costs and in terms of the impact of their manufacture on the environment.

Of course another and totally separate issue is that, from an aesthetic point of view, not all customers will be content to use a 'plastic' glass on all occasions.

Commercial dishwashers use between 70 and 500 gallons of water per hour – a cafeteria using disposables saves more than 71 gallons per 100 customers; if there are 500 customers per day, this is a saving of 1755 gallons per week. *Source*: Food Service and Packaging Ltd, USA.

Paper or polystyrene?
McDonald's in Europe ceased selling its burgers wrapped in polystyrene foam containers, albeit CFC-free, and sold them wrapped instead in waxed paper. The public perception was that this was far more environmentally responsible. But was it? What are the issues that need to be evaluated in making such a decision? Let us conduct a life-cycle analysis of the relative merits of each type of food wrapper using the disposable cup as a model.

PAPER

The raw material for paper is wood and this is a renewable resource. But forestry felling can have a negative impact on the landscape, and can create traffic problems during transportation of the logs to the pulp mills. The combustion of the diesel creates pollution, and also adds to carbon dioxide emissions. If we go back further, we could also include the environmental impacts of the manufacture of the lorry. Then we need to consider the damage caused to the road surface by the very heavy weight of the vehicle, plus the environmental costs of building the road (quarrying for aggregates, transport of aggregates, damage to the environment when building the road, etc.).

Extensive felling of virgin forests will allow the water table to rise which will affect the presence of other flora and fauna, and could also cause both flooding and drought as the established drainage pattern of the forest area is disrupted. There is also the issue of whether the wood is grown in a managed environment, or whether it has been felled from virgin, ancient forest, as can be the case in wood production in some parts of Finland and Russia.

Paper cups are made from bleached pulp which is manufactured from 50 per cent wood chips; some bark and waste wood are burned in the process to supply energy which adds to carbon dioxide emissions; on average 33 grams of wood plus 4 grams of fuel or gas or oil is required in order to produce a paper cup which will weigh 10.1 grams. If the paper cup is given a wax or plastic coating then there is an increase in energy requirements and other environmental demands.

In addition, a 1.8 gram mixture of the following chemicals is used per cup in the paper manufacture: sodium hydroxide, sodium sulphate, chlorine, sodium chlorate, sulphuric acid, sulphur dioxide and calcium hydroxide.

EXPANDED POLYSTYRENE

The raw materials for this material are hydrocarbons (oil and gas), and there can be considerable environmental impacts during the exploration for and the extraction of these materials, including accidental spillage and burning of waste gases during drilling, and spillage during delivery which can cause significant damage to the habitats of animals and plants. Despite this, however, the total environmental burden of the manufacture of expanded polystyrene is less than for paper.

Only one-sixth the volume of raw materials are used for the polystyrene cup as for the paper cup; this includes 0.05 grams of chemical per cup. Six times the volume of wood pulp is needed to manufacture the paper cup than a polystyrene cup of identical size, and the paper cup consumes twelve times more steam, 36 times more electricity, and twice as much cooling water as the polystyrene cup. In the case of the paper cup, 580 times more waste water is used in the pulping process than in the manufacture of the polystyrene cup; in addition, the waste water contains up to 100 times more contaminants from the paper bleaching and pulping operations than in the polystyrene manufacture.

The polystyrene is 'foamed' by the use of pentane; this is a gas which increases ozone concentrations both at ground and stratospheric levels, and it is also a greenhouse gas. However, the total contribution to global warming that this gas causes is far less than the methane that would be produced in landfill when the paper cups were rotting down.

One tonne of polystyrene will make the same quantity of expanded polyfoam cups as 6 tonnes of paper pulp would take to make paper cups. The 6 tonnes of used paper cups, if they degrade anaerobically, would produce 2370 kg of methane and 3260 kg of carbon dioxide. The greenhouse effect of methane and pentane are similar. Put another way, if only 2 per cent of the paper cups biodegraded anaerobically they would produce as much methane as all the pentane produced by 1 tonne of polystyrene.

Methane has a global warming impact between 5 and 20 times greater than carbon dioxide; rotting anaerobic paper cups produce twice as much methane as carbon dioxide. It would therefore be better to incinerate the paper cups as it would all be converted to carbon dioxide. If the paper cups were to be incinerated for heat recovery they would provide 20 MJ/kg, whereas polystyrene would produce 40 MJ/kg.

It is possible to recycle the polystyrene cups to produce packaging materials, insulation, patio furniture, etc. But paper cups are sealed with a non-water soluble and heat-resistant adhesive which cannot be removed during the pulping process, and which therefore makes them impossible to recycle. In addition they tend to be coated with wax or plastic film which also renders them unrecyclable.

When considering using traditional glassware and crockery it is equally important to take into account the environmental costs of *their* production, their maintenance (washing, heat, waste water, detergents, and their manufacture and distribution) and their final means of disposal – can they be recycled? However, if the life of one of these were long enough its total environmental cost would be less than that of either the paper or polystyrene cup.

McDonald's, Kentucky Fried Chicken and Burger King have all replaced their polystyrene foam packaging with biodegradable paper.

CONCLUSION

This chapter has investigated the range of packaging that is in use and the benefits to the consumer of that packaging. However, the benefits to the environment are less obvious, and the chapter has also addressed the intiatives that the various industries are undertaking to produce biodegradable packaging, or to minimize the use of packaging. There is no easy answer to the problem of waste generated by the use of packaging; it is essential to ensure the safety of food products, but at the same time it poses serious long-term environmental challenges. The following chapter will investigate the problem of waste disposal in greater depth.

QUESTIONS AND ISSUES FOR DISCUSSION

1 Test the issue of the environmental considerations of the glass versus plastic drinking vessels in a pub. What would be the results? Carry out a straw poll and ask the customers, and persuade the landlord to help you with a real project.

2 In what circumstances would it be more sensible to use plastic rather than glass drinking vessels? Why?

3 You are the assistant manager of the school meals service in a private school which has 300 boarders and 130 day students; in addition you must cater for 30 residential staff and 15 staff who work on a daily basis. There has been a substantial amount of money earmarked for the refurbishment of the kitchen and you have been asked to investigate the pros and cons of adopting a totally new style of service which includes the use of disposable tableware instead of the conventional reusables. Compile a report for your manager on the advantages and disadvantages of such a proposal, considering the effects on the catering budget over (a) five years, and (b) ten years.

Note that you will have to make certain assumptions including the number of meals served, and number of days the school operates each year. Include these and any other relevant factors in the introduction to your report.

Include in your report the following:
(i)   Current provision and cost of this.
(ii)   Capital cost of change to a system of disposables.
(iii)   Annual cost of running a service system based on the use of disposables, assuming costs run at a rate of inflation of 2 per cent per annum.
(iv)   Capital cost of completely updating the food service system based on traditional methods using reusables.
(v)   Annual cost of running a 'reusable' system.
(vi)   An 'environmental impact' analysis of each system.
(vii)   Your recommendations.

4 (a) Milk and cream portion packs designed for use with tea or coffee are a major source of waste. They are inadequate in size, and the cost of packaging is passed on to the customer. Compare the real costs of serving cups of coffee with cream pots and sachets with the cost of providing milk in jugs and sugar in basins. Note that you will need to consider the cost of the jugs, sugar bowls, wastage, washing-up and storage, and also work out the true net profit of each method of

service. You will also need to make assumptions about the expected life of any reusable equipment in order to come to a realistic conclusion.

(b) Create an environmental life-cycle analysis of the two different styles of service. How detailed does this report need to be? Why? Present your results in the form of a flowchart.

5 Draw a chart which illustrates the environmental burden of one disposable product versus a reusable one. What factors would you list? How would you obtain the information? Is selling price relevant?

6 Some revision: what are the temperatures at which (a) the washing cycle and (b) the rinse cycle should operate on a dishwasher? What are the reasons for the differences in temperature? In Chapter 4 we discussed energy-saving measures, and one recommendation was to turn down the temperature of thermostats on room sensors and water boilers. Would it be a good idea to reduce the temperature of the dishwasher thermostats in a similar manner in order to save energy? Give reasons for your answer.

7 Consider the claims made by the British Disposable Products Association on p. 141 about recycling plastics today. To what extent are these claims realistic?

8 Consider the argument that it is in fact more environmentally-sound to manufacture, use and dispose of polystyrene cups than waxed paper cups. The subject of noxious emissions during manufacture, use and incineration was not addressed. Carry out research to investigate to what extent noxious gases are or are not produced at these stages. Then construct a chart to describe a life-time analysis of the environmental burdens of the two products. As a result of your extra research and calculations, which one of the products is the more environmentally-friendly?

9 Carry out a similar analysis of glass and chinaware as in the above exercise.

10 Calculate the average 'life' of a glass in a bar, or a dinner plate in a restaurant (you will need to include some justification for the figure at which you arrive). Then compare the environmental burden of a once only use of each of these items of hardware. What conclusions do you draw?

Notes

1 C.W. Felix, C. Parrow and T. Parrow, 'Utensil Sanitation. A microbiological study of disposables and reusables', *Journal of Environmental Health*, September/October 1990. C.W. Felix, 'Foodservice Disposables and Public Health', *Dairy, Food and Environmental Sanitation*, November 1990.

The hospitality industry

2 Plastic film designed to be in contact with food safely is now widely available.
3 Although the subject of waste disposal may not appear to be a fascinating one, not only is it becoming increasingly important that we dispose of our waste safely, but there are a range of socially beneficial options available from which the hospitality industry can benefit!

CHAPTER 9

Waste management

We *can* protect the environment, but only if we work together. Gone are the days when 'somebody else' will take care of it. What's needed from everybody, is a life-long commitment, one big team effort. Then, and only then, can we hope to preserve the environment for future generations. Hand in hand we have the resources.

Biffa, *Environmental Report,* 1998

OBJECTIVES

1 To consider the social and environmental costs of waste generation.
2 To assess the contribution that the hospitality industry in general, and specific operations within it, make to the generation of waste.
3 To assess the opportunities to minimize waste.
4 To calculate how to carry out a waste survey and make recommendations for the minimization of waste generation together with financial projections of the costs and benefits of change both for that business and for the environment.

INTRODUCTION

This chapter will review a range of waste disposal methods and alternatives, discuss strategies to minimize waste and recommend strategies to benefit from waste. Most waste disposal in the UK is directly to landfill, but there is tremendous scope for waste reduction, recycling and energy recovery from most materials. Currently the costs of the various methods of waste disposal do not reflect the true costs of either their disposal or environmental impact.

Table 9.1 indicates that there is a range of choices for the disposal of waste. Currently only 5 per cent of household and commercial waste is recycled, and energy is recovered from an additional 4 per cent, yet potentially 50 per cent could be recycled. In addition:

- 85 per cent of all controlled waste goes to landfill
- 30 per cent of all household waste is compostable
- 30 per cent of sewage sludge is dumped at sea (due to end in 1998)
- 25 million tyres are scrapped annually – they are a considerable fire risk, yet many could be reprocessed or used for energy recovery.

Table 9.1 The hierarchy of waste management options

Reduce packaging; introduce technology which creates products with a longer life cycle and which are potentially less polluting.	*Reuse* returnable bottles and transit packaging (trays etc.).	*Recycle* waste materials to create a product which is usable; or *compost* organic materials for use as soil conditioners and nutrients; or practise *energy recovery*, either by burning waste or harnessing landfill gases.	*Disposal*: as a last resort in a safe and compact condition.

Put another way, the UK generates approximately 400 million tonnes of solid waste each year. Of this, commercial premises, which include the hospitality sector, produce 15 million tonnes or 4 per cent of the total figure. (Households produce 20 million tonnes or 5 per cent.) Of the commercial total waste, 70 per cent goes to landfill, 5 per cent is incinerated and 25 per cent is recycled or reused.

When choosing how to dispose of our waste we need to adopt the principle of the 'best possible environmental option' (BPEO). It is foolish to burn energy by sorting out products for recycling when they could be more easily and cheaply burnt for energy recovery. It is also impractical to collect more waste for recycling than the market can take. A recent comparison[1] between the environmental effects of landfill and incineration indicated that there is a net environmental benefit if waste is incinerated with energy recovery, although it is important to note that incineration, if not carried out at the correct temperature, can cause toxic by-products.

There are few direct economic incentives at present to reduce, reuse or recycle. However, in the case of reuse (returnable milk bottles is the classic example) we must remember that when the full energy costs of production, collection, transport and cleaning are taken into account this might not be the best option for all products. Recovery involves the recycling of paper, glass and aluminium and provides significant energy savings over virgin production.

Currently waste in the UK is disposed of in a variety of ways, none of which is particularly satisfactory. The two major methods are landfill, where the waste is buried under layers of soil which is eventually relandscaped, and incineration; 90 per cent of the UK's waste is placed in landfill sites, and 9 per cent is incinerated. The remaining 1 per cent is composed mainly of cardboard and plastic which is recycled. The Government has set a target whereby domestic waste will be reduced by 25 per cent and total packaging waste by 60 per cent by the year 2000. The EU is also working towards major improvements in waste reclamation and recycling systems, and many other EU countries have set themselves targets of 50 per cent recovery of municipal waste by the year 2000.

An EC framework Directive has been established concerning the collection, sorting, transport and treatment of waste, as well as its storage and tipping above or below ground, and the operations necessary for reuse, recovery or recycling.[2] Incorporating the 'polluter pays' principle, the Directive places a general duty on member states to encourage the prevention, recycling and processing of waste and to ensure that its disposal does not endanger human health or harm the environment. Member states are required to establish 'competent authorities' to control waste disposal by any company which 'treats, stores, tips or transports, collects, stores, tips or treats their own waste or on the behalf of third parties'. They must either obtain a licence or be supervised by the 'competent authority'. In the UK the 'competent authority' is the local authority.

The Department of the Environment estimates that 20 million tonnes of waste is generated from households annually, and 15 million tonnes from commercial premises. This represents 5 per cent and 4 per cent of the total waste generated in the UK respectively; the remainder is from industrial processes. Of the 15 million tonnes generated by commercial premises, 5 million tonnes are collected by local authorities from retail premises and small commercial premises, including catering.

Although there has been no official audit of the volume of waste that is generated by the catering industry in the UK to date, an analysis of samples of canteen waste in an unofficial study[3] suggested that the average composition of catering waste would be:

- 50 per cent compostable food waste
- 45 per cent packaging
- 5 per cent broken crockery.

THE ENVIRONMENTAL PROTECTION ACT 1990

The Environmental Protection Act 1990 came into effect on 1 April 1992, and it placed a new 'duty of care' on companies which were responsible for the disposal of 'controlled waste'. This includes waste from households, commercial and industrial premises. It is the duty of the caterer to store waste safely and securely, and hand it on to an authorized disposer in a safe and

---

Industry Case Studies

The French hotel group Accor, which owns Novotel and Sofitel, has introduced several environmental initiatives. Novotel has set up an ecology committee to focus on reuse, recycling, reducing and recovering materials. An ecology representative from each hotel is made up from staff, not management, and is a volunteer. Their task is to produce three monthly reports on planned and achieved savings, and to liaise with key staff.

In 1993 the Gleneagles Hotel in Auchterarder won first place in the Scottish Environment Awards for Business for outstanding efforts in environmental management. The hotel sent 3.6 tonnes of used soap and bathroom products, clothes and candles to Bosnia and Liberia, and recycling/reusing is standard practice: for example shortbread tins, coat hangers, glass and paper.

The Savoy and the Dorchester have established Green Committees to study the environmental claims of suppliers and to plan recycling and reuse projects. In 1991 the Savoy used 700,000 plastic cups of which it was planned to recycle 80 per cent.

In 1991 Trusthouse Forte launched a range of cruelty-free, environmentally-friendly toiletries in bedrooms in their hotels in London and Ireland. The company used vegetable-based soaps which were packed in recyclable PET bottles. Mending kits were made from recycled board and labels from recycled paper.

---

secure condition. This means no open or leaking containers. The waste must be removed regularly to minimize the risk of infestation by pests, and the risk to human health. Any movement of waste must be covered by the proper paperwork.

Section 34 of the Act imposes a 'duty of care' on the producer of the waste. They must ensure that only an 'authorized disposer' takes away the waste. 'Authorized disposers' include:

Council waste collectors
Registered waste carriers: these will have a certificate of registration from the local authority.
Exempt waste carriers: normally charities or voluntary organizations.
Holders of waste disposal or waste management licences: valid for only certain types of waste or certain activities. It is the caterer's duty to check that the licence is appropriate.

Exemptions from the above: if a disposer claims to be exempt, check this carefully.

Council waste disposers (Scotland only) are licensed by the local authority.

When disposing of waste the caterer must complete a written description of the waste and a transfer note, which can in fact cover multiple collections by the same collector over a given period of time up to a maximum of twelve months. These regulations also apply to outside catering.

Table 9.2 Cost comparisons of various methods of waste disposal[4]

	Cost per tonne
Incineration	£22–35
Incineration with energy recovery	£20–32
Removal of waste by road including landfill fee	
Uncompacted	£12–20
Compacted	£15–25
Removal of waste by rail including landfill fee	
Compacted	£24–32
Removal of waste by barge (river) including landfill fee	
Compacted	£25–35
Landfill gate fee	
Putrescible waste	£6–12
Industrial, non-putrescible waste	£4–10
Asbestos (bonded sheet)	£20–30
Special wastes	£10–80
Reclamation and recycling of household waste	
Bank systems	£5–16
Kerbside collections	£40–120
Composting	
Home (local authority supplied composter)	£5–20
Centralized composting facility	£12–28

Note: The reasons for the differences in price are due to costs of transport, duration and mode of handling and the need for capital investment, for example an incineration plant or a centralized composting facility.

Local authorities in the UK are responsible for the regulation of waste disposal, and waste regulation authorities are responsible for the licensing and inspection of waste management. Waste regulation authorities issue licences for the disposal of controlled waste and deal with recycling schemes and targets, and the National Rivers Authority is responsible for all discharges into the waterways.

There are two major options for the disposal of waste: either recycling or minimizing it from the source. Recycling involves separation, selling or saving for collection, reuse, composting, incineration with or without heat recovery, and landfill. Waste may also be compacted to save storage space before collection. Let us consider the issues surrounding each of these methods.

THE MINIMIZATION OF WASTE

This should be the easiest option. Costs incurred in the storage and disposal of food and other waste can be significant, depending upon the method of disposal chosen, so it is in the caterer's interest to work hard to minimize the generation of any waste. This includes reducing the amount of waste products actually entering the premises which are of no use to the operation of the business (the greatest culprit here is packaging).

Chapter 8 showed how companies have negotiated with suppliers to reduce the amount of packaging that arrives with goods, and how it is possible to have these delivered in returnable containers, so having achieved a reduction in the volume of waste that enters the premises, and organized operating systems so that there is little waste generated by the operation of the business, the next best option is to collect waste for recycling.

RECYCLING

Glass, paper, plastics, textiles and metals can all be recycled. Most people are happy to collect and sort bottles and newspapers to be placed in the recycling collection bins provided by local authorities, and staff in all types of operation are happy to sort bottles and cans into bins for charity, but it is vital that there is a market for these goods. As a cautionary tale: Germany introduced stringent laws on waste management and recycling so that in the early 1990s all local authorities were collecting every type of product that it was technically possible to recycle. However, there wasn't a market for all this recycled material. This was especially the case for paper. Prices of waste paper fell dramatically, and this was exported to other EC countries where the price of their recycled paper also fell making the saving and collection of waste paper equally unviable for those countries. Recycling can only be an attractive proposition if the price of the collection and processing of the raw material is substantially higher than that of collecting the recycled material, or if there is a sudden increase in the prices of the raw materials.

Currently only 3 per cent of UK municipal waste is recycled.

Table 9.3 Recycling levels achieved by some key industrial sectors (as percentages)

Material	1990 %	1992%	Target
Glass	20	26	50% by 2000
Plastics	2	5	—
Steel cans	9.3	11.9	—
Aluminium cans	5.5	16	50% by 1997/98
Newsprint	26.8	28.1	40% by 2000
Paper and board	31	32	—

Source: Sustainable Development – The UK Strategy, 1994

In addition, in 1990 the UK Government set a target to recycle 50 per cent of all household waste that can be recycled by 2000, i.e. 25 per cent of the total of all municipal waste.

Packaging

In July 1993 the then Conservative Environment Secretary, John Selwyn Gummer, set a challenge to the packaging industry to agree a way of organizing and funding itself to achieve recovery and recycling objectives.

Industry Case Study

In 1994 Linpac opened a second recycling plant which doubled the company's capacity to recycle used plastics packaging.

The European plastics manufacturers have formed a consortium called the Plastics Waste Management Institute to encourage research into the reuse of plastics. This is important because it is not possible to reuse returned plastic bottles as they cannot be sterilized adequately, so they have to be recycled for reuse.

Figure 9.1 Recycling bins in the UK

Life cycle analysis

Is it worth recycling or are the costs of collection, storage, and reprocessing in excess of the costs of using raw materials to create a new item? In the same way as it is important to compare the costs of production, use and disposal of reusable items compared with disposable items in order to arrive at a true comparison of their total costs, where straight costings invariably take no account of the environmental costs involved in production, distribution or use, it is equally important to carry out a similar exercise when considering the pros and cons of recycling. Consider the case of glass. Can you add anything else to the following list of issues which should be taken into account when considering recycling?

1 Mining the sand; transport; heat to convert sand to glass; various colours; shaping of final product; distribution and storage costs; use to include maintenance such as washing, heating water, detergents, etc.
2 The need for separate bins to sort out different items – these need to be well labelled, and staff need training.

Why recycle plastics?

By 1987 the average family in the UK was disposing of 40 kg of plastic materials each year. Although this represented in weight only 7 per cent of total household waste, by volume this was equivalent to 20 per cent. In other words, plastic waste is bulky. Estimates are that the figures for

Industry Case Study

In May 1990 a joint venture vending cup recycling scheme was set up by Dow Chemicals and the Autobar group of companies. The scheme aimed to show that it was possible to recycle vending cups and to investigate the costs that were involved. The pilot project was so successful that in March 1992 the Save A Cup Recycling Company Limited was created. This is a non-profit-making venture funded by major plastic cup manufacturers, importers of plastic cups into the UK, vending and food service companies, and polymer suppliers. Scheme participants include:

Vending and food service companies	Cup producers	Polymer producers
AVAB	Four Square Division	Elf Atochem Ltd
Autobar Industries Ltd	of Mars Ltd	Dow Chemical Co.
Gardner Merchant	Linpac Plastics	Huntsman Chemicals Ltd
Granada Vending Services	International Ltd	
Lyons Tetley Private Label Ltd	Mono Containers Ltd	
Nestlé UK Ltd	Polarcup Ltd	
Nichols Foods Ltd	Swiss Pack Ltd	
Premier Brands Ltd	Tedeco UK Ltd	
TM Group Ltd	Flo Spa	
Van Den Bergh Food Service Ltd		

Dow Chemicals estimated that in 1990 9.3 billion vending cups were used each year in Europe. This was equivalent to 40,000 tonnes of polystyrene with a value of £35 million. The UK used 32 per cent of these cups, or approximately 3 billion, making it the single biggest user in Europe and hence the ideal place for a recycling trial. It was estimated that if polystyrene cups which were not sold through vending machines were also included then this figure would increase to 6 billion, or 24,000 tonnes.

Polystyrene cups are easy to collect for recycling as they stack easily, saving on storage space, it is easy to remove contamination (i.e. food waste), and they are normally sold and disposed of in the same locality.

The project initially operated in an area which covered the whole of London north of the Thames, to Luton in the north and Reading in the west, but it has now spread to cover other areas throughout the UK. There are currently 1600 companies which participate in the scheme, including Boots, the Royal Bank of Scotland, IBM and Shell.

Collection bins are installed in areas where the drinks are purchased and consumed, and are designed so that the cups stack inside each other. They are collected at regular intervals and taken to the recycling plant where they are sorted to exclude major contaminants (including paper cups). They are then fed into a grinder which turns them into chips which are then washed and dried. The chips are extruded and formed into plastic pellets which are sold for use in non-food products such as coat hangers, video and radio cases, garden furniture, trays, office equipment, pallets, foamed egg boxes and foamed insulation, wood substitutes, horticultural containers, and industrial reels.

By 1993, 4 million cups had been collected annually, which represents 16.4 tonnes of plastic, and the company's objective is to collect 750 million cups by 1996.

commercial (including catering) waste are similar. But by reusing plastics there can be as much as 85–90 per cent savings in the energy used to make 'virgin' plastic. The advantages of plastics are that they are hygienic, resistant to mould, waterproof, and chemical and decay resistant. These same properties which make plastics so useful also make their disposal difficult. Used plastics take up a large volume of space in landfill sites, and most take centuries to decay as they are resistant to attack by the bacteria which decompose most waste. Yet the raw material from which most plastics are made, oil, is a finite resource and present scientific research estimates that it is likely that known reserves will run out in the next 50 years. If the technology to recycle used plastics were to be efficient, then this would lessen the pressures on these limited resources.

Current recycling technology

Problems arise with the recycling of plastics because it is vital that the different sorts of plastics are separated. If this is not done then the properties of the individual plastics are lost. Invariably there is no indication of what type of plastic a product has been made from, although some states in the USA have introduced legislation to ensure that this is labelled. Another problem is the use of multiple material packaging which cannot be separated, such as cardboard packs that have a combined aluminium and plastic lining.

It takes 20,000 PET[5] bottles to make 1 tonne of new plastic, and their collection and storage can create terrible space problems. In the USA it was found that it was necessary to recycle 2000 tonnes a year to make recycling financially viable; this is the equivalent of 40 million PET bottles! Another major problem is that of contamination: if just one PVC bottle in 10,000 PET bottles contaminates the load then the whole lot becomes unusable for recycling. There are currently no cheap or reliable methods of ensuring that the one rogue bottle can be identified, although researchers at Bradford and Hull Universities are developing a technique using ultrasound which will be able to detect the rogue polymer, based on the principle that each polymer has a different 'signature' as the sound waves pass through the material. Compared to other systems the process would be cheap, costing as little as £10,000.

In May 1989 an experimental plastics recycling scheme sponsored by Friends of the Earth, UK 2000, the plastics industry, the Department of Trade and Industry and the Department of the Environment was launched in Sheffield. Twenty-five plastic bottle banks were located in the city to collect PET bottles.

Milton Keynes Borough Council recycles approximately 1000 tonnes of PET, PVC and HDPE (High Density Polyethylene) using another technique for sorting involving X-rays. This is an expensive system which requires an initial investment of £140,000 and the labour costs are also high for the initial sorting process (which is done manually). The scheme also accepts deliveries from Glasgow and Manchester. The Council does not aim to make a profit – it sells the recycled plastic on at £100 per tonne whereas the costs of recycling are estimated to be £400 per tonne.

Shredders of plastic disposables are also available.

Incineration with energy recovery

An alternative use of waste plastics, disposables and packaging is to use them for energy generation or 'energy recovery'. This avoids the problems generated by food waste contamination or multiple coatings. Energy can be recovered either by incineration in a special plant or by burning methane produced by waste decomposition from sewage treatment plants or landfill sites. In this way heat can be provided for adjacent buildings, or power can be supplied to the National Grid. The Government has a target of 1500 megawatts of new renewable energy generating capacity by the year 2000. However, we should be aware of the high costs of investment in such a plant and also the greater potential for air pollution from incineration plants than from the burning of methane from landfill; 3 per cent of chlorine emissions are generated by burning municipal waste, most of which is due to the burning of plastics.

On the other hand incineration plants can generate higher volumes of energy when compared to the burning of methane. Methane is produced by the anaerobic decomposition of organic waste; it is potentially explosive if its venting is uncontrolled, and it is also a significant greenhouse gas. So it has a good future as a potential energy supply. It is usually possible to start exploiting it three years after the waste has been laid down, for a period of approximately ten to fifteen years.

Waste plastics can also be recycled by a process called pyrolysis (the thermal decomposition of plastics at very high temperatures in the absence of oxygen) which breaks them down into raw materials for reuse as raw petrochemicals.

Uses of recycled plastics

A company called Superwood in Ireland uses recycled plastic to make road signs and agricultural posts; it also manufactures posts for vineyards in France, and pipes and sheets for sale in Italy. Recycled plastic from PET bottles can be used for fibre-fill for pillows and sleeping bags, tensional strapping tapes, fence posts, paint brushes and rollers, fibres for filters, carpets, clothing, webbing, sails and tyre cords, and as extruded sheet for audio cassette cases and black plastic bags.

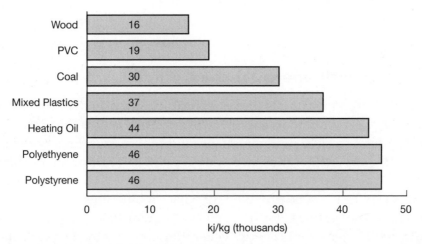

Figure 9.2 The calorific value of plastics compared with more conventional sources of fuel, in kilojoules per kilogramme

Source: *Plastics recycling*, Warmer factsheet, 1994.

Metals

The separation of metals into containers for collection can pose problems, particularly as staff need training so as to distinguish between metals, and they also require extra time to do this task. Thus the price of 'scrap' metals needs to justify the extra costs involved in recycling. However, there are a number of interesting schemes operating in the industry; Forte has operated a pilot scheme in one unit whereby the number of paladins requiring collection has been reduced by two a week. This saves on collection and disposal costs. A contractor collects all the cans, unsorted, weekly for no charge. They are sorted by the contractor who sells the aluminium content for recycling. Any profit is paid in the form of a monthly donation of £25 to a charity nominated by the staff of the unit. This acts as an incentive for the staff to ensure that they keep the metal separate from other waste. It is also good PR for the company.

Aluminium

For each tonne of virgin aluminium manufactured 4 tonnes of bauxite are used together with vast quantities of energy. The amount of energy required to melt down recycled cans for reuse is as little as 5 per cent of that used for the primary manufacture. As there are approximately 6 billion aluminium cans sold in the UK each year, and as in 1993 over 1 billion cans were collected for recycling,[6] there is plenty of scope for an increase in the volume of cans collected and in energy savings. Although 70 per cent of all drinks cans are aluminium, currently in the UK only 21 per cent of all aluminium cans are recycled, although worldwide 50 per cent of all aluminium drinks cans are recycled. Alcan estimate that if all the aluminium cans in the UK were recycled this would equate to 12.5 million less dustbin loads each year. The recycled cans are turned into aluminium ingots which are then used once more for can manufacture. The 1992 price for 'scrap' aluminium was 30–35p per kilo which benefits the collector, because for the can manufacturer there are significant savings on energy costs over that required to smelt primary aluminium. Alcan have a recycling plant that is so sophisticated it can recycle over 100 cans per second.

Glass

To make 1 tonne of glass, 1.1 tonnes of sand, limestone and soda ash are needed, together with an enormous amount of energy and water. In the UK alone over 6 billion glass bottles and jars are produced each year, and we generate over 1.5 million tonnes of glass waste.

163

Returnable glass bottles can be reused on average 30 times, although they do create problems for storage space while awaiting collection. In addition, it is in theory possible to recycle returned glass for ever. For every tonne of recycled glass used, 1.2 tonnes of raw materials are saved, and the equivalent of 30 gallons of crude oil in the form of fuel are saved.[7] It is obviously very profitable for the glass industry to collect glass for recycling, and there are significant savings to be made on landfill charges for the business which collects glass for recycling.

Bass has been heavily involved in the national glass collection and recycling service which was established in 1998 by the Brewers and Licensed Retailers Association (BLRA). Called Bottlebank, the scheme has appointed three national waste contractors (including Biffa) to collect clear, green and brown glass from licensed premises, whether pubs, bars, restaurants or hotels. Collections are made at least every two weeks, and much more frequently for busier outlets. The glass is then bulked up and taken for recycling.

Companies which normally compete with each other are co-operating to meet their packaging waste recycling targets. The industry plans to recover and recycle 350,000 tonnes of glass each year, all saved from landfill. There are plans to cover over 90 per cent of the UK with this scheme.

Paper

Over 30 per cent of the world's total paper production is made from recycled materials; in the UK this figure is over 50 per cent. However, we have already seen that the market for waste paper is erratic. It is important to note that not all types of waste paper are suitable for recycling; any that is contaminated by food waste cannot be used, so in the hospitality industry we are limited to saving office-quality paper and newsprint.

What is recycled paper used for?

There are a range of uses including cardboard of various grades, egg boxes, toilet rolls, paper towels, newspapers, good-quality typing paper and even coloured paper. In many cases good-quality paper is composed of a mixture of recycled pulp and virgin pulp.

Fort Sterling, the company which manufactures Nouvelle recycled toilet tissue for both domestic and industrial use, claims that its softness compares very favourably with the best quality tissue made of virgin pulp.

---

1 tonne of paper = 6 mature trees

Why recycle waste paper?

Only 10 per cent of land in the UK is forest, which is a very small percentage compared with most countries. We therefore need to import a substantial quantity of trees or paper. In Europe specific species of trees are specially grown for paper-making and the forestry commissions ensure that there are adequate supplies to meet foreseeable requirements. For instance, Sweden and Finland claim they have a greater stock of reserve forest than they did 100 years ago. It is important that all paper is produced from wood from properly managed, sustainable forests, where old trees are replaced on a regular basis, and where the foresters are careful to maintain the conditions which support and promote biodiversity. Finland has been criticized by environmental groups including Greenpeace and Friends of the Earth because some of its logging companies are razing whole areas of forest to the ground, making it almost impossible for plants and trees to regenerate. A report by the Finnish Government's Environment Ministry in 1991 estimated that as many as 692 species of plants and animals are facing extinction as the result of such practices. The logging companies' claim that they are operating sustainably is debatable. In fact, they are merely replacing one or two species of tree which are good for paper-making and are failing to address the overall sustainability of the forests. In addition, peat bogs are being drained in order to make room for more plantations, which means that even more species of trees face extinction.[8] This example highlights the fact that we should never take at face value any claims that a company may make to be environmentally responsible. We should ask questions and probe to discover the truth.

Virgin pulp is used to make paper where the properties of strength (wet and dry), colour and absorbency are prized, and also for good-quality printing. Pulp is often made from forest 'thinnings' and hardwoods are never used, but it still takes 2.2 tonnes of wood to make 1 tonne of pulp; in addition recycling is 40 per cent less energy intensive than the production of virgin pulp.

However, there are a number of problems with the principle of collecting paper for recycling within the hospitality industry. First, the paper needs to be stored until there is an adequate volume for collection, and this can constitute a major fire hazard. Second, the sorting process itself is labour intensive. Since it is not possible to recycle paper that has been used for food, the only type of paper suitable for recycling is newsprint and paper used for wrapping. It is likely that this job would be allocated to the chambermaids. For a variety of reasons, chambermaids have a high turnover rate, which means that any company committed to sorting paper would need to invest much time and money in staff training. In addition to these disincentives the productivity of those chambermaids involved in sorting paper would be reduced by up to 25 per cent, so if there is no money to be recovered on waste paper the exercise would not be economically viable.

The paper manufacturing industry is now more aware of the burden that some of its processes can place and have placed on the environment, and have adapted their processes so that paper colours are often based on vegetable dyes, and where glue is used and is appropriate, the glue is water-based and 100 per cent biodegradable. Current paper blending processes no longer use dioxins which can cause miscarriages, birth defects, and serious behavioural and neurological problems.

Paper itself is a naturally biodegradable material, although if placed in landfill it can take decades to completely biodegrade in anaerobic conditions.

Incineration of paper with heat recovery

Forte are considering the feasibility of incineration of paper as a form of heat recovery, or the use of paper pellets as fuel.

FOOD WASTE DISPOSAL

In landfill sites, where all oxygen is excluded from the waste as it is covered with thick layers of soil, food and other organic waste is broken down anaerobically (in the restricted presence of oxygen) and both methane and carbon dioxide are released. Methane can be used as a fuel but in the UK it is normally left to disperse into the atmosphere via vents which are strategically placed over the site. We should remember that methane is a greenhouse gas, like carbon dioxide, which has a greater global warming potential than does carbon dioxide.

The catering industry generates on average approximately 50 per cent of its waste as waste food. Much of this can be minimized if the caterer makes careful specifications to the supplier or even purchases ready-prepared meals, ready-trimmed meat and ready-prepared vegetables. This would only leave the problem of how to dispose of food waste left on the customer's plate, together with any unused or unwanted food from the kitchen.

Industry Case Study

In the past Forte had a policy whereby every item that was on the menu would be available throughout the opening hours of the unit. In the case of motorway service areas this meant 24-hour availability. Invariably this led to food wastage of items on display on self-service counters, due to deterioration in appearance and also because of the need to comply with food hygiene legislation. In the light of the new policy to minimize food wastage, the company decided to reconsider its 24-hour availability policy. The Environmental Services Director, John Forte, worked out that for every 8 oz of food served on the plate there was $3\frac{1}{2}$ oz of waste generated, either as the result of its production, or because the customer did not wish to eat it. As the company was producing approximately 2 million meals every day of the year this resulted in a phenomenal volume of waste – 437,500 lb, or 130 tons. This would need to be disposed of in landfill and also generated costs of collection and storage – think how many black plastic bags this represents, or how many gallons of water is needed to wash it down food waste disposal units!

Food waste placed in plastic bags can attract vermin. Some establishments dispose of their food waste in waste disposal units that are attached to the mains drainage so that the waste eventually ends up at the sewage works for disposal.

Another option to deal with waste food is to turn it into compost. This is a process in which the waste is broken down biologically under controlled conditions so that the end product can be used for horticulture. The decomposition is carried out by bacteria in the presence of oxygen and the food waste is broken down into water, carbon dioxide and humus which is returned to the soil to improve its structure and to add to the micronutrients in the soil. It is an odourless and fairly rapid process.

Mature compost can be used in horticulture in a variety of ways. It can be dug into the soil thus improving its structure. In clay soils it helps to break up the clay, and allow aeration of the soil and improve its drainage quality in the winter, and improve water retention in the drier summer months. It also helps sandy soils to improve their ability to retain moisture, and reduces the ability of the winds to blow the light soil away, hence preventing erosion. If compost is applied to the surface of the soil around plants it acts as a mulch: it prevents the growth of weeds, and it also helps to retain water around the plant. In all cases nutrients contained in the composted material will benefit the growth of plants. Compost is also used commercially as a peat substitute when making up potting mixtures.

On average as much as 3 tonnes per acre of topsoil is lost from the earth's agricultural land each year, so compost is an essential method of improving the structure of the remaining soil and replacing lost nutrients.

There have been few attempts to produce compost commercially in the UK even though as much as one-third of all domestic and commercial waste in the UK is compostable. The Department of Trade and Industry supported a pilot project which involved the joint composting of municipal waste and sewage sludge.[9] South West Water, Devon Waste Management and Focsa Services (UK) Ltd demonstrated that by composting up to 70 per cent by volume of municipal waste can be diverted from landfill sites, compared with more conventional recycling schemes where only 30 per cent can be diverted. The end product was designed to be used for tree planting schemes, the improvement of spoil heaps, land reclamation, the capping of abandoned landfill, quarry and mining sites, as a base material for turf growing and as a low-nutrient fertilizer for farmers. A widespread and successful scheme like this would mean that municipal waste could be disposed of as follows:

- organic waste to be composted
- non-organic and non-combustible material to be buried in landfill sites
- all other waste to be incinerated and the energy created to be recovered.

It was also estimated that if 80,000 tonnes of municipal waste were to be composted each year there are likely to be significant returns on the capital invested, together with significant environmental cost savings as the production of methane and leachate from landfill sites would be eliminated, and there would be less need for landfill sites.

Forte have set up a pilot scheme at their motorway service station at Birchanger Green whereby food waste is composted; the final product is designed to be used as a peat substitute in the surrounding grounds. The company has also considered harnessing the methane from compost generation for use as a biogas for fuel purposes. Forte's total annual waste disposal costs can be as high as £5 million, so any savings that can be made by the judicious sorting and reuse of waste are significant.

Industry Case Studies

Sheraton Hotels reduced waste tonnage by 13 per cent by implementing a recycling programme. This has meant savings of $7000 per month. The scheme recycles waste plastic cups which are turned into video cassettes, coat hangers and waste bins.

The Canadian Pacific hotel recycles waste soap by donating it to charity and has installed shampoo dispensers.

At the London Hilton in Park Lane empty wine bottles are divided into colours and collected twice a day for recycling.

Food waste disposal machines

Food waste disposal machines are usually plumbed into the cold water outlet in the wash-up area, and consist of an electrically-operated rotating blade which grinds up the food. Problems with these machines arise on a regular basis if non-food waste such as serviettes or cutlery is put into them. Even sticky food, for example cooked rice, has been known to jam machines. Newer models, such as Hobart's Ecolo, are more advanced and can even cope with bones!

Waste compactors

Packaging, cans, tins, bottles and cardboard are all safety hazards until they are removed from a business's premises. The waste can harbour dirt, it can attract vermin, it can be a potential fire hazard and pose a threat to safety if it blocks exits. A safe and hygienic way in which to store waste until it is removed is as a compressed block sealed in strong plastic bags in a separate storage area. Waste compactors are easy to operate, require little maintenance and operate quietly. These machines will compact every type of waste, from a ratio of five bags to one up to twenty bags to one, providing a substantial saving of up to 70 per cent on space and saving on disposal charges.

Waste compactors are electro-hydraulically powered. They are able to compact cans, glass, cardboard, food and plastic packaging to a mere 14 per cent of their original volume in a matter of seconds. The rubbish is then presented ready-wrapped as a cube ready for disposal. The bags are designed to hold half a cubic metre of compacted waste, weighing on average 25–30 kg. The compactors are supplied with a trolley for ease of transport. These machines are ideal for use in a range of catering operations including restaurants, hotels, guest houses, nursing homes, canteens and fast-food outlets. They are already used extensively on ships, in order to comply with new marine legislation which bans the dumping of raw waste at sea.

A waste disposal machine's motor power can range between .75 kW (750 watts) to 1.1kW, and they can operate in as little as 25 seconds. The initial investment in one can be substantial, but this plus the running costs can normally be balanced against the savings made on storage and waste disposal.

Some machines can also wash, sanitize and deodorize the waste before crushing or pulping, and again these can reduce waste by up to 80 per cent. Glass is pulped so that there are no sharp edges and the waste can be used as a component part of building materials and asphalt, for shot-blasting and for filling drainage ditches. A typical compactor has a motor rated at 2.2 kW, uses 45 litres of water per minute, and costs in the region of £6000.

For use in restaurants there is an under-counter glass crusher which crushes empty bottles quickly, quietly and with no vibration. This reduces the volume of glass by 95 per cent and saves on storage and waste disposal costs.

We should bear in mind that the landfill tax[10] means that the greater the volume of waste the greater the tax, so the purchase of a compactor is not only an environmentally responsible action but in the long term it will also pay for itself.

Industry Case Study

We have seen in this chapter how companies can run up some very large costs for waste disposal. Forte adopted the policy in the 1980s that it was better to minimize the volume of waste entering its premises. In the case of non-perishables, they negotiated with their suppliers to dispense with any unnecessary wrapping and packaging. Perishable foodstuffs, however, were another matter.

They looked at how production waste could be minimized, and came to the conclusion that the purchase of *all* foodstuffs in their raw state was wasteful. For instance, it made more sense to purchase only the heart of the lettuce, rather than to purchase the whole lettuce and to throw away the outside leaves. If waste were eliminated transport costs would be reduced as only the food to be used would be transported; disposal costs would also be reduced.

In order to ensure that the food was as fresh as possible and that no food would be wasted, or run out, the company decided on a policy of small but frequent deliveries so that any unit would not have more than a certain maximum level of stock. In order to minimize transport costs the company checked that its own delivery fleet was operating efficiently, by implementing a programme of regular maintenance and making sure that vehicles did not carry half loads.

CONCLUSION

In keeping with government policy of developing fiscal rather than regulatory incentives to encourage environmental responsibility, it is anticipated that the increased landfill taxes, imposed in the November 1994 Budget, will only be the start of many. Both the previous Conservative and the New Labour Governments have made it clear that they are very keen to apply the 'pollutor pays' principle to waste management.

The success of an industrial society has until recently been measured by the extent to which it can produce goods and services whose purchase in turn creates jobs and wealth. However, this short-term success has extensive long-term environmental effects. The use of non-renewable resources, such as energy and raw materials, will inevitably result in their loss. The perception that there is an endless supply of improved versions of consumer products has resulted in excessive waste and wasteful habits. Producers have encouraged the purchase of their products by the use of ever-increasing layers of wrapping to make the product look more attractive or hygienic. Sustainability means that society must readdress its values and adopt policies which will encourage people to reduce the amount of waste that is generated and to conserve those resources that are used for the production of goods and services, as well as to consider the reuse or recycling of waste products.

In the future there will be a steady trend towards encouraging the disposal of waste by the '4 Rs method': reduce, reuse, recycle, and recover; landfill will be seen as a last option. Government policy means that it will become increasingly expensive to dispose of all wastes, and these costs will have to be either assimilated by the business or passed on to the customer. Forte has shown how it is possible to negotiate with suppliers to reduce the volume of packaging that accompanies a product. There is no reason why every business should not take a similar approach; after all, the supplier adds the cost of the packaging to the selling price of the product, and it is the purchaser who is also compelled to pay for the disposal of the packaging!

Changes in behaviour take time to become established, so it is never too soon to start staff training, and to offer incentives for staff to sort waste for recycling, and to let them know the benefits of the extra work that this involves.

Industry Case Study

'Going for Green' is a Government sponsored scheme which was launched in 1996. The scheme aims to encourage people to protect the environment by reducing waste, saving energy, saving on natural resources, preventing pollution and taking care of the local environment.

To show its support, McDonald's has worked with its suppliers to reduce its packaging. Waste from ketchup and soft drinks packaging has been reduced by 25 per cent, and it has saved on hundreds of tonnes of packaging that used to be generated by its cheese and fruit pie suppliers. The company has installed waste compactors in 700 outlets in order to reduce waste volume by 40 per cent. More packaging is made from recycled materials, and the company will feature the 'Going for Green' message on its sugar packets.

QUESTIONS AND ISSUES FOR DISCUSSION

1 Work out the cubic capacity of the waste bins of a catering establishment where you work. Assume you have been asked to recommend to the manager whether it is worth purchasing a waste compactor. The technical specifications are:[11]

> Compaction force: 2000 kg f
> Compaction ratio: approximately 5:1
> Operating cycle: approximately 25 seconds
> Motor: 1.1kW (1.5HP) 3phase
> Voltages: 380/420
> Fuse Rating: 15 amp
> Bag Capacity: $\frac{1}{2}$m^3 uncompacted
> Bag Size: 500 × 500 × 450 mm
> Average bag weight: 25–30 kg
> Cubic metre: 1.455
> Price: £4450 + VAT

Work out the volume of waste produced each week by the restaurant/canteen. What are the current costs of its disposal? If this waste were to be compacted how would the costs be reduced? Taking into account the savings, how long would it take before the waste compactor paid for itself? What other advantages are there for the canteen/restaurant if it were to invest in a waste compactor?

2 In his Budget speech to the House of Commons on 29 November 1994, the Chancellor of the Exchequer Kenneth Clarke stated his intention to impose a landfill tax on waste disposal. The proceeds from this tax, however, would be used to subsidize employers' National Insurance contributions in order to reduce the costs of employing staff and to encourage companies to take on more staff. Comment on this with regard to Government policy to use 'economic instruments' as a way of encouraging people to change their behaviour towards waste.

3 Friends of the Earth argue that the Government should introduce a law which restricts the number of polymers that a company can use to make plastics, and that the claims placed on many bottles stating they are 'recyclable' should be checked. Comment on this.

4 You have recently been appointed Assistant Manager in a busy seaside hotel, with special responsibility for environmental management. The owners of the hotel have promised you a bonus of 5 per cent of any savings you make for the hotel as the result of your project. Having undertaken an environmental audit, you decide that the first and easiest course is to tackle the problem of waste. Using a local hotel or restaurant or similar catering establishment, carry out a waste survey and make recommendations for the minimization of waste generation. This should be accompanied by financial projections of the costs and benefits of change both for the business and for the environment.

5 In this chapter we have seen an example of a trial scheme in Milton Keynes on the feasibility of recycling PET bottles (see p. 161). The costs of recycling were £400 per tonne but the selling price of the recovered goods was only £100. What could the Council do to make this scheme more profitable?

6 Most waste disposal in the UK is directly to landfill, but there is tremendous scope for waste reduction, recycling and energy recovery from materials. Currently the costs of the various methods of waste disposal do not reflect the true costs of either disposal or environmental impact. An article in the *New Scientist*[12] has argued that it may be better for the environment if waste paper were to be burnt in municipal incinerators rather than be recycled,

depending on the price allocated to environmental 'externalites' such as carbon dioxide, methane, carbon monoxide, sulphur dioxide, nitrogen oxides and particulates. Read this article and comment on its implications.

Notes

1   Warren Spring Laboratory, *The Pearce Report*, 1993.
2   Directive 91/156/EEC; OJ L 78, 26 March 1991.
3   National Environmental Technology Centre, F6, Culham, Abingdon, Oxfordshire OX14 3DB.
4   Courtesy of the London Waste Regulation Authority, Hampton House, 20 Albert Embankment, London SE1 7TJ.
5   PET: polyethylene terephthalate.
6   Alcan Aluminium Can Recycling.
7   J. Elkington and J. Hailes, *The Green Consumer Guide*, London: Gollancz, 1988.
8   For a fuller explanation of the implications of such activities in Finland and Russia see Martin Wright, 'Death by a Thousand Cuts', *New Scientist*, 11 February 1995.
9   Department of Trade and Industry's Environmental Management Options Scheme. Project Information Brochure no. 2, 'Co-Composting of Municipal Solid Waste and Sewage Sludge'.
10   Introduced in 1994 by the Conservative Government.
11   Based on waste compactor model no. CP501SF. IMC, Croxley Green, Herts, WD3 3AX.
12   Fred Pearce, 'Burn Me', *New Scientist*, 22 November 1997, pp. 31–4.

CHAPTER 10

The Green consumer

> The government's role is to provide the correct fiscal, regulatory and financial framework for the UK strategy programme, and to ensure that advice and information are available on the actions that can be taken to make savings. But it is people in households and businesses who will make the decisions and take the actions.
>
> *Sustainable Development – The UK Strategy*[1]

OBJECTIVES

1 To investigate whether it is the increasing environmental awareness (in its broadest sense) of the consumer that drives the 'greening' of many businesses, or whether industry is shaping the environmental awareness of the consumer.
2 To identify the 'Green' consumer in the hospitality industry.
3 To analyse the recent growth of Green consumerism.
4 To examine the effect of recession on environmental attitudes.

INTRODUCTION

A survey by the Department of the Environment in 1993 found that 85 per cent of the UK population claim some level of concern over environmental issues. The major sources of concern included the destruction of the tropical rainforests and global warming, the dumping of chemicals and toxic wastes on land and at sea, traffic congestion, rubbish, and drinking water quality. These cross local and international areas of concern. Most people said that they obtained their information from the media, but considered that there was more that the Government could do to educate people about environmental issues.

A majority of the sample, 62 per cent, felt that the pollutor pays principle should apply even if this meant that the cost of goods might increase; 48 per cent claimed to recycle newsprint; 44 per cent took bottles to a bottle bank; and a staggering 77 per cent claimed that they tried to minimize the volume of noise that they generated.

Further research by the Department of the Environment indicates that children have particular concerns about the environment, probably as the result of work carried out for school projects and environmental issues and programmes targeted at young people in the media. They claim to be keen to contribute in some way, especially to local projects such as recycling, wildlife projects and clean-up schemes. However, whereas the 8–15 age group is particularly aware about environmental issues, other research indicates that the 18–24 age group shows less concern.

This chapter will examine the phenomenon of the 'Green consumer' and consider whether this market could be targeted by the hospitality industry. First we shall look at how this phenomenon came about.

GROWTH IN THE GREEN CONSUMER MARKET

Throughout the 1980s in the UK there was increasing public awareness of the importance of considering environmental issues when making purchasing decisions. Once regarded as eccentric and even a 'sub-sector' of society, Green consumers became mainstream, respectable and middle-class. The trend first showed itself in the under-40s, but as these people got older their values remained the same and the age span grew. One spectacular marketing success was The Body Shop, founded by Anita Roddick. This company, which sold cosmetics and associated products, built its reputation on the fact that none of its products had previously been tested on animals. This simple concept, combined with the new style of fun cosmetics and value for money, immediately found a niche with young people.

'The Green consumer avoids products which are likely to

- endanger the health of the consumer or of others
- cause significant damage to the environment during manufacture, use or disposal
- consume a disproportionate amount of energy during manufacture, use or disposal
- cause unnecessary waste, either because of over-packaging or because of an unduly short useful life
- use materials derived from threatened species or from threatened environments
- involve the unnecessary use – or cruelty to – animals, whether this be for toxicity testing or for other purposes
- adversely affect other countries, particularly in the Third World.'

Source: J. Elkington and J. Hailes, *The Green Consumer Guide*, 1988.

Books like *The Green Consumer Guide* (first published in 1988) sold in their hundreds of thousands, and the significant demand for recycling facilities for paper and glass was met by many local authorities. When it was discovered that CFCs, which were used as propellants in aerosol cans, could be responsible for the depletion of the ozone layer, people voted with their pockets and stopped buying aerosols. In turn, manufacturers responded to consumer pressure and substituted the propellants in their products or else reverted to more environmentally-friendly methods of delivery. During this period consumers were becoming increasingly concerned about the quality of their food. The book *E for Additives* by Maurice Hanssen was an instant success in the UK, and was followed by similar books, articles and rumours, so that eventually the public perception was that every food containing an E number was a potential carcinogen.

As a result of the adverse publicity, food manufacturers were legally obliged to modify the format which listed the ingredients in packaged foods. Ironically this misconception arose out of the requirements of an EC Directive that all ingredients should be listed in descending order of weight on the back of packaged goods, and that any chemical additives could be listed either by their full chemical name, their common name or by their EC code (if allocated). In the interests of space many manufacturers opted to use the EC code, or 'E' number, to their eventual detriment.

The public interest in food quality, although at times misinformed, blended well with the greater value system of the environmental movement. Attention was also directed to the volume of agricultural chemicals which were used in the production of food, not only because of the dangers of pesticide residues in food to human health, but also because of the long-term damage that was being caused to the countryside. The rural idyll of the British countryside as a patchwork of green fields dotted with happy animals had within a period of 40 years been transformed by the effects of monoculture. East Anglia had become one huge field, the dust-bowl of the UK, and was losing large amounts of topsoil to the North Sea. Animals had been selectively bred to ensure maximum production. The only type of cow one saw, and then only in the summer months, was the black and white Friesian. Owing to selective breeding and intensive farming techniques, pigs were kept indoors in cramped pens. The salmonella in eggs scare, in 1988, heightened public awareness of the way in which poultry was reared. The public were led to believe by the press that the reason why eggs were contaminated with salmonella was because hens were kept in cages in unhygienic conditions, and fed the processed remains of their own species.

Of course, the situation was not that simple, but the public voted with their feet. In the late 1980s and early 1990s public demand for organic fruit and vegetables and free range eggs was met by the supermarkets. However, although consumers were prepared to pay a premium price for free range eggs, there was considerable resistance to the premium demanded for organic fruits and vegetables, and some supermarkets stopped selling them. This coincided with the start of an economic recession at the beginning of the 1990s, and the fact that free range eggs continued to sell in part reflects the British consumer's concern with animal welfare, but is probably a greater reflection of the impact of the salmonella scare.

In 1989 the Green Party gained 16 per cent of the vote in the European elections in the UK. The Prime Minister Margaret Thatcher and her Conservative Government seemed suddenly to become far more committed to the environment. And public disillusion as a result of the exposure of a number of financial scandals in the City of London was accompanied by a surge of interest in ethical investments.

The late 1980s also saw an increase in a vast range of environmentally-friendly products on sale in the supermarkets. But 'Green' cleaning products soon met with consumer disappointment: not only were they more expensive, but they were not as 'effective', i.e. they weren't able to give the same standard of 'whiteness' as more conventional products. Customers felt that they had been misled, and this, accompanied by the pain of the recession in the early 1990s, meant that public involvement in environmental issues became less of a priority, sales of Green cleaners fell and less recycling took place. Other effects included a significant reduction in donations to charities and a drop in membership of environmental organizations, including Greenpeace, Friends of the Earth, the Soil Association and the HDRA (Henry Doubleday Research Association, an organization devoted to the promotion of organic methods of plant, fruit and vegetable production).

Table 10.1 Consumer priorities in the late 1980s/early 1990s (percentages)

Concerns to do with	1989	1992	1996
The environment	35	11	3
Health care	29	28	34
Unemployment	24	62	44
Law and order	16	16	22

Source: MORI, 1997.[2]

However, the business world had noted the change in consumer priorities, and despite the recession addressed these and developed long-term strategies to deal with the new breed of consumer; in contrast to the 'selfish 80s' the 1990s were branded the 'caring 90s'.

It is interesting to note that large PLCs, who at the beginning of the 1990s appeared not to have had an interest in environmental issues, were by the middle of the decade developing environmental policy statements and reporting their progress in environmental management systems, first as part of the company's Annual Report and then as a separate Environmental Report. Cynics might argue that this change in attitude was more to do with a company's concern for its reputation and desire to retain its market position than a genuine commitment to the environment. Realists could argue, however, that although those factors were persuasive it is also true that as trading conditions have become more competitive, the financial gains and improvement in working conditions and customer service that environmental management systems provide a company with make good business sense.

As the UK struggled out of the recession in the later 1990s, interest in the environment and similar issues re-emerged. Animal welfare protests took place in January 1995 at Shoreham in Sussex and Brightlingsea in Essex; here the middle classes and older people joined forces with young radical supporters of animal rights to prevent the export of live calves to Europe to be reared for veal. These protests were followed by similar demonstrations against the export of live sheep to Europe for slaughter.

The later 1990s also saw the involvement of the 'respectable' and the affluent in the protests against road-building schemes in areas of beauty such as Salisbury bypass over Twyford Down and the extension of the Lewes bypass through the South Downs. Although the Salisbury bypass went ahead, the public concern that manifested itself across all social strata made policy-makers reconsider road-building programmes. This also coincided with the election of the New Labour Government in 1997 who showed their concern about the impact of the motor vehicle on the environment by creating a new government department, the Department of Transport, the Regions and the Environment, headed by the Deputy Prime Minister.

In 1995 the CWS (Co-operative Wholesale Society) conducted a survey of 30,000 of its retail customers. Seventy per cent said that they had at some time boycotted either products or stores because of their opposition to the retailers' policies; 80 per cent stated that they felt it was the duty of retailers to provide more information on environmental and ethical issues in the production of individual products. Overall the survey indicated that animal welfare and issues to do with the environment informed consumer decisions when purchasing.[3] (The success of 'welfare meats' has already been addressed in Chapter 7.)

The surge in consumer commitment to the environment and associated issues in the late 1990s is evidenced by a range of phenomena:

- the animal protests at Shoreham and Brightlingsea
- the election of the New Labour Government in 1997 with a strong commitment to environmental issues in its manifesto
- renewed growth in the membership of environmental groups – combined UK membership of Green organizations in 1998 was 4–5 million.

DEFINITION OF THE 'GREEN CONSUMER'

MORI has defined 'environmental activists' as those people who indulge in five or more of the following activities:

- watch TV programmes on the subject of wildlife and conservation
- read books on environmental issues
- walk or ramble in the countryside
- contribute financially to environmental organizations
- join an environmental pressure group
- write to their MP or local councillor on environmental issues
- actively campaign on environmental issues.

Using these criteria, MORI identified that 14 per cent of the UK population were 'environmental activists' in 1988, 31 per cent in 1991, 23 per cent in 1992 (probably due to the effects of the recession) and 28 per cent in 1993.

Peattie[4] identifies a number of different ways to describe Green consumers. He cites a survey by Marketing Diagnostics which lists four types of Green consumer:

- Green activists – this includes people who are members of an environmental organization, making up 5–15 per cent of the population.
- Green thinkers – this group tries to identify new ways of helping the environment. They purchase Green goods and services, and make up approximately 30 per cent of the population.
- Green consumer base – this includes anyone who has changed their habits to consider the environment: 45– 60 per cent of the population.
- Generally concerned – this includes anyone who claims to be concerned about the environment: up to 90 per cent of the population.

Obviously there can be considerable overlap between categories, and it would appear from this list that everyone could claim to have at least some Green credentials. To be a credible environmentalist, however, it can be argued that it is what you do rather than what you claim to do that is of most significance. With this in mind, the four categories of population identified by Ogilvy and Mather[5] are probably more realistic:

- Activists: 16 per cent of the population. These people
1 are aware of green issues, likely to buy green products and services
2 are concerned for their children
3 believe in people
4 are optimistic about future technological development
5 place environmental protection above economic growth
6 are home owners with older children
7 vote Conservative
8 biased slightly towards upmarket consumers

- Realists: 34 per cent of the population
1 youngest group – biased towards those with young children
2 are worried about the environment
3 perceive a conflict between profit and environmental protection
4 are not confident that problems will be resolved
5 are sceptical of the 'green bandwagon'
6 vote Labour

- Complacents: 28 per cent of the population
1 biased towards upmarket consumers, with older children
2 are optimistic about mankind, business and government
3 see the solution as somebody else's problem
4 are not very aware of green issues
5 lean to the right politically

- Alienated: 22 per cent of the population
1 are less educated, downmarket consumers
2 are biased towards young families and senior citizens
3 are unaware of green issues
4 see green as a transient issue
5 are pessimistic about possible solutions
6 lean to the left politically.

Again, it is difficult to pigeon-hole individuals into a single category, but the above definition provides an indication of attitudes. However, membership of such groups will change over time, as people age and as the world is exposed to new environmental threats.

GREEN PURCHASING PATTERNS

Having examined the various categories of Green consumer, it is important to look at whether people really do put their principles into practice. Robens[6] argues that there is a gap between attitudes and behaviour, and gives the following explanations:

- Green products are perceived to be too expensive
- Consumers prioritise price, quality and convenience before the environment
- Consumers are confused about the plethora of 'green' claims
- Many businesses are reluctant to make green claims as they fear falling foul of legislation or consumer group pressure
- Consumers feel that there is a lot of green 'hype'.

His findings support other research that looks at false Green claims. For instance, an investigation by the National Consumer Council[7] in 1995 found that there were large numbers of products marketed with spurious environmental claims. The claims were either unsubstantiable, vague or deliberately misleading. They tended to be accompanied by a range of unfamiliar logos. The research found that shoppers were confused, sceptical and even ignorant about the claims that were made, even those who claimed to be 'Green' shoppers. The report concluded that to allow manufacturers and sellers of products and services to continue with misleading claims would go against government policy which is to encourage the purchase of more fuel-efficient and less environmentally-damaging products and services.

THE GREEN CONSUMER IN THE HOSPITALITY SECTOR

In this chapter we have considered a range of general issues associated with Green consumerism; let us now look at the hospitality sector specifically. This book has outlined several measures which the industry can take to improve its environmental performance, and the various industry case studies have shown how this can be put into practice. A book such as this one cannot hope to be definitive; and it should be remembered that new and exciting examples are to be found throughout the world. But do such initiatives help to increase a company's market share? Do customers deliberately choose to stay at a hotel or eat in a restaurant because of its environmental performance? What research has been undertaken in this area?

Probably the most successful campaign to date is not in the strictest sense an environmental one, but it is certainly associated with it – that is the provision of rooms and restaurant areas which are smoke free.

In practice, little research has been carried out on the Green consumer of hospitality products. However, a survey conducted in 1995 of 489 air travellers, by Virginia Polytechnic Institute and State University, published in *Lodging Hospitality*, on their views about hotels and the environment found that

- 70 per cent of the sample claimed that they were likely to choose a hotel with a strong environmental record
- 26 per cent did not care
- 3 per cent were antagonistic to environmental initiatives in the hospitality industry
- 91 per cent stated that hotels should use energy efficient lighting
- 86 per cent stated that hotels should provide recycling bins for guests.

It should be remembered, however, that the majority of the hotels that have taken a serious interest in environmental management issues are those which attract the corporate guest, who is more likely to choose the hotel for its convenience and standard of service than for its environmental performance. It will be interesting to see whether the new Scandic purpose-built Sjolyst Hotel in Oslo will prove to be more popular because of its environmental record than for its location.

THE EC ECO–LABELLING SCHEME AND THE EC ECO–LABEL LOGO

The eco-label is awarded to products which have been assessesed on a cradle to grave (i.e. life cycle analysis) basis. The first criteria for washing machines, dishwashers, light bulbs, soil improvers, and hair sprays in the UK have been published, and more will follow for other goods and eventually services.

The establishment of this award scheme should encourage more manufacturers to aim for it as it is likely to become a good marketing tool. However, experience with voluntary energy efficient labelling

The eco-label

schemes in the UK for domestic appliances indicate that people will only buy them if there is a price advantage – environmental factors come second to financial factors. Similarly, with unleaded petrol, it was only when the duty was reduced to below that of leaded petrol that consumption and purchase increased. These experiences support research that argues that consumers will often say one thing but do another. However, the Eco-labelling scheme is a voluntary one, and this should give credibility to any Green claims, if the consumer is educated about what it really means.

CONCLUSION

The conclusion that we can draw from this chapter about the Green consumer is that, in the UK at least, although people claim that environmental issues inform their purchasing decisions, value for money and convenience take priority. This could be to do with still-painful memories of the recession, and that the realities of day to day living will always take precedence over more ethereal issues. Having said that, there certainly appears to be an increasing awareness and concern about problems that modern consumer societies are creating for the environment. As public consciousness is raised by the plethora of international meetings on these issues, it may be that consumers will find that the environmental performance of products and services in every sector of their lives will become more important and that they will become more selective.

QUESTIONS AND ISSUES FOR DISCUSSION

1 Devise a questionnaire in order to discover people's 'Green' attitudes. Try it out as a pilot on at least five people. Rewrite the questionnaire in the light of your findings. Then apply the questionnaire to at least 100 people, and analyse the results to discover if there is such a things as a typical Green consumer profile. Are your results biased? If so, why?

2 Try applying the questionnaire to two distinct groups, for example 18–24-year-olds compared with the over-65s; or between different socio-economic groups; or between those in Higher Education and those who left school at 16. Are there any differences in attitudes? Why might this be the case? Are your results biased? If so, why?

3 In the light of your findings from either of the above questions, consider how you would promote a new hospitality operation, e.g. wine bar, bistro, hotel, coffee shop,tea room, sandwich bar/delivery service, etc., *or* a given product, e.g. a menu (this doesn't have to be vegetarian). Present your marketing strategy and be prepared to give reasons for your methodology and

decisions. How will your techniques/strategies differ according to which category you are targeting?

4 Read the section on the profile of the 'Green consumer' (pp. 180–1). Which category of consumer do you most closely identify with? Are these categories well-defined? Would you modify these in any way? Give reasons for your answers.

5 You have recently been appointed to the position of Food and Beverage Manager of a family hotel in the West Country which is heavily dependent on the tourist trade. Competition is very stiff, however, so you have been given the task of differentiating the product (or package) that this hotel sells from that of its competitors. You decide to aim at the ABC1 market who are members of the Royal Society for the Protection of Birds, the Ramblers' Association and other similar organizations. Explain how you would go about the task of differentiation, giving examples in each case.

6 Obtain a copy of a company's Environmental Report and write a critique of its environmental performance, what claims it makes and what the public perceives as its 'Green' credentials.

Notes

1 *Sustainable Development – The UK Strategy*, London: HMSO, 1990.
2 A. Martin, *Tourism, the Environment and Consumers*, paper presented at the conference, 'Environment Matters', Glasgow. Published by MORI, 1997.
3 Cited in *Environmental Business Management*, by A. Hutchinson and F. Hutchinson, London: McGraw Hill, 1997.
4 K. Peattie, *Green Marketing*, London: Pitman, 1992.
5 Cited in *ibid.*, p. 120.
6 J. A. Robens, 'Green Consumers in the 1990s: Profile and Implications for Advertising', *Journal of Business Research*, vol. 36, 1996, pp. 217–31.
7 National Consumer Council, *Green Claims*, London: National Consumer Council, 1996.

Further reading

K. Peattie, *Green Marketing*, London: Pitman, 1992.

CHAPTER 11

Transport

> Even allowing for technical improvements in vehicle design, the consequences of growth on such a scale would be unacceptable in terms of emissions, noise . . . and disruption of community life. . . . In our view the transport system must already be regarded as unsustainable . . . and will become progressively more so if recent trends continue.
>
> *Report of the Royal Commission on Environmental Pollution*[1]

OBJECTIVES

1 To discuss the major causes of environmental pollution generated by road traffic.
2 To discuss alternative methods of delivery that can be adopted by the industry.
3 To describe the effects upon human health of traffic pollution.
4 To describe a range of systems which a company can adopt to minimize the impact of its vehicle activity whether directly or indirectly, on the environment.

INTRODUCTION

In Chapter 1 there was a brief discussion of the social and environmental problems caused by acid rain. The two major contributors to its creation are power stations, which burn fossil fuels, and transport. Not only does acid rain affect delicate ecosystems, but there is an increasing volume of evidence to indicate that emissions from road transport are responsible for the rise in asthma and other diseases of the lungs. The effect on health and the environment obviously affects the quality of human life, particularly as the result of photochemical smog (see pp. 190–2) and poor urban air quality. It is the combustion of petrol and diesel fuels which produces carbon dioxide, nitrogen oxides, benzene, ozone, PM10s, and volatile organic compounds, all of which affect human and animal health and have an impact on ecosystems and contribute to global warming. Vehicles are now the major cause of urban pollution, and are the fastest growing source of carbon dioxide worldwide; half of this is from cars.

The World Health Organization's air quality target for 'Health for All' by the year 2000 is that air quality standards should be improved in all countries, thus reducing the threat to health by pollution. Obviously this is a very vague directive, and each country is allowed to set its own standards, thus making its own interpretation of what constitutes 'good' air quality.

THE EFFECTS OF TRAFFIC POLLUTION ON HEALTH AND THE ENVIRONMENT

Immediate effects include mild soreness and irritation of the eyes and throat, and heart attacks (possibly fatal) in people with pre-existing cardio-vascular and lung disorders. More chronic or long-term effects include bronchitis, lingering chest infections, emphysema, asthma and the possibility of lung cancer. Animals suffer similar effects to humans, and crops and forests suffer from restricted growth and even destruction. Rubber, masonry and paintwork can also be damaged severely.

Transport is the major cause of air pollution in the UK. The concentration of air pollutants often exceeds WHO guidelines.

Transport is a significant source of greenhouse gases; 24 per cent of the UK's carbon dioxide output is from transport, and road transport accounts for 90 per cent of this figure.

The number of road vehicles increased by 5 million between 1981 and 1991, from 19 million to 24.5 million. The volume of traffic in the UK is predicted to double in the next 25 years.

The wider environmental impact due to the continued and increasing use of road traffic and road building schemes is substantial. It includes ecological damage caused during building construction on the actual site, damage caused during the mining and transport of aggregates, oil spillages and the dumping of used tyres. Used tyres are a particular problem: 25–30 million tyres are disposed of each year, 25 per cent are recycled, either as 'retreads' or burnt under controlled conditions for fuel, or for the recovery of hydrocarbons. The remainder are placed in landfills where they can cause fires, water pollution or subsidence. In addition, water which runs off from roads means that waste oil can end up in waterways and aquifers. And finally, road noise increases as more vehicles take to the roads, contributing to the impairment of both urban and rural quality of life.

Some facts and figures

- The EU forecast in April 1998 that carbon dioxide emissions from all forms of transport in the EU will increase by 39 per cent between 1990 and 2010.

- In the UK in 1985, 14.8 per cent of carbon dioxide came from road transport (23 million tonnes); by 1995 this had risen to 20 per cent (30 million tonnes). If emissions targets are to be achieved, people must either use vehicles less or make them more efficient; a 1993 OECD report claimed that it is already possible to improve fuel consumption by 25 per cent.

- The EU has negotiated a voluntary agreement with car manufacturers to achieve a 40 per cent efficiency in fuel use for cars sold in the EU.

- In the UK petrol tax has increased by 6 per cent a year since 1993 – if this continues to 2002, it will achieve a 4 per cent improvement in fuel economy.

- The European Commission proposes that by 2008 emissions from new passenger cars will average 120 grams of carbon dioxide per kilometre – this is equal to 100 km per 5 litres of petrol and 4/5 litres of diesel. The current level is 8 litres, so there will be a 40 per cent improvement in emissions.

- If it becomes cheaper to run a car this may encourage more use.

- PM10s are microscopic particles from factory emissions and vehicle exhaust fumes. They have a diameter of less than 10 micrometres – and are associated with lung disease.

- PM2.5s are believed to cause heart disease.

URBAN AIR POLLUTION

The nature and causes of urban air pollution have over time changed. The Clean Air Acts of 1956 and 1968 created smokeless zones that did away with the smogs with which London was so infamously associated. In 1952 the smog led to an extra 4000 deaths in two weeks. As a result of the legislation people were forbidden to burn ordinary coal with the result that sulphur and soot levels were dramatically reduced. However, as this form of pollution receded it was replaced by other pollutants, including nitrogen oxides, carbon monoxide and volatile organic compounds (VOCs) generated by vehicle engines. The new 'photochemical smogs' (see pp. 190–2) are as dangerous to the more vulnerable members of society and have replaced the pea-soupers of the past.

DIESEL OR PETROL?

Diesel vehicles have been promoted as being more fuel efficient than petrol vehicles, and as having more robust engines. They also emit far less hydrocarbons and carbon dioxide than petrol cars without catalytic converters. Diesel does not contain lead – and this is probably where it gets its reputation for being more environmentally-friendly.

On the negative side, diesel engines emit twice as much nitrogen oxides and six times more sulphur dioxides than petrol engines; 40 per cent of the UK's total nitrogen oxide emissions are from diesel engines. Research has recently been published which indicates that diesel vehicles are a major source of PM10s – the tiny particles of soot that we sometimes find ingrained in our clothing, and which get embedded in the lungs and are very difficult to expel. It is claimed that PM10s and smaller particulates are related to the premature death of 10,000 people in the UK every year. Diesel engines also emit polycyclic hydrocarbons, which are carcinogens, and they are noisier than petrol engines.

So we need to understand that it is necessary to balance the benefits of fuel economy against the disbenefits of any substantial contribution to pollution.

In July 1998 EU ministers agreed to reduce the level of sulphur in diesel from 500 to 350 parts per million (ppm) by 2000, and to 50 ppm by 2005. The high sulphur content in diesel prevents catalytic converters from working effectively.

Petrol

Petrol is sold in the UK as either leaded or unleaded (leaded petrol is being phased out as of January 2000). Lead tetraethyl is added to petrol to improve the performance of the engine, but it is expelled in the exhaust fumes. Eighty per cent of lead compounds in the air are from motor vehicle emissions. In cities as much as 50 per cent of the lead that we breathe comes from car fumes, whereas this figure is as low as 20 per cent for people living in rural areas. Researchers have found that high levels of lead in the atmosphere can be highly toxic, particularly to the brain and central nervous system of young children. There are some who claim that lead can affect the intellectual development of children, that it is the cause of low birth weight in babies, and that it accumulates in the liver.

The UK Government has deliberately reduced the tax on unleaded petrol in order to encourage sales. This has been a successful strategy, and as the sales of leaded petrol decrease the volume of lead in the atmosphere will also drop.

Carbon dioxide

Emissions of carbon dioxide from cars are predicted to rise from 80 million tonnes per annum in 1990 to 130 million tonnes per annum in 2030; and from goods vehicles and buses, from 110 million tonnes in 1990 to 210 million tonnes in 2030. This rise in emissions will substantially contribute to global warming unless manufacturers develop engines which are more efficient, or the volume of transport use is reduced. Indeed, the greatest significant contributor to the UK's carbon dioxide emissions will be from transport.

Nitrogen oxides

Road transport contributes 51 per cent of the UK's nitrogen oxide emissions. Although the use of catalytic converters will by 2010 reduce the UK total by 14 per cent of 1991 levels, if predictions based on current road traffic usage are correct, then the benefits of the catayltic converter will be outweighed by the increase in traffic.

What is photochemical pollution?

In summer the warm air at ground level normally rises, taking with it any pollution, until it cools at higher levels and returns to the earth. This causes air circulation, and the pollutants tend to be 'exported' to other areas. On occasions, however, the air does not cool as it reaches higher altitudes, rather it increases in temperature. This is called a *temperature inversion*. On such occasions the cooler air at the lower altitudes is unable to rise and is trapped together with its pollutants at ground level.

In winter the air at ground level sometimes cools faster in the late afternoon than the air at higher altitudes. This usually occurs when there is a weak sun which warms the air at higher levels. Consequently the air at ground level does not rise, and the pollutants are trapped. To make matters worse this event often coincides with the evening rush hour which further degrades the air quality. This is also called a temperature inversion.

In December 1991 levels of nitrogen dioxide in major cities in the UK reached record highs, and were the major contributory factor to the 'smog' of Christmas 1991. Summer smogs in other major conurbations, such as Los Angeles, St Petersburg, Athens, Rome, Tokyo and Mexico City, are composed of the same constituents and cause serious respiratory problems including asthma, the incidence of which is increasing rapidly in the developed world, and which can sometimes be fatal.

Photochemical smog is composed of several ingredients. They are:

1 Airborne particulates (also known as PM10s) These are mainly produced by diesel exhaust fumes. The reduction in their emission has not been as significant as that achieved with nitrogen oxides and VOCs as the result of the use of catalytic converters in petrol engines. Studies in the UK, USA and Europe indicate that the high levels of emission of these particulates contribute to increased levels of morbidity and mortality from complications of lung disease, and they also cause general irritation of the surfaces of the lungs and eyes. Other fine particles include traces of metals including iron.

2 Nitrogen oxides These include nitric oxide and nitrogen dioxide. They are both created during the combustion of petrol and they react with other hydrocarbons to form ozone (see below). These gases dissolve in water droplets in the air or in the lungs themselves to form diluted acids which are breathed in as nitric acid. This can cause intense irritation of the lungs and bronchial tubes and in some cases bronchitis. Since 1970 the volume of nitrogen oxides emitted from motor vehicles has doubled – perhaps as a result of efficiency gains in the emission of carbon monoxide and VOCs due to improvements in engine efficiency.

3 Volatile Organic Compounds (VOCs) This collection of chemicals, collectively known as VOCs, can be found in cleaning solvents, glue and petrol. Some VOCs are understood to be toxic, and even carcinogenic. For instance, benzene is known to damage the genetic structure of cells which can lead to cancer. There is no known 'safe' level of exposure to this chemical which comes about due to combustion of petrol and losses during its distribution (both leaded and unleaded petrol in the UK have similar levels of benzene). Catalytic converters can reduce emissions of benzene by up to 90 per cent.

Butadiene, also a by-product of the combustion of petrol, is similarly a suspected carcinogen and is even more dangerous than benzene. Again, its presence in the atmosphere is significantly reduced by the use of catalytic converters.

The VOCs react with other products of combustion to produce a range of secondary pollutants including ozone.

4 Ozone at ground level Curiously, whereas ozone is desirable in the stratosphere because it protects against harmful ultraviolet radiation, it is undesirable at ground level as it can damage the health of humans and animals, and also harm crops. Although ozone occurs at ground level naturally, its concentration can be increased by human activity, especially by

motor vehicles. It is formed as the result of a series of chemical reactions between nitrogen oxides and VOCs in the presence of sunlight. Maximum concentrations are usually recorded in the afternoons as time is also an important factor in the equation. Scientific evidence indicates that ground-level ozone concentrations have doubled over the past century in the UK. Current UK levels are 30 parts per billion (ppb); this is twice the pre-industrial level, and 37 per cent of the UK concentration is estimated to be created by motor vehicles as the result of emissions from exhausts and evaporating petrol. Hence it is at the peak of summer heatwaves that concentrations of ozone become exceptionally high. The World Health Organization guideline on ozone concentration is no more than 70–100 ppb per hour, or 50–60 ppb over eight hours.

Southern England, and especially the south-eastern counties, are particularly vulnerable to high concentrations of ozone at ground level due to the drift in light winds and high temperatures of the precursors across the Channel from the Continent. In 1990 parts of south-east England exceeded 100 ppb ozone for over 45 hours. In a photochemical smog light winds and strong sunlight can increase these levels of ozone to over 200 ppb. Although this is a rare phenomenon in the UK, in hotter climates, e.g., Mexico City and Japan, this situation can last for weeks at a time.

In 1991 the UK signed the VOC protocol whereby each signatory country agreed to reduce the emissions of VOCs to 1988 levels by 1999.

5 Carbon monoxide: 83 per cent of all carbon monoxide emissions in the UK are from motor vehicles. This is the equivalent of 4.5 million tonnes, and this will increase as the volume of traffic becomes greater. High concentrations of this gas in the atmosphere affect the ability of haemoglobin to carry oxygen to the cells due to the fact that haemoglobin has a greater affinity for carbon monoxide than for oxygen. This results in headaches, poor mental and physical performance and dizziness. Excessive exposure to this gas can be fatal.

'GREEN' VEHICLE TECHNOLOGY AND GOVERNMENT ACTION

The catalytic converter

The catalytic converter is installed in all new cars which run on unleaded petrol. It is designed to reduce emissions of nitrogen oxides, carbon monoxide, benzene and butadiene by 90 per cent. The converter turns these noxious gases into carbon dioxide, nitrogen and water. However, the increased benefits of their use will be outweighed by the projected increase in vehicle numbers by 2010, and it should be remembered that carbon dioxide is a greenhouse gas. A converter is only effective if a journey is longer than five miles. On short journeys the converter does not have time to warm up to the correct temperature to be effective; indeed, for a journey less than a mile, it has been estimated that a petrol-burning car with a catalytic converter will produce up to fourteen times more pollutants than a diesel-burning engine. Finally, there is also the problem of how to dispose of them safely once their useful life is over. Catalytic converters, therefore, can only be regarded as an interim solution to the problems of pollution caused by excessive volumes of traffic.

Unleaded petrol

In 1987, sales of unleaded petrol in the UK were very small, but the differences in the duties levied by the Government on leaded and unleaded petrol meant that unleaded sales increased in 1993 to 54 per cent of all petrol sales. Government projections are that unleaded petrol will account for 90 per cent of all sales by 2000, and almost all sales by 2012. As a result of this change in fuel choice, lead emissions from petrol engines in the UK fell from 8000 tonnes in 1975 to 2000 tonnes in 1992 and will continue to drop pro rata over time.

Overall the prognosis for air quality, both in rural and urban areas, is not good, as the quotation from the report by the Royal Commission on Environmental Pollution at the beginning of this chapter clearly states. If the Government is to achieve the targets set by the conventions to which it is signatory, then additional incentives are increasingly likely to be deployed to reduce the volume of traffic. This will mean fiscal penalties (additional and increased taxes) on petrol and diesel prices, road tax and even the outright banning of some vehicles or journeys in city centres. The wise manager or company should already be taking this into account when making decisions about the size of vehicle to purchase, its age, the type of fuel it runs on, the number of projected journeys, etc. In addition, those companies which deliver goods may well start to pass on the increased costs to the purchaser.

The Transport White Paper 1998

In July 1998 the Labour Government published its long-awaited Transport White Paper on plans for an integrated transport strategy; this included plans to allow local authorities to impose charges on private transport users which could then be redirected back into schemes to promote the use of public transport and cycling and for traffic calming schemes. This was a new departure in public policy as in the past such charges would have gone directly to the Treasury. Sadly no time has been allocated for a Transport Bill to implement this in the timetable for the Government's busy legislative programme.

Road building

Approximately 1.2–1.5 per cent of the UK's total land area consists of roads. And there are always new schemes to improve on the current provision or to bypass towns or other bottlenecks. New road schemes often damage sites of special scientific interest and areas of outstanding beauty. Between 1985 and 1990, 9000 km of new roads were built by the Department of Transport and local highway authorities; not only does increased road building result in damage to the environment and wildlife habitats, but it also indirectly leads to more land being used to provide the necessary aggregates. Aggregates are made up of 32 per cent sand and gravel from land sources, 7 per cent sand and gravel from marine dredging, 51 per cent crushed rock (sandstones, limestone, dolomite and igneous rocks), and 10 per cent is from secondary wastes including china clay sand, slate waste, colliery spoil, pulverized fuel ash and blast furnace slag. Approximately 30 per cent of all aggregates extracted are used for road construction (another 30 per cent are used for property development). It is anticipated that if current projections of road building (and property) continue, demand for aggregates will increase from approximately 240 million tonnes in 1993 to over 400 million tonnes by 2010. Friends of the Earth estimate that each mile of motorway uses 10.52 hectares of land; this includes the land taken for junctions and the number of junctions. Motorways alone in the UK take up 200 square kilometres.

Freight traffic

The hospitality industry is largely dependant on road transport for its goods, and also for its customers. The growth in total road freight in the UK over the past 40 years is shown in Table 11.1.

In 1981 freight transport mileage as a percentage of passenger transport was 23.42 per cent, and by 1991 this had decreased to 21.7 per cent. However, this apparent decrease can be accounted for by the large increase in permitted HGV size.

An increase in traffic carrying goods is associated with improved economic growth, and individual purchasing power, and hence a demand for

Table 11.1 The growth in road freight in the UK, 1950–90

Year	Road*	Rail*
1950	30	33
1960	50	30
1970	85	25
1980	92	20
1990	140	15

*in billion tonne kilometres
Source: Department of Transport figures.

improved and increased road networks. Over recent years the pattern has been for the increased use of very heavy vehicles where operators can carry huge loads cheaply, and the use of light vehicles in the service industries.

Fiscal incentives

It is Government policy that environmental costs will in future be included in the goods and services that we consume, although it has also expressed its intention to balance environmental costs against the need for industrial competitiveness. It is therefore likely that increased fiscal incentives to reduce the number of journeys by road will become increasingly tough.

The forward-looking manager will already be taking steps to ensure that there is sufficient storage capacity if deliveries are to become less frequent. Although this means that stock levels need to be kept at a higher level, and this means increased capital outlay and tying up more capital, considerable savings can be made as there will be less paperwork to process, and staff time will be saved as fewer deliveries mean less time spent checking-in and storing. An additional consideration is that it may well be possible to negotiate larger discounts for bulk purchases as fewer deliveries will save the supplier time as well. Obviously this will entail greater care when placing an order, but some companies have already very successfully implemented such schemes.

Any measures to increase prices will have to weigh the benefits, some of which may only be felt in the future, against the potential costs now.[2]

The previous Conservative Government committed itself to an annual increase of 5 per cent on fuel duties which will eventually increase the price to above the all-time high 1980 prices. This policy has been continued by the New Labour Government. The 1998 Transport White Paper has also considered the policy of road pricing, especially of motorways and in urban areas as a form of rationing.

The Royal Commission on Environmental Pollution

In October 1994 the Royal Commission on Environmental Pollution produced a report for the Government[3] which, *inter alia*, made 110 recommendations for the reduction of vehicle traffic in the UK. The main recommendations are

- To achieve WHO air quality standards by 2005
- To improve fuel efficiency of new cars by 40 per cent by 2005
- To double the price of petrol by 2005
- To reduce carbon dioxide emissions by 80 per cent of the 1990 levels by 2020
- To increase the proportion of rail freight from 6.5 per cent to 10 per cent by the end of the century and to 20 per cent by 2010
- To tax aircraft fuel
- To halve the £19 billion road building programme, and the money saved to be spent on public transport.

Industry Case Study

Transport issues present a major environmental dilemma. Forte developed a policy whereby in order to minimize wastage, and to keep stock holdings at their minimum, units were built with very small storage areas. This meant that they needed to take small but frequent deliveries of their produce. This involved a large number of journeys by lorry.

In common with other large national companies, Forte operates a system whereby a central distribution depot takes delivery of a range of goods from suppliers, in order to obtain the best price and also in order to ensure that quality is maintained. Individual units will then order directly from the central distribution unit. This means that longer journeys are made by lorry, and that at least two journeys are made for each item – the first from the supplier, and the second from the company's own distribution depot.

In considering the above case study, the question is, does this make for good environmental practice? In addition there are the costs to the environment of transport – air pollution, road building, traffic jams in city centres, the effects on human health, and so on.

The company fleet

If you need one, ensure that

1 Vehicles purchased/driven are the smallest equated with need.
2 The company operates a car pool so that employees can select a car from a well-maintained stock. This means that the company will require fewer vehicles.
3 Use unleaded petrol only. Consider whether you need a diesel engine or not.
4 Purchase/use vehicles with manual gear boxes – automatics consume more fuel.
5 Service the car regularly. A well-tuned engine uses far less fuel.
6 Keep the tyres pumped up to the correct pressure. This will reduce any resistance or 'drag'. Fit radial tyres which also reduce drag and can produce a fuel saving of as much as 10 per cent.
7 Drive steadily – a steady speed of 50 mph will provide a 30 per cent fuel saving over a speed of 70 mph!
8 Ensure that any chemicals or waste oils produced during servicing are safely disposed of.
9 Investigate the idea of using electric vehicles for short or inter-site runs as appropriate.
10 Ensure that coach or taxi drivers or drivers of delivery vehicles switch off their engines while waiting for customers outside the hotel or business.

Industry Case Study

Forte devised an incentive scheme for all employees entitled to a company car whereby they were able to 'trade down' to a cheaper, less energy-guzzling vehicle. The savings made were then invested in their pension.

An environmental conundrum

The catalytic converter is fitted to all new cars in Europe and North America to clean exhaust emissions. However, new research published by the US Environmental Protection Agency indicates that the amount of emissions of nitrous oxide from vehicles in the US rose by 49 per cent between 1990 and 1996 as the number of cars fitted with catalytic converters increased. Nitrous oxide is a by-product of the cleansing process; it has a global warming potential (gwp) 300 times greater than carbon dioxide (note that nitrogen based fertilizers also produce nitrous oxide). The converters also reduce the efficiency of motor vehicle engines, causing increased fuel consumption and thus increased carbon dioxide emissions. However, they do reduce chemicals which make ozone at low levels – ozone is a greenhouse gas at low levels, is a danger to human health and reduces crop yields. Note that ozone can stay in the atmosphere for several days, compared with 120 years for nitrous oxide.

If a hospitality business runs its own transport, for instance if it is involved in deliveries or outside functions, or even if the management run a company vehicle, action can be taken to make energy and cost savings. If possible vehicles should be fitted with a catalytic converter and be able to run on unleaded petrol. Only essential journeys should be made in the vehicle, and it should preferably be fully laden and the trip should be made at times when traffic congestion is likely to be at a minimum. This should minimize the contribution to pollution the vehicle makes, and at the same time efficiently save on both time and fuel.

CONCLUSION

This chapter has examined the issues of commercial transport and the environment. It has shown how significant volumes of pollutants are generated by traffic, and also how the use of vehicles has increased over the past fifty years. It has considered the impact of pollutants caused by traffic on public health and on the environment, and finally, it has suggested ways in which a business can minimize this damage. The message that comes across is that the greatest benefit to the business is a saving in costs.

The next chapter will examine the range of business tools that can be employed to implement and improve upon environmental performance.

QUESTIONS AND ISSUES FOR DISCUSSION

1 Carry out an audit of transport use at a catering establishment of your choice. The audit should include a survey of private and company vehicle use, together with the pattern of deliveries using vehicles to and from the premises. Write a report which describes the vehicle, type of fuel it runs on,

engine power, age of vehicle and journey pattern. Work out its contribution to global warming. Make recommendations for change and give reasons for these. What are the likely financial implications of your recommendations? Illustrate your report with charts and/or graphs as appropriate.

2 Find a newspaper article which says that traffic pollution is not a problem. Give a critical analysis of its argument.

3 Industrial economies are dependent on the rapid transport of goods and services. Is it reasonable for environmentalists to call for a ban on traffic growth, or even for its severe restriction? What would the likely effects be for economic growth should the Green Party win the next General Election?

4 You are the general manager of a national company which provides a grocery delivery service to caterers. The Board of Directors is concerned that over the next decade there will be increasing financial pressures on transport to such an extent that the current policy of deliveries on demand to customers will increasingly make the business non-viable. You have been asked to write a report for the next meeting in which you make recommendations for change. Write a report using the following headings as guidelines:

Current activities
Size and type of fleet of delivery vehicles
Implications of change to monthly delivery pattern
Strategies to assist customers to accept change
Financial benefits to the company (this needs to be in general terms rather than specific figures).

As an example use a case study of deliveries to a small restaurant in a town 30 miles away, and look at their stock list and delivery records.

Notes

1 *Report of the Royal Commission on Environmental Pollution*, London: HMSO, November 1994.
2 Department of the Environment, *Sustainable Development – the UK Strategy*, London: HMSO, 1994.
3 *Report of the Royal Commission on Environmental Pollution*, London: HMSO, November 1994.

Part 3

The business environment

CHAPTER 12

Environmental business tools

We offer assistance and encouragement to other restaurants as well as private citizens who wish to review their policies in the face of environmental issues. We suggest options for the use of polystyrene products, give advice and recommendations on establishing recycling programmes and share information that we have collected from such institutions as the United Nations, Earth Island Institute and many more.

Hard Rock Café company statement

OBJECTIVES

1 To identify a range of strategies which can be employed by the hospitality industry to respond to environmental targets.
2 To be able to devise a plan whereby continuous monitoring can be implemented in order to achieve success.
3 To devise an environmental policy for a hospitality operation.

INTRODUCTION: THE IMPORTANCE OF AN OVERALL BUSINESS STRATEGY

In Part 2 we examined the wide range of responses made by many hospitality operations to the increasing public concern over the environment. These companies have in many ways been pioneers; they have tested the market, discovered what is feasible, responded sensitively to customer feedback, and to the opinions of their staff, and they have developed strategies whereby the business can improve its profitability, but at the same time improve its record on environmental issues. This chapter will look at the systems that a company can adopt so as to be able to incorporate environmental policies. If attention to environmental issues is kept separate from the main trading exigencies, then the policy will not be successful. The need for a business to act in an environmentally-responsible manner should be as important as the need to ensure that the company itself remains viable.

Core 'tools' used to manage and to monitor environmental performance:

- The initial environmental review
- The environmental policy statement
- The environmental audit
- The environmental report

Additional 'tools' used by companies or legislators to encourage good environmental performance:

- Environmental taxes
- Environmental labelling
- Information management
- Insurance requirements
- Pressure from:
   investors
   shareholders
   leaseholders
- Health and safety information
- Site management procedures
- Awards and/or grants
- British Standards Awards
- Environmental management awards

From the above list we can see that there are a range of tools that can be used to develop a strong environmental track record; some are voluntary, such as undertaking an environmental audit, introducing an environmental labelling scheme, using information technology to monitor performance, and establishing good site management procedures.

There are, of course, other 'tools' whereby a company has little or no choice but to conform. These include legislative requirements, including health and safety laws, taxation, the requirements of insurance companies and of shareholders; in addition there is consumer pressure and the demands of the market. The undertaking of environmental audits and the publishing of environmental reports is of such vital importance that a separate chapter is devoted to each (see Chapters 13 and 14); this chapter will consider some of the other options listed above.

The emphasis on incorporating environmental practice into good business practice is the challenge we must meet as we enter the new millennium. The business that successfully achieves this will anticipate legal requirements as they become increasingly demanding, will automatically select the most   up-to-date and appropriate technologies, and will undertake regular environmental reviews as a normal part of monitoring business performance, and will act upon the results of these reviews. It will also regularly evaluate the impact of the products and services that it provides using a life-cycle assessment.

In their book *Environmental Business Management*, Hutchinson and Hutchinson (1997) list the ten stages that a company must go through to improve its environmental performance:

1 Secure the commitment of senior management.
2 Undertake an initial environmental review.
3 Develop objectives and policy aims and an action plan.
4 Develop an environmental management system.
5 Implement the system.
6 Undertake an environmental audit/eco audit.
7 Gain independent verification and standard accreditation.
8 Market and communicate the changes.
9 Continuously review procedures and progress and assess the target attainments set.
10 Consider new innovations in strategy and operations.

This list differs from the one on p. 204 in that it does not discuss the importance of establishing an environmental policy first of all. As we have seen throughout this book, there is no right or wrong way to implement an environmental policy, and there are different, equally valid, opinions.

THE ENVIRONMENTAL REVIEW

It is generally recognized that the first stage in the implementation of a company environmental policy is to carry out an initial environmental review in order to determine the company's current impact on the environment. This can be either a relatively brief investigation of the company's current activities in the areas of waste, energy use, water use and perhaps purchasing, or an in-depth investigation which can take the form of the first part of an environmental audit (for more details, see Chapter 13). The results of this investigation will then act as a framework for any discussions. What are the issues involved? Does the company wish to improve its environmental performance? What advantages are there in devoting time and perhaps resources to this issue? Are there potential savings to be made? What are the legal requirements? Will these be the minimum standards, or the maximum? What steps are your competitors taking? Do you want to be a leader in your field?

Having considered these issues, the next step is to decide on specific policies, and to translate these into targets and tasks and to communicate these both to your staff (at all levels in the organization) and to a wider audience – after all, this could be good PR!

THE ENVIRONMENTAL POLICY STATEMENT

The next stage is to decide on the company's environmental policy and to communicate this in the form of a statement. There is no standard format for this, and there are no limits as to what can or cannot be included. The environmental policies of most companies tend to outline general principles which the company aims to embody in all its activities. However, as these statements are designed to be in the public domain, it should be remembered that over-optimistic or unrealistic principles can leave an organization open to criticism. An astute company will therefore use such caveats 'normally', or 'wherever possible' or similar phrases – certainly in any early drafts – until a definite policy has been established throughout the company.

Note that it is important to regularly review and redraft the environmental policy statement to ensure that it complies with the company's thinking and with its activities. Each new version should reflect the maturing of the company's environmental activities and attitudes.

Examples of environmental policy statements from a number of companies are included in this chapter to serve as an illustration of the variety of ways in which the issue is interpreted. For instance, Ecover, the manufacturer of environmentally-friendly detergents, publishes an environmental policy statement that details the extent to which it implements environmental and ethical standards into its operations; it states that it complies with legislation, and that it carries out regular environmental reviews of its activities, and that it will improve on its environmental activities as a result of these reviews.

In contrast, the environmental commitment statement of Inter-Continental Hotels and Resorts incorporates six general principles which include the interests of the customer and the local community; it acknowledges the differing environmental issues within the world, and emphasizes the importance of education and training.

Table 12.1 considers the issues that are addressed in the environmental policy statements of two companies – Ecover and Inter-Continental Hotels – and it can be seen that although they are very differently worded, they share common themes.

Table 12.1 A comparison of the environmental performance of Ecover and Inter-Continental Hotels

Issues addressed in environmental policy statement	Ecover	Inter-Continental
Supplier compliance	yes	yes
Customers	yes	yes
Energy conservation		yes
Local community	yes	yes
Staff	yes	yes
Waste management	yes	yes
Materials	yes	yes
Training	yes	yes
Fair trade	yes	
Legal compliance	yes	
Environmental reporting	yes	yes
Pollution control	yes	
Environmental audits	yes	
Regular reviews	yes	

The following section lists the environmental policy statements of a number of companies.

Inter-Continental Hotels and Resorts' Environmental Commitment (source: *Inter-Continental Hotels and Resorts Environmental Review*, 1986)

Inter-Continental Hotels and Resorts strives:

- To conserve natural resources and energy within its hotels without sacrificing safety standards or jeopardising guest satisfaction
- To select only products and materials from environmentally responsible sources, whose use – wherever possible – has positive, beneficial effects
- To minimise and efficiently manage waste production, ensuring the least possible negative impact on the environment
- To acknowledge regional differences in environmental needs and practices by establishing adaptable local programmes, designed to improve the performance of each individual hotel
- To identify ways to participate in local community action on the environment worldwide
- To develop awareness of environmental issues internally and externally through a variety of education and training initiatives.

It is of interest to note the very general and idealistic wording of the Scandic environmental policy statement.

Scandic's Environmental Policy (source: *Scandic Annual Report*, 1997)

No company can avoid taking environmental responsibility and focusing on environmental aspects in all parts of its operations. Scandic will take the lead and constantly improve its contribution to reducing or eliminating environmental damage. Scandic's objective is to become one of the most environment-friendly companies in the hotel industry and to operate in accordance with the conditions of Nature.

Another way of looking at an environmental policy statement is to consider it as an alternative company mission statement, or as the company's *environmental* mission statement.

Bass Policy Statement (source: *Bass Annual Reports*, 1998)

Bass will ensure that Group companies:

- undertake a thorough risk and hazard analysis
- are sensitive to environmental issues and consider their potential impact in all new projects and development
- implement their company environmental policies
- have management accountability and responsibility for environmental matters
- develop management programmes and set quantified targets where appropriate
- monitor and report on performance on a a regular basis
- communicate with those affected by their actions; and train and involve employees at appropriate levels and functions within the organisation.

Forte Hotels' Environmental Policy (source: *Environmental Status Report*, January 1998)

Forte Hotels recognises and accepts its responsibility to respect the environment.

We believe that everyone has a duty to care for the environment and to seek ways to conserve natural resources. Our aim is to be conscious of all environmental issues.

In pursuit of our business goals, we seek to minimise the wastage of raw materials and energy and to minimise harmful emissions resulting from our activities.

We will comply with all laws and regulations concerning the environment and will actively co-operate with the authorities on environmental protection matters. Where regulations do not exist or where we feel that they are inadequate, we will set our own standards of environmental performance.

We will inform all our suppliers and contractors of our environmental policies and will monitor their performance to ensure that the goods and services they provide meet our environmental objectives.

Granada Group PLC Corporate Environmental Policy
(source: *Corporate Environmental Policy and Environmental Management Framework*, Granada Group, 1997)

Granada Group PLC recognises the need to balance business plans and operations with the allocation of adequate resources to prevent pollution and provide sustainable developments in the future. In this respect the Company is committed to the integration of environmental management issues into all parts of its business and will strive to improve environmental performance for the benefit of customers and other stakeholders. The Company will:

- comply with all statutory and mandatory requirements and will strive wherever practicable to achieve standards of performance which are better than the legal minimum
- seek to minimise the impact of its operations on the environment
- seek to conserve energy and water and minimise the wastage of consumables in a manner which is compatible with the needs of its customers
- monitor and impose standards on suppliers, contractors and advisers to encourage them to provide services and products to its businesses in a manner which satisfies its environmental standards
- minimise the risk of environmental accidents by preparing emergency plans and procedures
- communicate its policy to employees and, where appropriate to the public
- train employees in order to meet the obligations of this policy
- encourage the development, evaluation and implementation of cost effective environmental initiatives where there are environmental benefits to be achieved

The Company will achieve such standards by delegating to the Managing Director of each division full responsibility for preparing, implementing and reporting progress on the adopted environmental management systems.

It is important to note the varying sizes and scope of the policy statements shown here, and to remember that there is no right or wrong way in which to compose one.

Finally, it is important to ensure that the company's environmental policy statement is written clearly and is widely disseminated, so that staff, customers, suppliers and other stakeholders are aware of the principles which govern the company's actions.

THE SETTING OF PERFORMANCE TARGETS

The next step after publishing an environmental policy statement is to establish a series of performance targets so that progress can be monitored. If they are to have any real meaning, these performance targets should be specific and able to be measured.

It is important to establish a *standard* for the targets and also a *date* by which these standards must be achieved. It is important that a monitoring system is implemented to check progress.

The targets must be realistic, but if the company's policy is to have any credibility there is no point in making them too easy. The most appropriate option is to set a variety of targets which can be met in the short, medium and long term. In this way, those targets which are easy to implement can be quickly achieved and monitoring will show immediate progress, while targets set for medium- or long-term achievement can be started at the same time, and their effects will 'kick in' at a later stage. Such a system will suggest that progress is continuous and cumulative.

Examples of short-term targets
- Replace standard light bulbs with low-energy bulbs. This involves an initial outlay but repayment in terms of reduced energy costs will take immediate effect.
- Reduce the central heating thermostat by 1 °C – this will immediately provide an 8 per cent saving in heating costs without affecting customer comfort.
- Ask customers to place their towels in the bath only if they want clean ones, otherwise they should reuse their towels; this should immediately save on laundry costs.

Examples of medium-term targets
- In co-operation with the Food and Beverage department, work towards replacing any portion control packs with normal-sized supplies of milk, cream and preserves. This will save on waste and packaging.
- Replace old kitchen equipment, including cooking equipment, refrigerators and freezers, with more energy-efficient models.

- A review of the menu should be incorporated with the above point so that the purchase of energy-draining appliances for a limited menu range or a dish with limited appeal can be avoided. A menu should not be devised on the basis solely of equipment, but if the environmental costs of preparation of a dish are taken into account, or even the energy costs, then it is possible that a very new style of menu could appear!

Examples of long-term targets

- Consider the purchase of a number of waste compactors, for example for packaging waste, and even for the crushing of glass. The initial purchase costs will take some time to be recovered from the savings made from waste collection, so it is important to work out a realistic timescale, perhaps as much as five years.
- A large user of energy might consider the installation of a combined heat and power system, which again may have a payback period of up to five years.
- If considering building a new extension or even a new property, then choose an environmentally-friendly style of construction. There are a number of architectural firms who specialize in this style of construction. Judicious design and construction will more than pay for itself in energy savings, reduced maintenance costs and excellent PR.

STAFF TRAINING AND ENCOURAGEMENT

With all successful companies the degree of time and money invested in staff training will pay for itself many times over. You don't have to be told that well-trained staff are content and confident staff, have good relationships with customers and with each other, use their initiative, and remain with a company. This is good for business.

If your environmental policy is to be successful, then it is vital that staff are trained in how to work in a more environmentally-friendly manner. They must not only know the 'rules', but they need to understand why they are being asked to do something, and hopefully to accept that this is a better way. One successful technique is to get staff as part of a training programme to implement some of the more simple energy-saving processes in their own homes. They will soon see a saving in their fuel bills, and water savings for those on a water meter.

Ensure that environmental awareness is part of every induction programme, that it is part of regular training sessions, that staff effort is reinforced by positive feedback, and that environmental awareness is as much a part of the company culture as, say, is customer service.

Finally, appoint one member in each section to be responsible for environmental activities, so that they can play their part in planning and monitoring work in this area. One of the best known examples is John Forte, who was responsible for all environmental policy in the Forte group, and who implemented a range of excellent policies which not only saved the company large sums of money but also substantially reduced the impact of its activities on the environment.

FEEDBACK

The previous section mentioned the importance of feedback to staff. Feedback to the wider community can be achieved through the publication of environmental reports, which we discuss in Chapter 14, but further discussion of the success of staff feedback is necessary here.

The companies which have been particularly successful in encouraging staff to implement environmental actions in the workplace are those which have involved staff from the very beginning. Although there must be 'top-down' commitment for success, such a policy must not be regarded as yet another imposition. Regular information on the savings made, and feedback on what is done with those savings, is important. For instance some companies ask staff to nominate a charity to which a certain percentage of the savings are to be donated, or some of the money is used for a staff party.

> ### Industry Case Study
>
> Ramada Hotels have established environmental committees which are run by the staff. The company gives an annual Chairman's Award for each region, hotel and employee with the most outstanding environmental performance. This includes cash incentives.

Feedback from staff is also useful; not only do the staff feel that they are being consulted, and that their opinions and experience are of value, but they are invariably the individuals best placed to observe the impact of new policies, or to suggest a new environmental measure, and also to provide feedback on customer reactions. Some companies award an annual prize to the member of staff who makes the best suggestion for changing a policy or way of working which improves the quality of working life or productivity of the business.

THE COMPANY MANAGEMENT STRUCTURE

If the senior management of a company is not totally committed to an environmental policy then the strategy is not likely to be very successful. It is therefore essential that there is a senior member of staff present on the decision-making team who has responsibility for environmental issues. All members of staff who have environmental responsibilities should report to this senior person. S/he must have as much influence on the company board or management team as the Chancellor of the Exchequer does in the Cabinet. To take this analogy further, in the same way as the financial implications of every Cabinet policy decision are taken into account by the Treasury, the environmental implications of every company action should be carefully weighed.

A cautionary tale

Royal Dutch Shell became embroiled with environmental lobby groups over a number of decisions that the company made in 1995. Its decision to dump a defunct oil-rig, the Brent Spar, in the North Sea, together with its activities in Nigeria in an environmentally-sensitive area (opposition to which led to the execution of the political activist Ken Saro Wiwa by the Nigerian military government) resulted in a worldwide boycott of its service stations. Since the international outcry, Shell has published an environmental report (in 1998) and has placed ethical issues in the forefront of its policy-making. But it was an expensive lesson.

Bass is a good example of what can be achieved. It has established a company-wide environmental working group; this is made up of a Board Member or senior manager from each division and legal, communications and risk management specialists. It is chaired by a member of the Executive Committee of the Bass Board. In turn, all divisions have established working groups to share best practice methods.

PUBLIC RELATIONS

The example of Shell indicates the importance of good public relations. If a company makes environmental claims for its activities then these must be seen to be made in good faith. The public is prepared to forgive a genuine mistake, but is not prepared to accept cynical 'jumping on the bandwagon' of the environmental movement. During the 1980s and at the beginning of the 1990s so many companies were making 'Green claims' for their products that the public rapidly became disillusioned. Friends of the Earth even invented the 'Green Con' award.

Notwithstanding the above, it is essential that the improved environmental impact of the company or of its products are promoted both to the customer and to the press.

A good way to promote environmental performance, and to attract staff committed to this ethos, is to mention the company's record in this area in recruitment adverts. Yet another 'free' method of promoting activity is in any form of advertising: on the menu, displaying any awards in prominent positions, printing on stationery, paper napkins, labels, and even on company vehicles.

Astute targeting of the company's environmental track record at the 'Green consumer' is sure to pay dividends.

COMMUNITY INVOLVEMENT

Some companies become involved in schemes to improve the local community as a way of showing an environmental commitment. They either donate money, or they lend staff to a given project, or they encourage their staff to become involved in their spare time. Companies which have done this include Marks & Spencer, Forte and Bass.

Bass has committed itself to donating £100,000 per year for three years to fund projects in the Millennium Greens scheme, run by the Countryside Commission. The Greens are to be 'peaceful havens in rural and urban areas, designed to be breathing spaces for the local community'.[1] The company plans to support 80 Millennium Greens during the sponsorship period, and each Green will be run by a local trust to be a permanent reminder of the millennium celebrations for the local community.

INSURANCE REQUIREMENTS

It is important to ensure that the company is adequately insured for any environmental infringements. The leakage of sewerage, the build-up of fat in sewers which causes mains blockages, the inappropriate disposal of waste materials, are all matters which are likely to be costly.

The greenhouse effect appears to be causing extreme global weather conditions; floods, hurricanes, gale-force winds and droughts are occuring more regularly than in former years in the UK. This is not helped by planning permission being granted for building in areas which have been liable to flood in the past, and the fact that adequate flood defences are not constructed by the developers.

Properties need to be well maintained to resist the effects of extreme weather conditions, and the importance of adequately insuring for the full cost of rebuilding and refurbishing cannot be stressed enough.

MONITORING PROGRESS

Continuous and rigorous monitoring and the reviewing of progress and setting of new targets is germane to the success of the implementation of an environmental policy. This issue will be discussed further in Chapter 13 on the environmental audit. However, it is worth considering here the frequency of such reviews. Should they take place on a monthly, quarterly or annual basis? And who should undertake the reviews – internal company employees, or external and independent 'auditors'?

The process of monitoring and reviewing progress should in turn lead to the production of a report publicizing the findings of the audit, and comparing these with the set targets. Annual publication of progress will eventually build up a record of the company's environmental achievements.

Industry Case Study

The manager of the Inter-Continental Hotel, New Orleans, believes that the implementation of environmental initiatives works due to a number of reasons. These are:

1 There is commitment from the very top.
2 There is an environmental operations manual for reference.
3 There is an environmental committee which is composed of employees from all departments who meet regularly to discuss problems and successes.
4 Both the purchasing director and the chief engineer are committed to the initiative. This is considered critical to the success of the programme.

▶

5 An environmental purchases specification sheet has been drawn up which guides decision-making. In one year the company saved US$28,000 by buying recycled products, which in many cases can be cheaper.
6 Suppliers have been chosen specifically because participation in the scheme guarantees business.
7 There is a constant review of products used and purchased. For example, Image packs, toiletries, and containers are all environmentally-friendly. This policy is made clear to the customers, and it makes a statement about the company.
8 The hotel group disseminates positive national and international publicity.
9 There is a recycling centre in the hotel which is equipped with compactors, glass crushers and a baler. This saves US$500 each month through recovering cutlery, and since the scheme has been operating has saved $10,000 from recovered operating equipment, and $50,000 from reduced transport costs. In addition, it has generated $3,000 in sales of recyclables.

MEMBERSHIP OF TRADE/INDUSTRY ORGANIZATIONS

Joining an organization that has common objectives and which can offer support and advice is often a way for companies to achieve objectives. Although there are a range of organizations to which a hospitality company can become affiliated, there is one organization which is concerned specifically with the environment: this is the International Hotels Environment Initiative (IHEI).

The International Hotels Environment Initiative

Steered by the Prince of Wales Business Leaders Forum[2] the International Hotels Environment Initiative (IHEI) was launched in May 1993. The aim of the initiative is to promote environmental awareness within the hospitality industry and was the outcome of co-operation between a number of major international hotel chains, including the Inter-Continental, Ramada, Forte, Accor, Hilton International, Holiday Inn Worldwide and Marriott. An environmental charter was drawn up and hospitality companies were invited to sign. In August 1994 the membership of the IHEI comprised ten hotel groups which represented 6574 hotels and approximately 1.2 million bedrooms.

A working group staffed by a representative from each company meets regularly to co-ordinate the campaign. On an international basis regional co-operation and action programmes are planned for different parts of the world; for instance the Asia-Pacific region has formed its own association which co-ordinates activities within its own region. In addition, the IHEI works closely with the World Travel and Tourism Council and its environmental research centre.

It remains to be seen whether this ambitious initiative can be implemented at the level of the individual hotel or by small chains of hotels, and whether eventually those companies in the Third World and the former Eastern bloc become involved, especially as there is little environmental infrastructure in place in these countries (for example regulated waste disposal, recycling, environmentally-friendly facilities, etc.).

The origins of the IHEI

In the late 1980s the Chief Executive of the Inter-Continental Hotel group, John Van Praag, commissioned research into how its 101 hotels could meet the environmental challenge. The result was a policy manual which covered:

energy efficiency
recycling and reuse
purchasing policy to influence activities of suppliers
water conservation
cleaning materials, and
chemicals used in grounds.

This manual was converted into 'The Industry's Guide for Best Practice'.

INDEPENDENT VERIFICATION

Another initiative that a company can take to improve its environmental performance is to seek independent verification. There are a number of organizations and schemes which have been established to set standards in this area and to make awards to those who fulfil the criteria. It should be noted that membership of these various schemes is voluntary and that failure to belong does not mean that a company does not have a good environmental track record. It is the issue of independent verification of 'Green claims' that is important.

Voluntary schemes include Eco-labelling, Eco-management and Audit, and BS 7750.

BS 7750

The Environmental Management Standard is awarded by the British Standards Institute (BSI). It was launched in 1994 after a preliminary pilot period beginning in 1992 to discover any inherent shortcomings; 140 companies from 25 different industrial sectors in the UK tested out the Standard for twelve months, although no hospitality companies were included in this list.

The Standard is designed to run in parallel with the Standard for Total Quality Management, BS 5750 (ISO 9000), and is designed so that its provisions can be applied to every type of business and every industry sector.

Entry to the scheme is voluntary and accreditation is achieved through fulfilling targets which the company itself establishes. This is a major weakness as no independent standards of environmental performance or targets are set, no dates by which changes should be implemented are established, and there is no requirement for the general public to have open access to the information which a company makes about its environmental claims. Critics argue therefore that this scheme allows a company to set, and thus maintain, low environmental standards.

There is concern that there will be a wide variation in the rigour with which companies pursue their environmental objectives, and it has been argued that it is possible for the less ethical company to achieve and display the Standard without much effort and to use it as a cynical marketing tool.

BS 7750 is modelled on a positive feedback loop, so that as the result of continuous monitoring of performance improved standards are set to be achieved by the next review period.

Companies which successfully achieve the BS 7750 award are allowed to display the Standard on their letterheads in the same way as many companies currently display BS 5750 to indicate that they have implemented systems to ensure Total Quality Management (TQM). In order to gain the award the environmental performance of the company is rigorously reviewed by a number of external verifiers to ensure that the standard is consistent between and within different industry sectors.

When applying for the BS 7750 a company can choose to either

- consider the environmental impact of its site, or
- consider the environmental impact of the goods it sells, or
- consider the way in which its business operates, or
- all of these or a combination of some.

The standard is based on a number of basic criteria:

1 The company must devise an environmental policy which is open to public scrutiny. The statement can be as long or as short as a company wishes.
2 A fully documented environmental management system must itemize those processes and products that it is monitoring, and include data on emissions, smells, waste, noise and energy use.
3. The company must draw up a schedule of the effects of its activities upon the environment, and indicate all the potential hazards that may result from accidents or emergencies created by its operations.

   Using this schedule, a company will then set its own targets, such as the reduction of waste or energy use by a given percentage each year, or by a certain date; there is no requirement to publicly disclose these targets – the reason given for this is that this might reveal sensitive trading information to competitors.
4 The company must summarize its past environmental record.
5 The company must also record the environmental activities of other companies with which it deals.
6 The company must carry out a regular programme of internal environmental audits which will build on each other, in the expectation that there will be a rolling programme of improvements in its environmental activities.

The BSI instigates a series of regular checks to see that the company is complying with the standards and targets that it has set itself.

Supporters of the scheme maintain that this 'cradle to grave' approach, which covers all aspects of the company's current, past and future behaviour, is its major strength.

The BSI claims that any company which achieves the BS 7750 Standard, or any company working towards it, will derive a wide range of benefits including savings in costs: in energy use, in insurance premiums against damage as risks are reduced, and in waste disposal costs. In addition, the company's reputation with its customers, shareholders and suppliers will be enhanced, and equally important, any company involved in the BS 7750 scheme will have little difficulty in complying with a host of environmental legislation which is expected to be imposed as the UK attempts to meet its international commitments.

This is a good scheme in principle but it raises a number of questions: to what lengths is a company expected to go in order to implement the Standard? For instance, should it insist that all its suppliers or the companies which it supplies possess the Standard? Should the transport company which delivers the company's groceries also possess the Standard? Would it be adequate merely to inform the suppliers about the BS 7750 criteria? These are issues about which individual companies and directors will make different decisions.

Many companies have to date had a very poor environmental record and so the BSI was really compelled to permit the secrecy clause if it was to persuade companies to work towards change. In the future it is almost certain that the worst polluters, once they have cleaned up their operations, will be more than happy to indicate to the public just how great their change of heart has been. But in the interim, as many industries and companies work through the process of change, it is important that some sensitive information remains confidential. Some environmentalists have argued that this is the wrong approach, and that it is important to shame companies into more rapid and responsible action. Fortunately the hospitality industry is by no means a major environmental polluter.

In contrast to the BSI, in the USA all companies are legally required to file a 'toxic releases inventory'. Ironically, this provides extensive information which is available under the Freedom of Information Act on the activities of US companies operating in the UK; some pressure groups are campaigning for similar legislation to be introduced in the UK.

BS 7750 meets most of the requirements for registration in the European

Industry Case Study

ARA Food Services has worked to get BSI 7750 accreditation for six ARA sites in the UK. The company has for some years worked to its US 'Earthsense' standard: 'reduce, reuse and recycle'. In the USA freshmen are given an Earthsense mug at the start of their university career in the hope that they will use this in preference to disposables.[3]

ARA uses 38 million vending cups each year. In the Netherlands it is a legal requirement that all new vending machines are designed so that they are capable of using a china cup.

EMAS Scheme.

EMAS: Europe-wide Eco-Management and Audit Scheme

This voluntary scheme was introduced in 1995. It is administered by the various member states of the European Union. It requires companies to develop schemes and policies on a site-specific basis; this means that large or multinational multi-site companies need not improve the environmental performance of all sites. Another weakness is that there is no requirement to comply with industry best practice, or with environmental legislation; a company merely needs to indicate that it is implementing environmental improvements.

The strengths of this scheme are that validation of the company's claims is independent, and that the company is required to publish quantifiable targets to achieve, and that the company must permit public access to any documentation that establishes the targets, and that the results of the independent audit are made public.

ISO 14000 series

Another system of environmental validation is offered by the International Standards Organization, based in Geneva. This is the ISO 14000 series:

- ISO 14001 – Environmental Management Systems – specification with guidance for use.
- ISO 14004 – general guidelines on principles, systems and supporting techniques.
- ISO 14040 – life cycle assessment, general principles and practice.

The 14000 series is designed to replace BS 7750, but to comply with the EMAS scheme. There are concerns that this scheme has been developed by industry for industry and that it could lead to a reduction in standards as a company has only to comply with local regulations. The argument is that if a company is located in a country with poor environmental legislation, the ISO standard could be awarded to that company whereas it would not gain the standard in another country with more demanding criteria. It is feared that companies will choose this standard in preference to the EMAS system, as there is no requirement for independent verification.

Finally, the ISO 14000 series addresses few of the Agenda 21 issues which were endorsed at the Rio Summit in 1992.

Biffa Waste Services is working towards obtaining ISO 14001 certification for its subsidiary Island Waste Services Ltd by 2000. It already has six other operational sites certificated to this level.

Redhill landfill site has the EMAS registration, the only working landfill site in Europe to achieve this.

The Small Company Environmental and Energy Management Assistance Scheme (SCEEMAS) is a UK-based scheme. Small and medium enterprises (SMEs) have been slow to become involved in environmental issues as they are wrongly perceived as needing huge capital investment. This scheme was launched in 1995 and is targeted at firms with up to 250 employees. The Department of the Environment offers grants for the following activities:

- To undertake an environmental review, create an environmental policy and to develop a programme of environmental improvement – 40 per cent of the total cost to the company.
- To establish an environmental management system – a 40 per cent grant. This will cover the costs of hiring consultants.
- The publication of an environmental report, the contents of which must be open to public inspection – a 50 per cent grant. In this case the standards are required to be consistent with the EMAS scheme.

This scheme was initially restricted to companies in the manufacturing, power generation, recycling and waste disposal sectors.

CONCLUSION

This chapter has examined the vast range of tools which a business can use to monitor its environmental performance and to set targets for improvement. Some tools, such as taxes, are compulsory, but the majority are voluntary. A number of environmental policy statements have been printed in full for examination; here we can see that there is no one way to produce such a document. The issue of performance targets has been examined, and the importance of independent verification of environmental claims has been stressed. In the next chapter a major environmental business tool, the environmental audit, will be examined in depth.

QUESTIONS AND ISSUES FOR DISCUSSION

1 Draft an environmental policy statement for a hospitality operation with which you are familiar.

2 Devise a strategic plan which can be used by a hospitality business in order to monitor its environmental performance. Identify the size of the business and the nature of its operations so that you can be as precise as possible.

3 Set some environmental performance targets for a hospitality business of your choice. These may be in the short, medium or long term, or all three. Supply costings with your rationale for these targets, and also costs and benefits to the environment.

4 You have been appointed to a new position as the officer with responsibility for environmental issues of a leading hospitality trade association. Your brief is to establish a new environmental industry standard for the hospitality industry, which is intended to be a valuable and respected award. Set out in detail the criteria that you would establish and write a rationale for your decisions.

5 BS 7750 is a new standard designed to indicate a company's environmental performance. Using the criteria briefly mentioned in this chapter, and basing your answer on a catering company of your choice, describe how you would proceed in order to achieve this standard if you were the proprietor of that business. What does its possession by a company signify? Alternatively find out more details about the BS 7750 criteria and apply these to the same question.

6 What are the objections that some people have to BS 7750? What is your opinion of self-regulation?

7 What are the business advantages of possessing BS 7750?

Notes

1 Bass Environmental Report, 1998.
2 Prince of Wales Business Leaders Forum. An international network of Chief Executive Officers which promotes corporate citizenship, business involvement in the community and the practice of sustainability.
3 For more information on the debate over the use of disposables and reusables, see Chapter 8.

Further reading

A. Hutchinson and F. Hutchinson, *Environmental Business Management*, London: McGraw-Hill, 1997.

CHAPTER 13

The environmental audit

At Granada, we care about the communities and environments in which we operate. We have a responsible approach to the care of our customers, employees and the communities we serve, and towards the earth's resources. These are important accountabilities in which we fully involve all the employees in Granada worldwide.

Granada PLC, *Annual Report and Accounts, 1998*

OBJECTIVES

1 To discuss the contents of a checklist in preparation for an environmental audit.
2 To examine the process of the environmental audit.
3 To discuss the analysis of the results and make recommendations based on these results.
4 To distinguish between an environmental audit and an environmental impact assessment.

INTRODUCTION

The previous chapter discussed the range and importance of certain 'tools' which can be employed by a business to assess and improve on its environmental performance. A core tool, central to all progress, is the environmental audit. So what is an environmental audit?

In the same way that a limited company, and all other sensible businesses, carries out an annual and independent review of all financial transactions which have taken place in the previous tax or financial year, a company which is keen to monitor and to improve on its environmental performance will at least annually also audit its track record in this area.

The objectives of carrying out an environmental audit are:

● to assess the company's current environmental performance;
● to identify areas where improvements can be made;
● to develop a structured programme in order to implement these improvements;
● to identify the environmental costs and benefits which will result;
● to identify the resources necessary to achieve the above.

HOW TO CONDUCT AN ENVIRONMENTAL AUDIT

It is important that this procedure is carefully organized and planned, with an itinerary of *what* will be monitored, *when*, and *how*. So as to limit any disruption caused by the audit, it is important that the full support of the senior management, or the equivalent, is assured, and that those involved in either carrying out the audit or being audited are provided with the time and other resources for it to be done properly.

The following list is just one way in which to break down the audit into manageable areas; it consists of a schedule of issues to consider in each major area to be examined. Note the significant cross-referencing of a number of issues in the schedule.

1 Environmental Policy
- Does the company have a policy on its environmental performance?
- If it does have a policy, is this written in a statement for public scrutiny, or is it just a vague, unwritten policy?
- Who knows about the policy? The staff? All staff? Customers? Suppliers?
- Is the policy extensively publicized?

2 Performance Targets
- Has the company set itself specific environmental performance targets?
- Does the company conform to current environmental legislation?
- Has the company set itself a mixture of targets which are short/medium/long term or a combination of all three?
- Are the targets measurable?
- Are the targets realistic?

3 Management Structure
- Does the company management structure enable the successful implementation of an environmental policy?
- Has a senior member of staff been nominated to be responsible for this area?
- Does that individual have full and appropriate support from their colleagues?
- Have other members of company staff been allocated environmental responsibilities?
- Are all members of staff aware of the objectives of these appointments?

4 Staff Training and Education
- How much money is spent on this area of training?
- Is there a regular 'environmental' slot in the training programme?

- Do environmental issues form part of induction sessions?
- Is the company's environmental policy and performance mentioned, and emphasized, when recruiting staff?
- Are staff given environmental responsibilities?
- Are staff encouraged to play an active role in the development of the company's environmental policies (i.e., through suggestion schemes or by becoming environmental representatives)?
- Do staff have adequate information about the company's environmental performance? Its policies? Its future plans?
- Are staff encouraged to promote the company's environmental profile in the community generally?
- Does the company have a fund to provide staff with the opportunity to take part in voluntary environmental activities?

5 Public Relations
- Does the PR department (if relevant) and company publicity adequately promote the company's environmental policies?
- Is the positive environmental impact of the business and the products that it sells promoted to customers? To the press? To suppliers?
- Does the company's packaging, paperware, labelling, company literature, etc., promote its environmental policies?

6 Community Involvement
- Is the local community involved with the company?
- Does the company promote environmental projects in the community?

7 Investment
- Does the company have a policy on ethical investment of company capital?

8 Finances
- Can the costs associated with minimizing the company's impact on the environment be reduced (i.e., water rates, waste disposal, investment in new technology, recycling, energy, etc.)?

9 Purchasing Policy
- Does the company purchase or use environmentally-friendly products (e.g., transport fitted with catalytic converters, diesel versus unleaded petrol, etc.)?
- Does the company monitor the environmental performance of its competitors (i.e., collect environmental information about their performance, products, materials, processes and policies)?

The business environment

- Does the company establish environmental criteria for the assessment of suppliers?
- How will these criteria be applied?
- To what extent will preference be given to those companies which meet them? Will the criteria be mandatory?
- Over what timescale will these criteria be implemented?
- Does the company require or encourage suppliers to carry out an environmental review of their operations?
- Is the company prepared to offer financial, technical or management assistance to its suppliers in order that they achieve an improved environmental performance?
- Are specific environmental criteria established as a guide?
- Does the company provide the supplier with purchasing specifications?
- Is the purchase necessary?
- Is the potential toxicity of a product considered?
- Is packaging minimized?
- Are products sourced from a local supplier?
- Is the recycling potential of the purchase/packaging considered?
- Is the quality and durability of the product considered?
- Are sustainable resources used wherever possible?
- Is the use of recycled/recyclable paper specified?

10 Market Pressures
- Does the company target the 'Green consumer'?
- Are consumers made aware of the company's environmental beliefs?
- Are products labelled to promote this stance?

11 Contingency Plans
- Do any company activities have the potential to cause environmental problems (i.e., pollution, noise, litter, etc.)?
- Are staff trained in the minimization of these actions?

12 Insurance
- Is the company adequately insured for any environmental damage which might be costly to correct?

13 Property Management
- Is the property well maintained?
- Are all repairs and modifications planned on the basis of their potential to damage the environment, and decisions made accordingly?

- Are the environmentally best options always considered first when choosing replacement equipment, paint and other maintenance items?
- Is there a regular programme of monitoring the use of heating, lighting, ventilation and waste disposal procedures?
- Are environmental factors of design, landscaping, odour, noise and overall tidiness considered?

14 In the Office

(i) Use of Paper

- Is it efficient?
- Is recycled paper used in preference wherever possible?
- Is waste paper recycled?
- Photocopies: are they necessary? Are they double-sided?
- Internal circulation of memos: who receives them? Do they need to? Is electronic mail a substitute? Are staff trained in the minimization of hard copies?

(ii) Equipment and Furniture

- Are all choices of equipment and furniture ecologically-sound wherever possible?
- Is a life-cycle analysis of these products carried out before purchasing decisions are made?

(iii) Ecological Activities of Suppliers

- To what extent are these considered?
- Any of the items from the following list?

    Energy: Is it efficient? Can any measures be taken to reduce consumption?
    Buildings: Is there adequate insulation/draughtproofing?
    Lighting
    Air-conditioning
    Energy-efficient equipment
    Transport
    Alternative sources of energy
    Waste: Is it minimized? Can it be categorized and recycled?
    Water: Is it metered?
    Is the method of sewage disposal legal?
    Use of flow-meters and flow-restrictors, spray taps, showers, dual-flush toilets, leaking pipes, the disposal of hazardous chemicals?
    The product: consider design, raw materials, packaging, process operation, water use, energy sources/use, storage, emissions/discharges, waste disposal, transport and distribution, noise, etc.

15 Ambience
- Is there a pleasant and attractive working environment?
- Do the company's buildings match the local environment?

16 Landscaping and Site Management
- Are the grounds and gardens sympathetically landscaped?
- Are they in harmony with the local ecology?
- Are they planted with native plants?
- Are non-native, environmentally-damaging/demanding plants kept to a minimum?
- Is there a minimal use of chemicals?
- Are there wildflower areas?
- Are perfectly mown lawns essential?
- Are garden materials and furniture made from recycled plastics, sustainable woods, local and untreated materials?
- Access to the site: is it safe? Is it adequate?
- If roads to the site pass through residential areas, are speed limits complied with?

17 Health and Safety Issues
- Are these taken fully into consideration (e.g., phosphates, use of solvents, COSHH regulations)?

18 Transport and Distribution
- Are company cars supplied for employees?
- Are the cars essential for their work?
- Are the cars fitted with catalytic converters?
- Are there restrictions on the engine size?
- Is there a fuel allowance?
- Is private mileage paid for?
- Are vehicles regularly maintained?
- Is there a pool car system?
- Do people have to travel long distances for meetings? Can they tele-conference or telephone?
- Are staff encouraged to share cars on long journeys rather than take cars separately?
- Are commercial vehicles regularly serviced?
- Is the use of alternative modes of transport – rail, bikes or other forms of public transport – encouraged in preference to cars?
- Is car use discouraged by placing restrictions on parking? Or even charges?

- Distribution routes and methods of distribution of the company's goods and services – are these the most appropriate?
- What is their environmental impact?
- Choice of location of offices and production areas – what are the implications for commuting and distribution?
- What are the effects on the local community of any vehicle movements?
- Are vehicle emissions monitored and minimized?
- Are vehicle noise levels minimized?
- Are vehicle mileage rates considered and monitored?
- Do vehicles always run with a full load?

19 Packaging
- Is the packaging of goods intended to be transported or sold minimized?
- Can packaging material be reused or recycled?
- Is packaging designed to be refilled, reused or recycled?
- Are suppliers and customers encouraged to recycle any used packaging?
- If so, is this feasible (e.g., bottle banks, reuse of plastics, refillable containers, etc.)?
- Is the packaging adequate? Excessive? Too heavy?
- Can packaging be reduced?
- Can products be distributed and sold in bulk, or loose?
- Can its materials of construction be modified to assist waste disposal?

20 Energy Management
- Is energy used efficiently?
- Have measures to reduce consumption been investigated and put into operation?
- Are there regular reviews of energy use?
- Are energy efficiency practices encouraged?
- Are buildings designed and used to promote energy efficiency?
- Is the efficiency of heating and air-conditioning systems carefully monitored?
- Lighting: is it energy efficient in design and operation?
- Is the use of natural light maximized?
- Are all electrical items the most energy efficient?
- Have integrated energy management systems been installed? These can control heating, lighting, air-conditioning and electrical loads.
- Transport and distribution – has the most efficient use of fuel been determined?

- Are emissions from energy sources on site controlled (i.e., generators, boiler houses, etc.)?
- Are there plans to reduce the use of energy derived from fossil fuels?
- Is the use of alternative energy sources considered (e.g., methane from landfill gas, refuse-derived fuel, combined heat and power systems)?

21 Water Management

- Is sewage disposal efficiently managed?
- Is water usage monitored and controlled?
- Are the water supply and sewerage costs monitored?
- Are the quantities of water used and sewage discharged regularly monitored?
- Can the usage and costs of the above be compared across and between sites?
- Is the water supply metered?
- Are flow-meters and flow-restrictors installed to control consumption?
- Have all measures been taken to reduce consumption (i.e. the fitting of spray taps, reducing the quantity of water needed for showers and toilets, placing flow-restrictors on taps)?
- Are leaks quickly mended?
- Can recycled or 'grey' water be used?
- Are sewage costs correctly calculated?
- Are no hazardous chemicals discharged into drains or onto surfaces where they can run off?
- Are water-sprinkler systems correctly maintained?

22 Waste Management

- Is waste of all types minimized?
- Is any residual waste recycled or reused?
- Is all waste disposed of correctly?
- Are waste disposal costs properly controlled?
- Does waste disposal comply with statutory controls?
- Does the company know how much waste it produces?
- Are precise details of the content and source of the waste recorded?
- Are there records of waste production, disposal routes and costs?
- Is waste segregated to facilitate collection/recycling?
- Have all recycling possibilities been explored?
- How much recycling is actually carried out?
- Are there local waste exchange schemes?

- Is waste minimized by using less, or alternative materials (e.g., reusable ribbons, cartridges, etc.)?
- Are commercial waste disposal contractors properly registered, cost efficient and environmentally responsible?
- Do the waste disposal contractors recycle the company's waste? If so, how much and what benefit is this to the company?
- Do the waste disposal contractors use licensed sites?
- Do contractors dispose of waste as efficiently as possible and in an environmentally-friendly manner?

23 Noise

- Does the creation or use of the company's product create noise?
- Do customers/staff create excessive noise?
- Does the company's transport make excessive noise?

24 Recycling

- What? How? When? Why? How much?
- See item no. 22, 'Waste Management'.

25 Use of Materials and Processes

- Are all the business processes designed to minimize usage of energy and waste, and consumption of raw materials?
- Are energy, water and raw materials recycled wherever possible?
- Are appropriate environmental monitoring systems in place throughout these processes?
- Is the best technology available used to prevent excessive damage to the environment?
- Are developments in technology regularly reviewed to identify possible improvements?
- Are processes designed and operated to minimize effluents, emissions and solid wastes?
- Could processes be designed to be waste free?[2]

IMPLEMENTING THE ENVIRONMENTAL AUDIT

The above list will not be appropriate for every business, so the first step is to decide which areas are to be audited. In a business that is new to conducting an environmental audit it may be sensible to choose only one or two of the above sections, and then to increase the numbers of areas addressed over time. Probably the best areas to select to begin the process are items no. 20, 'Energy Management', and no. 22, 'Waste Management'. Within each sector, identify which issues relate to the business in question and list these for audit.

The next stage is to decide how each step will be evaluated. How will each area score? How can an objective assessment of achievement be decided? One solution is to award points on the basis of 0–5, 5 being the grade for excellence.

Gradings for the Environmental Audit
0   no effect
1   very poor
2   poor
3   satisfactory
4   good
5   excellent

Figure 13.1 is an example of a simple environmental audit of water use using a 0–5 scoring system. The questions were selected using item no. 21 on the list, 'Water Management', and modified to suit the particular circumstances of the business. The chart could be further modified to check whether the monitoring of water use, or bills, is carried out on a weekly, monthly or annual basis.

It can be seen that the maximum possible score that can be achieved in this instance is 60, therefore a score of 33 is a good indicator that improvements could be implemented.

Year ending April 1999	*Score*
Water usage monitored?	3
Water costs monitored?	5
Sewage volume monitored?	0
Are sewerage costs correctly calculated?	0
Water supply metered?	5
Flow-restrictors installed?	2
Spray taps installed?	2
Leaks quickly mended?	3
Can recycled or 'grey' water be used?	0
Any hazardous chemicals discharged into drains or on to surfaces where they can run off?	3 5
Are water-sprinkler systems correctly maintained?	5
Total score (maximum possible = 60)	33

Figure 13.1 An example of a score system for an environmental audit

So how can this first audit be used to improve environmental performance? Let us review each entry separately.

1   Is water usage monitored? This scored a satisfactory grade. If possible it would be interesting to monitor which sections of the business used the most water. Is it possible to install water meters on the piping entering the kitchen or the residential area? Is it possible to read these meters on a weekly basis? In this way a pattern of water use in each area can be established and acted on if necessary.

2   Is the volume of sewage that is discharged monitored? Is it possible to do this? If not don't audit it!

3   Are the sewerage costs correctly calculated? These are normally based on 95 per cent of the water use. Check this. How can sewerage costs be reduced?

4   Are flow-restrictors installed? These can reduce the amount of water travelling to taps and showerheads. A score of 2 indicates that some are installed. Set an objective so that by the following audit, 50 per cent of all taps/showers will be fitted with flow-meters. If by the next audit the target has not been achieved, award a low grade and set a more realistic target for the following year.

5   Are spray taps installed? Again, set a target of a rolling programme of tap replacement. Remember that taps can be expensive so replacements might only be cost effective when refurbishing rooms or washrooms. Always aim to cover the capital costs of installation from savings in water charges over 3–5 years.

6   Are leaks quickly mended? A score here of 3 indicates that there is room for improvement. Decide how this can be achieved; for example through staff training in the importance of reporting leaks quickly, and set targets to have them fixed within twelve hours.

7   Can recycled or 'grey' water be used? The fact that this item is included in the audit list suggests that it might be possible to do so. Water from baths and showers can be reused to flush toilets, for use in the dishwasher pre-wash cycle, for watering grounds, and for outside cleaning of hard surfaces, etc. Investigate how much it would cost to install a separate level of plumbing and water storage. Is this only practical for a new building?

8   Are hazardous chemicals discharged into drains? This scored 3. What constitutes 'hazardous chemicals': cleaning fluids, bleach, dishwasher chemicals? How can their use be minimized without risking the health and safety of guests? Set a target to investigate the selection of equally effective but less hazardous chemicals by the following audit. Perhaps by the following year set a target to fully implement their use.

9 Are any hazardous chemicals discharged onto surfaces where they can run off? Are any weedkillers or chemical fertilizers used in the grounds? A score of 5 suggests not.

10 Are water-sprinkler systems properly maintained? This should always earn a score of 5.

The important point to be made about environmental audits is that they should be carried out regularly, preferably annually, and that the results should be used to set targets to be achieved for the following year's audit. They are also another useful management tool for monitoring the general operating systems of the business from a different angle, perhaps by different personnel. They assist in the achievement of high standards and hence business success.

Bass has conducted detailed environmental audits with the assistance of independent consultants in all its divisions and, of course, each audit was tailor-made to meet the conditions of each site and its activities. This company measures its performance by using key performance indicators (KPIs). At present these relate to legal compliance, energy management and the implementation of the systems. There are plans, however, to extend their scope as the company's environmental management scheme becomes better established.

Industry Case Studies

In 1991 Inter-Continental Hotels established a '134 Action Points Programme' as a benchmark by which the company can judge its environmental performance. This is the same system as the points listed in this chapter for environmental auditing. By 1994 the company had set improvement targets based on the findings of this 'audit'.

Targets for 1995 were based on the 1994 achievements and these concentrated on the areas where the greatest improvements could be achieved and which could be reliably audited. Each hotel carries out its own audit which is independently checked by the company's financial audit team. These are carried out every 12 to 18 months.

Scandic Hotels measures its environmental performance on a quarterly basis against its own 'Environmental Index'. The Environmental Index is a 'target controlled benchmarking tool for measuring how a number of priority environmental activities are progressing at each hotel'.[1] In 1997 the company achieved a 5 per cent improvement, with an overall point score of 76 per cent.

In Chapter 14 we will examine the way in which Inter-Continental Hotels used the results of their environmental audit for their environmental report.

THE DIFFERENCE BETWEEN AN ENVIRONMENTAL AUDIT AND AN ENVIRONMENTAL IMPACT ASSESSMENT

There can be some confusion about the difference between an environmental audit and an environmental impact assessment. The latter is a statutory requirement which must be undertaken when there is a planned development such as a motorway, a housing or industrial estate, a large supermarket or similar major building development. The process assesses the direct and indirect effects of a project on:

- human beings, fauna and flora;
- soil, water, air, climate and the landscape;
- the interaction between the above; and
- material assets and the cultural heritage.

The Environmental Audit, on the other hand, is a close examination of the impact on the environment of a range of activities which a business carries out; these may be one or all of the following:

- the office environment
- the products of the business
- the processes whereby the business produces its goods
- distribution of its products
- installation of its products
- the end use of its products
- the dismantling or destruction of its products at the end of their useful life
- the raw materials that are used to make the products
- the sourcing and transportation of the raw material
- the working conditions of those who harvest the raw materials/transport them.

The stage at which an environmental audit can start or finish, and its scope, must be established. In the first instance it would be wise to work within narrow and immediate parameters and gradually widen the scope as the efficacy of the annual audits is proven.

CONCLUSION: THE NEXT STEP

Having carried out an environmental audit, which is an expensive process in terms of resources, the next step is to publish the results. We have seen how those companies which possess or aim to be awarded an environmental quality mark are required to make these results public. There are many companies, however, who feel – rightly or wrongly – that to do this might compromise commercial confidentiality. A compromise for a company which might wish to promote its environmental credentials without revealing all its company business, is to publish its environmental performance progress in the form of an annual environmental report. The next chapter will consider the form that such a report might take, and analyse the statements that a number of companies which have published an environmental report have made.

QUESTIONS AND ISSUES FOR DISCUSSION

1 Devise a checklist in preparation for an environmental audit in a hospitality operation of your choice.

2 (a) Carry out an environmental audit of a hospitality operation of your choice.
   (b) Analyse the results and make detailed recommendations based on your findings.

3 Choose one of the categories in the checklists in this chapter and change it from being quite a general outline into a more specific application to the hospitality industry.

4 A large multinational hotel company plans to develop a motel complex in a national beauty spot. It realizes that in the present climate it will be an inspired plan to build the complex according to environmental principles. You have been employed as the environmental expert with the remit to successfully steer the plan through to completion. Compile a report listing the stages of your working plan, including a rationale for each step.

Notes

1 Scandic Hotels, *Scandic Annual Report*, 1997.

2 Adapted from *Your Business in the Environment*, London: Legal Studies and Services Ltd, 1991.

CHAPTER 14

Reporting on environmental performance

A commitment to environmental issues enhances competitive strength.

In accepting its responsibility towards the environment, and by seeking to reduce the environmental impact of its operations, Scandic reinforces the values shared with its staff and with its customers and business partners. Moreover, a more efficient use of resources has a positive effect on the financial results and enhances the company's competitive strength.

Scandic Annual Report, 1997

OBJECTIVES

1 To examine a range of company environmental reports.
2 To evaluate the claims made in these reports.
3 To examine the range of issues that are addressed in the environmental reports.

INTRODUCTION

In the previous chapter we looked at how a company might thoroughly investigate its environmental performance by undertaking an environmental audit. This chapter will examine the ways in which companies report their environmental performance and how valid these claims are. Publication by businesses of these details is entirely voluntary, but it should be regarded as one way of improving or promoting a company's public profile, particularly if it is a leader in its sector, or if it has in the past been criticized for its environmental performance.

The law requires that public limited companies (PLCs) publish annual reports for their shareholders; the report contains financial information and a discussion of the company's activities over the past year. The content of the report is then raised at the annual shareholders' meeting. Annual reports do not normally contain detailed information on the company's environmental performance, although this may be mentioned if there is a particular issue, or if the company is planning to publish in the future fuller details of its performance. One example is Scandic Hotels; brief information about the company's environmental performance is given in their 1997 annual report. There does appear to be a pattern that as companies become more successful in their performance in this area, they then publish more extensive information in a separate report.

Hutchinson and Hutchinson argue that it is important to make public one's environmental performance for the following reasons:[1]

- So that the company can be seen to be conforming to its stated policy towards the environment.
- To provide the information for other companies, whether customers or suppliers, who are also working towards more sustainable business practices and with whom the company might wish to collaborate.
- To conform to public pressure to act in a more environmentally responsible manner.
- To show that the company is complying with the increasingly demanding regulatory environment on environmental issues.
- To promote the company's 'Green' image.
- As another tool for the company to use in its pursuit of high standards.
- To maintain its market leadership within its own sector.
- To meet increasing demands by investors for 'ethical' funds in which to invest.

What is an environmental report?

In contrast to the annual report of a PLC which outlines a company's financial situation, an environmental report details a company's environmental performance over the past year, and sets the company targets in this field for the following year. As more and more companies publish such reports, it will be possible to construct a profile of a company's long-term environmental performance. The reports are a relatively new phenomenon, and are usually published annually on, of course, recycled paper.

What factors should be addressed in an environmental report?

There is no standard format for an environmental report, but an examination of reports from a cross-section of industry suggests that the following points are popular:

- environmental targets and target dates
- the extent to which these targets have been achieved
- financial data relating to the company's environmental performance, e.g., investment policies, expenditure on health and safety, contingency funds for environmental disasters
- site reclamation issues (if relevant)
- legislation as it affects the company
- waste and recycling
- energy
- emissions
- purchasing
- training
- aesthetic, visual issues
- initiatives taken to support the local community.

An analysis of recent environmental reports by a number of companies, none of them from the hospitality industry, shows a certain format pattern and an emphasis on the following issues:

- A foreword by a famous person, e.g., Jonathan Porritt (S); or by the Board member with special responsibility for the environment (BT, BA); and/or the Chairman's introduction (S, IBM, U)
- Environmental policy statement (S, BA, IBM, U)
- Independent verification of the claims made (BT, BA, IBM)
- Compliance with legislation (U)
- A discussion of the company's activities and their impact on the environment (S, BT) e.g., planning and store development (S)
- Store design and operation (S)
- Waste management (S, BT)
- Transport (S)
- Suppliers – indirect impact (S)
- Integrated crop management (S)
- Organically-grown produce (S)
- Animal testing (S)
- Animal husbandry (S)
- Timber and forest products (S)
- Peat (S)
- Nutrition strategy (S)
- Labelling and customer information (S)
- Future actions and targets (S)

- Procurement (BT), i.e., purchasing, and improvement targets (BT)
- Fuel and energy (BT, IBM)
- Emissions to air and water (BT, IBM)
- Impact on the local environment (BT) – visual, ecological disturbance, grounds maintenance, their community programme (BT, IBM)
- Product stewardship (BT)
- Employee involvement (BT)
- Development of its environmental management systems (BT, IBM)
- Extensive description of environmental activities (BA, IBM)
- Noise (BA)
- Emissions, fuel efficiency and energy (BA, IBM)
- Waste, water and materials (BA, IBM)
- Congestion (BA)
- Tourism and conservation (BA)
- Pollution prevention (IBM)
- Plantations policy (U)
- Speciality chemicals (U)
- Detergents (U)
- Foods (U)
- Worldwide perspective (U)

Key
S   J Sainsbury
BT   British Telecom
BA   British Airways
IBM   IBM
U   Unilever

Reports by some other companies

B & Q

B & Q has published two separate environmental reports: the 'Timber Report' and 'How Green is my Front Door?'. The latter discusses its supplier environmental audit, the sourcing and use of timber, paper, issues of product and packaging disposal, retail operations, international issues and future action.

Marks & Spencer

Marks & Spencer did not use to publish a separate environmental report. Instead, it included a section on its role in the community in its annual report and also a section entitled 'Green policies make commercial sense', where it described its waste management and packaging policies, and its development of a code of practice for suppliers worldwide on the use of chemicals in textile production, especially dyeing, printing and finishing. Also mentioned was the work that it was doing with its transport fleet, such as improved refrigeration, better route planning and the use of double-decker lorries.

In 1998, however, the company published a separate account of its environmental activities entitled 'The Environment'. This discussed issues of waste minimization and recycling, food safety, building and construction, use of natural resources, energy saving, refrigeration, noise reduction, transport, animal welfare (including product testing and tuna sourcing), supplier partnerships, crop management, timber sourcing, dyeing and finishing of fabric, involvement in the community, and the future.

The Body Shop

The Body Shop is of course a leader in the field of business environmental awareness. It currently publishes a Values Report (aka 'The Green Book', cost £10) which is divided into sections on social, environmental and animal protection statements. The report can be accessed free of charge on the Internet.

PepsiCo (includes Pepsi, Frito Lay, Pizza Hut, Taco Bell, KFC)

This company publishes a special report on its environmental commitment, and its record on waste, packaging recovery, recycling and solid waste. It addresses its use of and recycling of aluminium, PET, glass and water. Also discussed is the company's environmental policy on transport and shipment, air quality, fertilizers, and the composting of site organic waste. The report also describes the companys' philanthropic activities'.

The above examples show a range of environmental reporting styles presented by non-hospitality-industry companies. Let us now examine the types of reports, and the issues that they address, produced by the hospitality industry itself.

REPORTS BY THE HOSPITALITY INDUSTRY

Inter-Continental Hotels and Resorts

This company played a major role in the establishing of the International Hotels Environmental Initiative. It was the first hotel company to create an environmental management system and to publish a company environmental manual. To celebrate the fiftieth anniversary of the company, an environmental review was published in 1996 based on figures for 1995.

The review took the following format:

- Introduction containing the company's six-point environmental commitment (see p. 207)
- An executive summary
- Environmental management at ICH
- Natural resources and energy
- Products and materials
- Waste
- Regional environmental needs and practices
- Local community action
- Education, training initiatives and awards
- Environmental awards
- 134 Action Points Checklist

Although the company had developed its environmental policies over a long period, it was not until 1991 that these were formalized into the six-point statement (see p. 207) and a management programme to implement them was introduced. The 1996 review therefore assesses the progress made since 1991.

The company claimed the following successes:

- the energy management programme reduced energy consumption by 27 per cent between 1988 and 1995
- the water management programme reduced consumption by 6.6 per cent in 1995
- the company negotiated a contract with Ecolab to supply environmentally-friendly chemicals which 'meet or exceed the very toughest environmental regulations'
- 50 per cent of all staff have been involved in some form of environmental training.

Future plans include:

- to establish systems to measure and monitor waste disposal
- to involve all hotels in the company in environmental awareness

- to include the corporate offices in the environmental programme
- to implement the main provisions of Agenda 21 into the company operations over the next five years
- to develop partnerships with other travel and tourism companies and
  to encourage them to implement the objectives of Agenda 21 into their
  own operations.

The environmental review discusses in detail the company's environmental
activities and progress since 1991, showing results where appropriate, and
indicating the set targets for future progress. It highlights particular success
stories, and ends by listing a number of environmental awards won by
hotels within the group.

Scandic Hotels

Scandic Hotels has 109 hotels throughout Scandinavia, and 17 hotels in the
rest of Europe, providing 18,196 rooms and 3,652 rooms respectively. Fifteen
of Scandic's hotels outside Scandinavia are operated under a franchise
agreement with Holiday Inn. Its environmental report is contained within
the main body of the 1998 annual report, so it is not as detailed as Inter-
Continental's report. However, four pages are devoted to environmental
issues. The first part is a general discussion of the company's approach to
the environment, together with its environmental policy statement. It
stresses the importance of staff training and of regular monitoring of
progress – in this case once every quarter. It introduces its 'Resource Hunt'
scheme, which is a three-year programme to 'make Scandic the most
resource-effective hotel company by reducing consumption of energy and
water by 20 per cent and the amount of unsorted waste by 30 per cent'.

The report details the results of the first eleven months of the scheme,
showing that the average consumption of energy at its Nordic hotels was
reduced by 7 per cent, water consumption by 4 per cent and waste by 15 per
cent, achieving financial savings of 6 million Swedish kronor in 1997.

It stresses the importance of the company's 'Eco rooms', and outlines its
co-operation with suppliers to develop less harmful products and
processes. The second half of the report is concerned with more detailed
facts and figures which address certain issues such as:

- Comprehensive environmental work
- Basic outlook
- Energy and water
- Waste

- Hotel rooms
- Scandic's environmental index
- Chemicals.

It will be interesting to see if this company, which has made great strides in a short period of time, will eventually produce an environmental report separate from the company's annual report.

Bass

Bass is a large international hotel and leisure group, one division of which is Bass Hotels and Resorts. This includes the Inter-Continental, Crowne Plaza, Holiday Inn, Holiday Inn Express and Staybridge Suite brands. Its other divisions are Bass Leisure Retail, which includes the Harvester, Toby, Vintage Inns, O'Neill's, All Bar One, Edwards, It's a Scream, Hollywood Bowl and Dave and Buster's brands; Bass Brewers, which includes Carling, Bass, Caffrey's, Tennent's, Worthington and Hooper's Hooch; and Britvic Soft Drinks, for which it has management responsibility.

The company published its first environmental report in 1998. It covers the activities of the company as a whole and discusses the following issues:

- environmental policy
- the Bass environmental management system
- taking care of waste – risk register, waste management and packaging reduction tables and the national glass collection service
- conserving and using water – risk register and consumption tables and water supply management
- taking care of surroundings: locally, nationally and globally – risk register, utilities consumption and use of process gas, improving energy efficiency
- compliance (with legislation) record
- verification statement
- Bass environmental management structure
- Millennium Greens – supporting local communities.

The report outlines the hiring of an independent firm of consultants in 1996 to evaluate the company's activities and to identify their environmental impact. They established action plans, targets and defined responsibility for environmental management. Good progress has been made by the company in that it has moved from the fifth quintile in the Business in the Environment Survey in 1997 to the third quintile in 1998.

The report discusses the importance the company attaches to staff training and also to working with suppliers. The importance of marketing the company and the minimization of packaging is also highlighted, as are purchasing specifications.

One very important aspect of the Bass environmental report is the inclusion of a 'verification statement'. This is a short paragraph written by the consultants who were the advisers on its environmental actions. It states that Bass has shown by its activities that it is committed to the principles of environmental management. The verification is validated by an independent consultant who has not previously worked with Bass.

Biffa Waste Services

This company plays a major role in the collection and disposal of waste in the UK. As such it is ideally situated to respond to environmental issues particularly as waste disposal has become a serious problem in our society. It is not surprising then that its environmental report (1998) is dedicated to describing its overall business activities. The report starts with a foreword by its managing director, and then addresses the following issues, *inter alia*:

- the Biffa environmental action plan and its progress in the year 1997/98
- the Biffa environmental action plan for 1998/99 and the expected environmental benefits
- the national and international position
- the UK's waste legacy
- sustainability in practice
- recycling
- waste collection and disposal
- energy
- transport
- environmental management
- conservation
- new alliances
- new services
- helping customers
- the Biffaward (an award to 'divert money back into the wildlife and environmental research projects')

The report concludes with both an independent benchmarking statement and an independent verification statement. The former is provided by AEA Technology Environment which assessed the company using the

Business in the Environment Index of Corporate Environmental Engagement. This measures commitment to environmental management and involved 74 FTSE companies in the 1997 survey. Biffa was placed in the second quintile.

The verification statement indicates how the company's claims were verified and supports those claims. However, the credentials of the verifying company are not established!

Biffa plans to publish an environmental report every two years.

Biffa Environmental Policy (source: *Biffa Annual Review*, 1997)

As a leading waste management company, Biffa has a strong commitment to the prevention of pollution, the safeguarding of the environment and the protection of public health underpinned by the concept of sustainable development.

To meet this commitment we have established an Environmental Management System which enables us to operate in accordance with environmental legislation, Severn Trent Group Protocols, ISO 14001 and EMAS. This system, which was first introduced during 1996, is being implemented throughout Biffa's operations in accordance with a programme set by the Board of Directors.

Each facility operating within the Environmental Management System will, on a regular basis, review its activities for their effects on the environment and the local community, in conjunction with the objectives and targets specified in the Biffa Group Action Plan. As a result of this review, objectives and targets will be established as part of a process of continuous environmental improvement. Biffa will publish the Action Plan within its Environmental Report and the Severn Trent Plc 'Stewardship' Report, together with current performance levels.

To ensure the achievement of this policy Biffa has identified personnel within the Company with the necessary responsibility, authority and resources to implement the Environmental Management System.

Granada

This large company owns and operates the following hospitality operations and services:

- Forte (UK) Ltd
- Granada Food Services Ltd
- Granada Hospitality Ltd
- Granada Purchasing Ltd
- Granada Services Group Ltd

- Granada Entertainments Ltd
- Sutcliffe Catering (UK) Ltd
- Forte France SA (France)
- Forte Hotels (Deutschland) GmbH
- Forte USA Inc
- Forte Hotels UK Ltd
- Forte Holdings Ireland Ltd
- Forte International BV
- Granada Travel PLC
- Heritage Hotels Ltd
- Lusotel Industria Hoteleira Ltda
- Meridien Hotels Ltd
- Posthouse Hotels Ltd
- Société des Hôtels Meridien SA (France).

Throughout this book we have seen how Forte developed its environmental policies and management systems before being taken over by Granada in 1997. In its 1998 annual review, which covers the activities not only of the above companies, but also of its rental, consumer electronics and broadcasting operations, Granada for the first time devotes a section to 'Community, charitable and environmental initiatives'. Two-thirds of the section outlines the community work undertaken by its TV companies, its work in education and the arts, support for young people, and charitable donations and similar work. It describes its attitude to the environment in the following statement:

> A responsible attitude towards the environment often yields benefits to our businesses too, by eliminating wastage and reducing consumption of resources. We continually review our procedures to seek out ways to improve our environmental performance.

The section describes in brief the work done in Forte Hotels, the IHEI association, Le Meridien, Granada Food Services and Granada Motorway Services, and Granada Home Technology.

A separate report on the environmental status of the Forte Hotel Group was published in January 1998.[2] This report was intended mainly for internal consumption, and was based on a sample of 10 per cent of its UK hotels. The conclusions reached in the report are that the company's activities do not unduly threaten the environment, although there is substantial room for improvement. The report identifies the lack of environmental management structures and concludes that examples of good practice are more to do with the commitment of individuals rather than with company policy. The report maintains that the company has higher environmental standards in its housekeeping and kitchen operations. It identifies the fact that efficient use is made of energy and water, mainly as a result of investment in new technology, but that the implementation of systems for continuous monitoring is inadequate, making it impossible to establish targets or to monitor annual efficiency gains.

The report draws the following conclusions:

- The company must establish clear management structures with clear lines of communication and identified areas of responsibility.
- Performance benchmarks and league tables need to be established.
- Manuals of good practice must be published.
- Staff training in environmental performance is essential.
- All decision-making processes at senior management level must consider environmental issues.
- An executive environmental management team must be created to co-ordinate policies and management structures. This should include a consortium of regional managers plus other staff.
- Each hotel should establish an environmental management team.
- The company should require 'supplier compliance' in environmental issues.
- The publicity-raising activities of the company with regard to its environmental performance should also be used to inform the wider public of environmental issues in the leisure and tourism sectors.

The reader will note that the style of the Forte report differs from the other reports considered in this chapter in that it is self-critical. The other reports are intended for public consumption and as such are far more self-congratulatory, even though they have independent evaluations of the veracity of their claims. The ability to be self-critical is the strength of the Forte report.

TWO MODELS FOR AN ENVIRONMENTAL REPORT

Model 1[3]

Executive Summary and Recommendations: Detailed Report
a. Objectives of review and project outline
b. Current defined company policy and practices
c. Key environmental issues for the business
d. Current performance

e.   Strengths, weaknesses and opportunities
f.   Priorities: short-term goals and costs and benefits
g.   Priorities: medium-term goals and costs and benefits
h.   Priorities: long-term goals and costs and benefits
j.   Recommendations
k.   Performance targets
l.   Action plan
m. Timetable

Model 2[4]

Qualitative information
Foreword by a senior person
Profile of the enterprise
Environmental policy
Environmental targets and objectives
Views on environmental issues
Community relations

Management information
Environmental management systems
Management of environmental risks
Office and site practices

Quantitative information
Environmental indicators and targets
Use of energy and natural resources
Compliance with regulations and permits
Financial indicators

Products
Products, processes and services
Additional information

We can see from the above two models, and also from the examples that we have examined in this chapter, that there is no one model for an environmental report. A company can have free choice in the range and quantity of information that it decides to publish.

CONCLUSION

This chapter has examined the range and variety of environmental reports published by companies. Particular attention has been paid to those published by the hospitality industry. It can be seen that there is no standard format for the structure of an environmental report, and that a company can choose to omit any embarrassing information if it so desires. However, the company which is serious about its environmental performance will ensure that it does not gloss over difficult areas, and that the information contained in a report is independently verified. In addition, it is important that the format of an environmental report remains consistent from year to year so that data can be easily compared. Targets for the coming year should be set, and their achievement or otherwise should be disclosed in the following report.

QUESTIONS AND ISSUES FOR DISCUSSION

1   In view of your current understanding of the impacts of your particular industry sector on the greater environment, should the British Government consider the making of environmental performance reporting mandatory? Give reasons for your answer.

2   What factors should be addressed in an environmental report? Give examples of what companies include in their reports. Evaluate the extent to which these companies are truly open about their performance.

3   Do you agree with the statement published in The Body Shop's 'The Green Book' that it is not possible for any business to be environmentally-friendly? Using an example from your own industry sector, discuss this issue.

4   Where and when should environmental reports be published? Give reasons for your answer.

5   Examine the environmental report of any company and write a critique using the following headings:
    1 The company's business – an assessment of its current impact on the environment.
    2 What are the environmental claims made in the report?
    3 Are these claims valid?
    4 What room is there for the company to improve its environmental performance?
    5 How is the report presented?
    6 Does the company take the issues seriously or is this just good PR?

6 Compare and contrast the environmental reports of two hospitality companies.

7 Using the company for whom you carried out an environmental audit exercise in Chapter 13, consider how you would evaluate its impact on the environment
   (a) in the past year;
   (b) in the past 5 years; and
   (c) since it was formed.

8 Examine the balance sheets of a number of companies, together with the history of these companies. Choose one company, and
   (a) assess the environmental impact that the company has had over the years, listing the major activities/impacts;
   (b) consider how these impacts could be incorporated into the Company's balance sheets.

9 What are the main provisions of Agenda 21? How could a hotel company implement these into its operations? Over what timescale would this be possible?

10 Discuss whether a company should report its environmental performance over the previous year in a separate report, or whether this should be included in the standard annual report.

11 To what extent should the reader believe the claims that a company makes in its environmental report? What should be included in the report to give it greater credibility?

12 Examine the environmental report of one company. Consider the claims that it makes and analyse them critically.

Notes

1 A. Hutchinson and F. Hutchinson, *Environmental Business Management*, London: McGraw-Hill, 1997.
2 Forte Hotel Group, *Environmental Status Report*, 1 January 1998.
3 Business in the Environment, 'Structuring the Report – An Example', *Your Business and the Environment*, London: Legal Studies and Services (Publishing) Ltd, 1991.
4 World Industry Council for the Environment 1994, cited in Hutchinson and Hutchinson, *Environmental Business Management*, London: McGraw-Hill, 1997.

CHAPTER 15

Conclusions

> The days when individual companies were judged solely in terms of economic performance and wealth creation have long disappeared. Today, companies have far wider responsibilities to the community, to the environment and to improving the quality of life for all.
>
> *Chris Fay, Chairman and Chief Executive, Shell UK, May 1998*

In this book we have examined, albeit briefly, the environmental issues which challenge the hospitality industry at the turn of the millennium. By its very nature such a book can only take a cursory look at each issue, but it is hoped that it has provided enough case studies, enough examples of good practice, and enough ideas for the committed student or business to take the investigation further. Technology is improving rapidly, and lighting which was once 'state of the art' has already been superseded by more efficient materials and equipment. The pace of technological change is so great that a new edition of this book would contain a range of different examples.

However, the issues which were highlighted in the first chapter of this book will be with us for decades to come. The projected growth of the world's population, particularly in developing countries, means that human demands upon the natural environment can only increase. Even if the world population stabilizes within its 'carrying capacity', the desire of all people to achieve a standard of living comparable to that of the developed world will place huge pressures on natural resources. If the whole world were to use resources at the same rate as the industrialized world currently uses them, then these resources would run out very rapidly. Therefore we have a number of choices:

- to do nothing and hope matters will sort themselves out
- to start to consider the impact of human activities on the environment and to attempt to minimize them
- to develop new technologies to allow for the eventual loss of natural, non-renewable, resources
- to assist developing countries to achieve improved standards of living while at the same time minimizing their impacts on the environment
- to co-operate across and between national borders, political and religious beliefs, cultures and generations to work towards a more equitable distribution of resources.

We have only recently woken up to the realities of environmental degradation and its long-term implications, as evidenced by the fact that it took until 1987, when the Brundtland Report was published, for world leaders to embrace environmental issues into their national agendas. The subsequent squabbling at the regular international conventions on how to reduce national impacts on the environment indicates just how difficult it is to achieve an international consensus. Developing nations feel that they should be allowed a longer time in which to phase out their polluting activities, and yet the effects of climatic changes do and will hit them the hardest. The USA, the world's greatest polluter per capita, is extremely reluctant to reduce its global warming emissions for fear of electoral defeat, and also because of inter-party strife. The EU is finally working as a bloc to commit itself to reducing its impact on global pollution, but there are arguments between the member states as to how the targets that the EU has agreed to will be allocated; again the poorest members demand the greatest pollution quotas. China, the most densely populated and most rapidly growing nation in the world, refuses to agree to any international agreements to reduce pollution. The countries of the former Soviet Union are too poor to invest in less polluting technologies.

On an individual basis, we are very reluctant to reduce a standard of living which we have come to accept as the norm. How many people are prepared to give up the use of their motor car? How many people are happy to pay VAT on domestic fuels? How many people approve of the compulsory metering of domestic water? Repeated surveys have shown that many of us claim to be concerned about the environment, but if we are truthful does this concern inform every action that we take?

On the other hand, how easy is it for an individual to be 'Green' in today's world? In the modern throwaway, live for today consumer culture it takes quite an effort to be 'Green'. But if everyone became more concerned then it becomes much easier. Evidence from Germany and Scandinavia shows that a judicious mix of legislative coercion combined with a change in attitudes can create a more environmentally-caring society. In the UK, the diversity of people who combined together in opposition to road building and animal exports in the late 1990s shows that there is a grass-roots movement which cares about the environment and its associated causes.

At the end of the twentieth century the only report that the world community can receive for its efforts to prevent environmental disaster is to say that it 'could do better'! But at least it has started to consider the issues and to take threats seriously and to act upon them. Action in the coming century will need to be more rapid, more focused and more consensual if we are not to deprive future generations.

As far as the hospitality industry is concerned, it is to be congratulated on the steps that it has already taken. The formation of the International Hotels Environment Initiative (IHEI) and the tremendous support that this organization can provide is a significant sign that things are changing. The fact that it has been the major companies in the industry which have been its primary supporters is also heartening. These companies have been able to afford to take the risk to invest in new technologies in order to improve their environmental performance. Even if these risks were carefully evaluated in advance to ensure that they were likely to pay for themselves, this does not diminish their importance. Successful technology leads to increased purchasing and encouragement of innovation in the area of environmental technology. As prices come down, the new technologies can be afforded by more companies who will in their turn be able to reduce their impact on the environment.

The quarterly publication of the IHEI, *Green Hotelier*, which is available at a very affordable price,[1] contains excellent case studies, advice and supplier information which is of invaluable use to all members of the industry.

The large companies have shown that considering the environment makes sound business sense. Time and again actions to minimize a company's impact on the environment have brought significant savings in company expenditure, in addition to improving its public profile. They have embraced the use of environmental business tools, have carried out environmental audits, have set targets to achieve, have trained and involved their staff, they have monitored their targets, and have reported on their progress. Each company will no doubt admit that there is still a long way to go, but they have made an excellent start.

But what about the rest of the industry? The number of small and medium-sized hospitality enterprises far outnumbers the combined operations of the large multinationals, and it is these companies which need to start considering their contribution to environmental degradation. Unfortunately these operations have the least interest in minimizing their impacts, and they are going to be the most difficult to convince. Why is this? Consider the following list.

- They are often run on very tight staffing schedules and the managers/ owners do not have the time to think about such 'luxuries' as the environment.
- The managers/owners may well have not had the benefit of as much education as those employed by the large companies.
- There is a misconception that it will cost too much money to invest in more environmentally-friendly technology.

- They are unaware of the fact that they will save money as well as save the environment.
- They think that to trade in an environmentally-friendly manner would be too time consuming, on top of an already demanding schedule.
- Their suppliers are not well informed about environmentally-friendly equipment/techniques.
- They think that becoming a 'Green' business will involve such radical changes that it would alienate their customers.
- They are misinformed about the pressures on the environment and feel that it is 'scaremongering.'
- They don't care about the environment.

There are bound to be more reasons than the ones listed here, and it is worth carrying out a survey to discover what are the attitudes of hospitality SMEs towards this issue.

Although the impact on the environment of the hospitality industry is low when compared with that of heavy industry or transport, it must be stressed that it is the contribution of individuals and of small companies which when added together can be equally severe; small savings by every company can have a huge impact on the reduction in environmental degradation. The conservation of resources is not only responsible behaviour in the wider community, but as we have seen, it makes sound business sense.

We need to bear in mind that not all environmental initiatives will have significant economic paybacks, but as customers, staff and investors increasingly expect companies to take environmental issues into consideration, then it is important that a company is open about what it is doing, and that all claims should be verifiable. Companies should include quantifiable targets, or other performance indicators, and results of their environmental audits. The environmental annual report is the ideal medium through which to publish such information. Obviously there will be concerns about the disclosure of confidential business information, but if PLCs are able to publish annual financial reports, and some PLCs are able to publish environmental reports, then all businesses should follow their example.

The provision of some environmental information will often lead to pressure from staff and customers to do more – this is positive feedback which should be taken on board.

It is the usual practice in the UK to encourage the business world to 'police' itself through the development of industry guides to good practice or voluntary agreements. As international pressure increases on countries to improve their environmental performance it is more than likely that we will see the development of such codes for the hospitality industry; and in the

long run if voluntary encouragement does not work then legal requirements will be brought in. The tax on fuel is just the beginning.

We have seen how companies can take part in a number of voluntary
schemes to encourage positive environmental action. This will be seen as
good commercial practice and is a positive form of marketing. In addition to
the environmental management standard BS 7750, there is the EU Eco-
labelling scheme and the 'Making a Corporate Commitment Campaign'.
This latter scheme is based on good business practice and it enables companies to introduce environmental management systems, make environmental
claims about products and/or services, and to set targets for future performance which are instantly recognizable and verifiable by customers and
competitors. The EC Eco-labelling scheme will enable producers to make
genuine environmental claims about their products, and the customer will
be able to make comparisons and informed choices when making purchases.

In 1994 over 1500 companies had joined the 'Making a Corporate Commitment Campaign', which is run by the Energy Efficiency Office to
encourage energy efficiency. In 1995 the Eco-Management and Audit
Scheme was introduced. This scheme requires that companies make public
their environmental policies and these must be externally validated. There
is also the new Queen's Award for Environmental Achievement, a competition which encourages high standards of environmental responsibility. In
addition, the UK Government has funded pilot projects in an attempt to
encourage and support small business to include environmental systems
and innovations in their operations. Called Green Business Clubs, the projects have so far been undertaken in Blackburn, Sheffield, Amber Valley,
Dudley, Newcastle, Wearside, Hemel Hempstead and Plymouth.

STAFF INVOLVEMENT

One of the most heartening factors in all of this is the way in which staff
right across the sector and throughout the world have committed themselves to the issues of environmental management. Staff have not only been
instrumental in making useful suggestions in energy use and waste minimization, but they have been enthusiastic about the community support
schemes that so many companies have become involved in. They have vol-
unteered their spare time for these causes and have nominated charities to
which to donate money raised in energy-saving schemes. Like any other
aspect of a business, the extent to which staff are trained is reflected in their
commitment to that issue.

Consider the following strategies which have been used to maximize staff involvement in environmental programmes:

- incentive schemes, run either for individuals or for departments
- regular training sessions on the importance of taking action to save the environment and its practical application in the workplace
- environmental concerns as part of recruitment and induction programmes
- empowering and encouraging staff to put their ideas together, and awards for the initiatives
- to show how staff can educate guests to help to protect the environment, and to take part in the hotel's environmental initiatives
- donation of leftover resources to community projects chosen by the staff – this will include used soap bars, unwanted or used linen and towels
- earnings from the sale of waste paper, plastics and metals are placed in a special employee fund, or donated to a community initiative selected by the staff
- encourage staff to collect any rubbish, and clean up graffiti to improve the working environment.

If all levels of staff are committed to environmental issues in the workplace, the chances are that they will apply these principles in their own homes. Their small domestic contribution will combine with all the similar tiny contributions worldwide. They will also be setting a good example to relatives, friends and neighbours and perhaps also placing pressure on local authorities to take greater steps to protect the local environment.

THE FUTURE

It is impossible to predict what will happen in the future. However, there are some factors of which we can be sure. Population will continue to grow for decades before stabilizing, and this will place increasing pressure on the earth's resources. The effects of global warming will continue to increase and scientists will produce stronger evidence to support their claims that human activity threatens our existence. Politicians will continue to challenge such evidence in the fear that if they have to take unpopular decisions to counter these threats they will lose their positions of power. Politicians, after all, think only in terms of winning the next election. Yet politicians will be forced to bring in increasingly stringent legislation and taxation to encourage people to act more considerately towards the environment. It would therefore be reasonable to predict that the wise business is the business that anticipates such action and has minimized its impacts well in advance. The costs of compliance will be much reduced and will be staggered over a longer time period. The issue of threats to the environment will not go away. The incorporation of the concept of environmental stewardship into everyday business practice should be second nature.

A recent survey of businesses in Canada found that the five most frequently used materials were those which were most frequently wasted: paper, cardboard, wood, oil and electricity.[2]

Notes

1 *Green Hotelier* is published four times a year; an annual subscription costs £25 (1999 price).
2 Michael Allen, 'Ecosystems for Industry', *New Scientist*, 5 February 1994.

Index

acid rain 17
   damage 4, 186
addresses 89
Agenda 21, 32, 35, 39, 42, 221
agricultural land quality 23–4
air pollution
   causes 187
   urban 188
air-conditioning 57–8
aircraft emissions 14, 35
Alcan 163
aluminium recycling 163
ambience 230
animal welfare 118–21
   protests 179, 180
aquifer, 29 n12, 187
Asian Development Bank 34

B & Q environmental reports 242
Bass
   community involvement 214
   policy statement 208, 213
   reports 246–7
baths, water consumption 100
Best Available Techniques Not Entailing
      Excessive Cost (BATNEEC) 41–2
Best Possible Environmental Option
      (BFPO) 152
Biffa waste services 13, 164, 222
   policy 248
   reports 247–8
Biodiversity Convention 39
Birchanger Green 126
Body Shop 176
   reports 243
Bottlebank 164
Brewers and Licensed Retailers
      Association (BLRA) 164

British Antarctic Survey team 15
British Board of Agreement (BBA) 127
British Medical Journal 122
British Standards Institute 218–21
   BS5750 (ISO 9000) 218, 220
   BS7750 218–20, 258
Brundtland Report
   effects 34–5
   publication 32, 255
building
   design and insulation standards 64
   environmental considerations 126–8
   generally 63
   heating and ventilation 71–3
      air-conditioning 72–3
      combined heat/power systems
        (CHP) 72
      costs savings 71–2
   hotel bedrooms 79–80, 128–9
   lighting requirements 65–70
      costing formulas 69–70, 77
   location 64
   long–term objectives 79
   new 62, 126–8
   operational areas 63
      dish-washing and hot water 76–8, 102
      equipment usage 77
        running costs 78–9
      food production/service, 73–9;
        see also food preparation/
        service
   refurbishment 126–8
   temperature control mechanisms 64
building regulations 63
Building Research Establishment
      Environmental Assessment
      Method (BREEAM) 127

Index

business
  'Environment Business
      Management' 205
  strategy
      importance of overall 203
  tools 204–22
Business in the Environment Survey 246

carbon cycle 7–8
  facts and figures 4
carbon dioxide emissions 186, 187, 188,
      189, 190, 198
  building construction 127
  fossil fuels contribution 7–8
  global warming contribution 10
  greenhouse gas 6–12, 193
  major factor affecting
      temperatures 9
  new cars 39, 188
  percentage in UK 14
  sea reservoir of 13
  taxation to reduce 40
carbon monoxide emissions 192
  reduction 192–3
carbon tax
  proposals 4, 39
cardboard
  recycling 152–3
'Caring for the Earth' 33–4
cars
  new 39
  producing greenhouse gases 4, 186
case studies
  ARA Food Services 220
  Canadian Pacific Hotel 169
  Chewton Glen Hotel, Hampshire 72
  Considerate Hoteliers Scheme 128
  Dow Chemicals and Autobar 159–60
  Earth Communications Office (ECO) 128
  Forte Hotels 15, 56, 83–5, 99, 128, 129,
      137, 154, 167, 170–1, 196, 197
  Gleneagles Hotel 154
  'Going for Green' scheme 172
  Grand Hotel,Brighton 64
  Hilton International Hotels 103

Inter-Continental Hotels 85, 101, 102,
      103, 215–16, 236
Jamaica 101
Kalundborg, Denmark 43
Linpac 157
Little Chef 123
London Hyde Park Hilton Hotel 83, 169
McDonald's 81, 172
Novotel Hotels 154
Ramada Hotels 212
Sainsbury 54
Savoy and Dorchester Hotels 154
Scandic Hotels 107, 236
Sheraton Hotels 128, 169
catalytic converter 192–3, 197–8
chlorofluorocarbon (CFC)
  alternatives 53–5
  disposal 56
  effects 15
  emissions 50
  man-made 11
  Montreal Protocol 33
  refrigerant 49, 58
  types 51
  use 50–1
Clean Air Acts 1956, 1968 188
Clean Development Mechanism (CDM)
      36–7
Climate Change Convention 35, 39
Climate Conference in Buenos Aires 1998
      36–7
COMA Report recommendations 124–6
  cooking methods 125
  equipment 125–6
  ingredients 125
community involvement 214
  audit issues 227
compact fluorescent light bulbs 67–9
Compassion in World Farming (CIWF) 121
computer software
  Appraise 100+ 81
conclusions 254–60
Consultative Group on International
      Agricultural Research 24
consumer priorities 178

contingency plans 228
conversions 88–9
cooking equipment
    combination microwave/
        convection ovens 111–12
    combination steamers 110–11
        baking 111
        delicate dishes 111
        grilling 111
        roasting 110
        vegetables 111
    fat-free chip production unit 112–13, 126
    generally 114
    purchasing policies 114
    ware washers 113–14
Countryside Commission 214
cryptosporidium
    pollutant of drinking water 97

definitions 42–3
Department of the Environment survey
        1993 175–6
Department of the Environment,Transport
        and the Regions 14–15, 40, 179
detergents
    concentrates 106
    custom-made 107
    toxicity 105–6
diesel
    advantages and disadvantages 189
dishwashers
    energy consumption 76–8
    water consumption 101, 145
disposable products
    advantages/disadvantages 135–6, 143
    extent of use 134, 143
    generally 134–5, 147
    glass 144
    packaging 136–40
    paper 145–6
        versus polystyrene 145
    plastics 140–2
    polycarbonate 144
    polystyrene 144
        expanded 146–7

reusable versus 143–5
    SAN 144
Diversey Ltd 106
Drinking Water Inspectorate (DWI) 96
drinking water quality
    pollutants 96–7
drought
    effects 92, 94

E for Additives 177
Earth Summit in Rio *see* Rio Earth
        Summit 1992
EC Drinking Water Directive 96
EC eco-label logo 183–4
EC eco-labelling scheme 183–4, 258
Eco-Management and Audit Scheme 258
Ecover group 107
    environmental policy statement 206
    Inter-Continental Hotels compared 207
electricity rates
    economy 7 business tariff 80–1
    evening/weekend/night business
        tariff 81
    generally 80
    standard business tariff 80
Elkington J. and Hailes J. 164 n7, 176, 177
Energy Efficiency Office 62
    'Best Practice Programmes' 72 n10, 88
        n15, 127
    'Condensing Boilers', 71 n9
    'Making a Corporate
        Commitment Campaign' 258
energy management
    audit issues 231–2, 234
    generally 60–3
    new buildings 62; *see also*
        building, building regulations
    non-renewable sources 61
    objectives 60
    old buildings/established
        businesses 63
    planning 82–3
    renewable sources 61
energy-saving strategies 82–3

environmental audit
conduct 226–33
generally 225
impact assessment distinguished 237
implementing 233–7
objectives 225
Environmental Management
Standard (BS 7750) 218
application for 219
benefits 219–20
'cradle to grave' approach 219
criteria 219
questions raised 220
environmental policy statement
audit issues 226
corporate examples 206–10
generally 206, 209–10
Environmental Protection Act 1990 41–2,
51, 56, 153–6
environmental report
company analyses 241–3
conclusions 251
construction 240
form 240–1
generally 239–40
model examples 250–1
environmental review 205–6
erosion 23–4
EU Packaging Waste Directive 130, 139, 140
Europe-wide Eco-Management and Audit
Scheme (EMAS) 221
European EMAS scheme 221
European Environment Agency (EEA)
functions 38–9
European Environment Information and
Observation Network (EEION)
functions 38–9
European Union (EU)
Common Agricultural Policy 38
consolidating legislation 37–8
environmental protection in 37–9
framework Directive 153
international Treaties
implementation 38
polluter pays policy 37, 153

facts and figures 4, 188
family planning 24–7
fast food, pollution 123–4
finances 227
Finnish Government's Environment
Ministry 165
fiscal incentives 195
Food and Agriculture Organization
(FAO) 33
Food Hygiene (General) Regulations
1970, 65 n5
food poisoning 135–6
food preparation/service 73–6
electrical equipment
fan-assisted ovens 75
forced-convection ovens 75
induction hobs 75
initial costs 76
microprocessor ovens 75
energy consumption
ratings 74
strategies to reduce 74–5
wasted 76
gas appliances 73–5
bains-maries 73–4
fryers 73
initial costs 76
multi-energy tunnels 76
purchasing specifications 130
'RoFry' 112–13, 126
water consumption 97–8
food production
world 21–3
Food Safety Act 1990 136
food waste disposal 166–9
machines 169
Forte Hotels
'Community Chest' scheme 128
community involvement 214
policy statement 208–9, 212
waste disposal sceme 168
fossil fuels 6–7
burning,effect of 10–11, 17
Framework Convention on Climate
Change 9–10

freight traffic increase 194–5
Friends of the Earth 161, 165, 178, 194
   'Green Con' award 214
further reading 30, 44–5, 59, 89, 133, 185,
   224
future happenings 259–60
gas rates 81–2
glass, recycling 163–4
global warming 8–15
   counteraction 14
   effects 12–14
      UK 14–15
Government Consultation Paper 'Using
   Water Wisely' 95
Government Panel on Sustainable
   Development 41
Granada Group PLC
   policy statements 209
   reports 248–50
Green Business Clubs 258
Green consumer
   categories 181
   conclusions 184
   definition 180–2
   generally 175–6
   in hospitality sector 182–3
   market growth 176–80
   purchasing patterns 182
Green Consumer Guide 176, 177
Green Party 178
green purchasing patterns *see* Green
   consumer
Green Revolution 22 n8, 24
green technology *see* technology, vehicle
   technology and
   government action
Greenfreeze fridge 55
greenhouse gas emissions
   carbon dioxide 6–12
   chlorofluorocarbons (CFCs) 11
   effects 9, 12–15
   European Union 35
   major producers 4, 187
   methane 11
   nitrous oxide 11
   production 12
   reduction 3, 10, 35, 36
   stabilization 4
   transport major cause 187
Greenpeace 53, 55, 165, 178

Halon Users' National Consortium 56
Hanssen, Maurice 177
health
   ethical issues 124–6
   safety issues 230
Henry Doubleday Research
   Association (HDRA) 178
high density polyethylene (HDPE) 161
Horniman Museum 126
hotel bedrooms
   energy consumption 79–80
   'greening' 128–9
Hutchinson and Hutchinson 205
hydrofluorocarbon (HCFC) 49, 50, 52

incineration 152
   energy recovery 161–2
   paper 166
independent verification 217–22
industrial growth, implications 5–6
insurance requirements 214–15, 228
Integrated Pollution Control (IPC) 41–2
Inter-Continental Hotels and Resorts
   Ecover group compared 207
   policy statements 206, 207
   reports 244–5
Intergovernmental Panel on Climate
   Change (IPCC) 9, 12, 13, 14
International Conference on
   Population and Development in
   Cairo 1994 24–6, 35
International Hotels Environment
   Initiative (IHEI) 216–17
   'Green Hotelier' 256
   origins 217
International Institute for
   Environment and
   Development 34
International Labour Office 34

International Monetary Fund (IMF) 19
International Rice Research Institute
(IRRI) 24
International Standards
Organization (ISO)
ISO 14000 series 221–2
investment 227
Istituto Superiore di Sanita 34

Kyoto Conference, 1997 3
EU response 35
ratification 35–6
UK response 41

landfill
charges 137, 171
waste disposal 151, 152
landscape and grounds maintenance
audit issues 230
water consumption 104
laundry 102–3, 105–7, 129, 130
lead, pollutant of drinking water 96
local authorities
waste disposal obligations 155–6
London Wildlife Centre 126

management structure 226
market pressures 228
Marks & Spencer
community involvement 214
non-caged eggs 120
reports 243
materials and processes 233
metals, recycling 163
methane
burning from landfill 161
greenhouse gas 11, 162, 166
production 162
Millennium Greens scheme 214
monitoring progress 215
monoculture 29, n11
Montreal Protocol
EC implementation 38
ratification 50

responses to 33, 52
UK as signatory 39, 51
morbidity
meaning 29 n4

National Consumer Council 182
National Rivers Authority 156
nitrates
pollutant of drinking water 96–7
nitrogen oxides emissions 186, 188, 189,
190, 191–2
reduction of 192
noise 233
nuclear power 4, 60, 61

office materials/equipment/
procedure 130, 229
Ogilvy and Mather 181
organic
beverages 123
definition 122
produce 121–2
Ozone Depleting Substances (ODS) 49
ozone layer 15–17
CFCs, effects of 51–2
depletion 15–16
ground level 191–2, 198
role of 49

packaging
audit issues 231
constituents 138–9
disposable
advantages/disadvantages 135–6, 143
expanded polystyrene 146–7
paper 145–6
reusable versus 143–5
extent of use 134, 147
generally 134–5
multi-journey 142–3
outside the UK 139–40
plastics 140
banning proposals 141
degradability required 141–2

excessive use 130, 141–2
    recycling 141
unnecessary 136
waste 137
    sources 137–8
wasteful 130, 141–2
    solutions 141–2
paper
    incineration 166
    recycling 152–3
        reasons for 164–6
        uses 164
Peattie, K. 180
PepsiCo, reports 243
performance
    reporting 239–53
        generally, 239–40; see also
            environmental report
    targets
        audit issues 226
        setting 210–11
pesticide, pollutant of drinking water 97
petrol, unleaded encouraged 189
photochemical pollution
    components 191–2
    occurrence 188, 190
photovoltaics see solar energy
plastics
    excessive use 141–2
    recycling 141, 152–3
        reasons for 158–60
        uses 162
    types 140
PM10s
    diesel vehicles 189
    fast food restaurants 123
    lung disease association 188
    meaning 17, 191
polar ice caps 9, 12
polluter pays principle 37, 43, 109, 153,
        171, 175
pollution
    air 187, 188
    causes 6–17

fast food 123–4
photochemical 188, 190–2
water 96–7
polyethylene trephthalate (PET) 160,
        161
population growth
    agricultural land quality 23–4
    family planning 24–7
    generally 18–19
    inverted pyramid 20 n7
    replacement level 20 n5
    Third World countries 19, 20–1
    traditional checks 21–3
    UK 21
    world 20–1
Porritt, Jonathon 26
Potato Marketing Board 126
product 'greening' 118–33
    bedrooms 128–9
    building 126–8
    conclusions 131–2
    false claims 131
    fast food 123–4
    food and beverage sales
        animal welfare 118–21
        generally 118
    'freedom food' 119–21, 130
    generally 118
    organic produce/beverages 121–3
    supplier management 129–30
    trading policy 131
    vegetarian dishes 122–3
property management 228–9
public relations 213–14
    audit issues 227
purchasing policies
    audit issues 227–8
    products/materials 114

Queen's Award for Environmental
        Achievement 258
questions/discussion 27–8, 43–4, 58, 85–7,
        108, 115–17, 132–3, 148–9, 172–4,
        184–5, 198–9, 223, 238, 252–3

recycling
  audit issues 233
  cardboard 152–3
  current technology 160–1
  generally 156–7
  glass 163–4
  levels 157
  life cycle analysis 158
  metals 163
  packaging 157
  paper 152–3, 164–6
  plastics 141, 152–3, 158–60, 162
refrigerants 49–59
  availability 49
  chemistry 50
  conclusions 58
  energy efficiency 56–7
  hazards 50, 52
  transient 53
  types 52, 53–5
  use 50–1
regulatory authorities
  powers 42
renewable resources 32, 42
Restaurant Association 121
Rio Declaration on Environment and
      Development 35
Rio Earth Summit 1992 9–10, 34–3, 221
  UK response to 40–1
road-building schemes
  effects 194
  impact 187
  protests against 179
Robens, J.A. 182
RoFry 112–13, 126
Royal Commission on Environmental
      Pollution 186, 193, 196
Royal Dutch Shell
  policy statement 213
RSPCA
  'Freedom Food' scheme 119–21

Safeway, non-caged eggs 120
Scandic Hotels
  policy statement 208

reports 245–6
Sjolyst 79, 128, 183
sea
  carbon dioxide reservoir 13
  increased level 9, 12, 13
Secretariat of the Organization of
      Amercian States 34
sewage disposal 99–100
showers
  water consumption 101
Single European Act 1986 37
sink 7
  carbon 10
  meaning 29 n2
Small Company Environmental and Energy
      Management Assistance Scheme
      (SCEEMAS) 222
small and medium-sized enterprises
      (SMEs) 222, 257
Soil Association
  membership drop 178
  Symbol 121–2, 130
  wood labelling scheme 130
soil microbiology 29 n10
solar energy
  harnessing 60–1
staff
  feedback 212
  involvement 258–9
  training 211–12
    audit issues 226–7
Standard for Total Quality Management
      (BS 5750, ISO 9000) 218
sulphur dioxide emissions
  effects 11–14
supplier management 129–30
sustainable development 32
  meaning 32
  principles for achieving 31, 35
  UK strategy 39, 40–1
sustainable living strategy 33–4

taps
  water consumption 101
  dripping 103

taxation examples 40
technology
  combination microwave/
      convection ovens 111–12
  combination steamers 110–11
  fat-free chip production unit 112–13, 126
  generally 109–10
  ware washers 113–14
temperature
  inversion 190
  measurement uncertainties 9–10
Third World debt 19
toilets, water consumption 98, 99
Total Equivalent Warming Impact (TEWI)
      53–4
toxic releases inventory 220
trade/industry organizations
      membership 216–17
transport
  audit issues 230–1
  company fleet 197–8
  diesel 189
  generally 186–7
  green vehicle technology 192–8
  petrol 189
  pollution effects 187–8
Transport White Paper 1998 40, 193–4, 195
tropical rainforests, destruction of 4, 10

UK2000 161
ultraviolet light, effects 16
UNESCO 33
United Kingdom (UK)
  deregulation 39
  international treaties
      implementation 39
United Nations Centre for Human Settle-
      ments 34
United Nations Conference on
      Environment and
      Development (UNCED) see Rio
      Earth Summit
United Nations Development
      Programme (UNDP) 33

United Nations Environment
      Programme (UNEP)
  'Caring for the Earth' 33
  functions 32
United Nations Framework
      Convention on Climate Change
      Protocol 35, 39
United Nations Population Conference in
      Mexico City 1984 24
United Nations Population Fund
      (UNFPA) 33–4
urinals
  water consumption 98–9

VAT
  domestic fuels 3, 255
  insulation 3
vegetarian diet 22–3, 122–3
Vegetarian Society 123
vehicle technology and government action
  catalytic converter 192–3, 197–8
  company fleet 197–8
  conclusions 198
  fiscal incentives 195
  freight traffic 194–5
  road building 194
  Royal Commission on Environmental
      Pollution 186, 193, 196
  Transport White Paper 1998 193–4
  unleaded petrol 193
Virginia Polytechnic Institute and State
      University survey
  'Lodging Hospitality' 183
volatile organic compounds (VOCs) 123,
      188, 191–2

Waitrose, non-caged eggs 120
washing machines
  water consumption 101–2
waste disposal 137, 147
  '4 Rs method' 171
  authorized disposers 153–4
  compactors 169–70
  cost comparisons 155
  duty of care 153–4

(waste disposal continued)
    food 166–9
    generally 151–3
    incineration 152
    landfill 151, 152
    minimization 156
    recycling, 152–3, 156–66; *see also*
        recycling
    regulation of 155
waste management
    '4 Rs method' 171
    audit issues 232–3, 234
    EC framework Directive 153
    minimization 156
    options 152
    'polluter pays principle' 37, 43, 109,
        153, 171, 175
water
    audit 104–5, 235–6
    climate change, effects 93–4
    consumption benchmarks 100
    cost of 107
    cycle 91–2
    demand for
      baths 101
      dishwashers 102
      effects of excessive 92–3
      food preparation 97–8
      landscape and grounds
        maintenance 104
      meeting increased 94–6
      showers 101
      toilets 98, 99
      urinals 98–9
      washing machines 102–3
    detergents in 105–6
    drinking 96–7
    drought occurrence 92
    generally 90, 103
    'grey' 101, 104
    industrial and commercial users 95, 97
    Jersey 93
    management audit issues 232, 235–6
    sewage disposal 99–100
    sources in UK 92–3
    sustainable supplies 96
    taps 102
    'Using Water Wisely' 95
wave power 60
Wheat and Maize Improvement Centre
    (CIMMYT) 24
wind power 3, 60, 61
wood 130
World Bank 24, 34
World Commission on Environment and
    Development to the United
    Nations (UNCED) 32
World Conservation Union (IUCN) 33
World Health Organization (WHO) 34,
    96, 97, 187
    'Health for All' 186–7
World Meteorological Organization 34
World Resources Institute 34
World Travel and Tourism Council 217
World Wide Fund for Nature (WWF) 33